# Monsters and Mad Scientists

*For Elizabeth*

# MONSTERS AND MAD SCIENTISTS

*A Cultural History of the Horror Movie*

Andrew Tudor

Basil Blackwell

First published 1989

Basil Blackwell Ltd
108 Cowley Road, Oxford, OX4 1JF, UK

Basil Blackwell, Inc.
3 Cambridge Center
Cambridge, Massachusetts 02142, USA

*British Library Cataloguing in Publication Data*

A CIP catalogue record for this book is available from the British Library.

*Library of Congress Cataloging in Publication Data*
Tudor, Andrew, 1942–
    Monsters and mad scientists: a cultural history of the horror
movie/Andrew Tudor.
        p.   cm.
    Includes index.
    ISBN 0–631–15279–2
    0–631–16992–x (Pbk)
    1. Horror films—History and criticism.   I. Title.
PN1995.9.H6T78   1989
791.43′616—dc20          89–32084
                         CIP

Typeset in 10 on 12 pt Sabon
by Setrite Typesetter Ltd, Hong Kong
Printed in Great Britain by The Camelot Press, Southampton

# Contents

# Preface

The worst thing about writing this book has been admitting to it. Few conversation-stoppers have quite the force of a well-timed 'Well, yes, actually I'm working on horror movies', a response to solicitous research inquiries that provokes pity and disbelief in about equal proportions. After 10 years or so I can report back to all those who have been concerned about my mental health ('Doesn't it de-sensitize you?', one genteel lady asked, as if viewing horror movies functioned as a kind of condom of the conscience) that I have no desire to kick kittens, drink blood or disembowel members of the moral majority. Mind you, I have been enjoying horror movies since, at the age of 14, I discovered that long trousers and an appropriately casual cigarette would gain me admission to the X-certificated *The Quatermass Experiment*. It was a mixed blessing. The film was fine, but the hawk-eyed cinema cashier charged me adult rates thereafter.

Still, I did not embark on this project either to defend horror movies from uninformed attack or to celebrate their pleasures. The study grew, rather, out of my concern to develop a systematic ap-proach to analysing popular film, a context in which the horror movie appeared to have the virtues both of familiarity and of simpli-city. Had I realized in 1977 quite where this would lead, I would have approached the task with far less equanimity. The book has taken much longer to complete than I expected, as much as anything because self-imposed requirements of method have proved hugely time-consuming. Consequently, I am haunted by the fear that what has resulted might turn out to be more than anybody reasonably wants to know about the horror movie! To ease the reader's task, therefore, I have kept to a minimum that last refuge of scholarship, the footnote, as well as avoiding lengthy quotations from other texts.

This does not reflect a cavalier attitude to existing studies of the genre — inevitably, I have learned from many of them — though it does follow from my desire to view the development of the horror movie from a somewhat different perspective from that of other histories. For similar reasons I have not reproduced here the bibliographic information that is readily available in such texts as James Twitchell's *Dreadful Pleasures* or Gregory Waller's *American Horrors*. Interested readers would be better advised to consult those excellent sources. I am certainly grateful to them, for their content as well as their bibliographies, and to all the unmentioned others whose work has made the task of writing this book that much more rewarding.

I am also grateful to Elizabeth Shove, who was always willing to encourage or admonish me back to work when energy and inspiration flagged, and who generously found time to read and comment on the whole text.

Andrew Tudor

# 1

## Introduction: Horror-Movie Histories

Histories are plainly reconstructions. However much their authors might protest that they are simply telling the story of events – and, these days, there are few historians who would be foolhardy enough to make any such claim – they are always and inevitably retelling it. Indeed, the very notion of what constitutes a properly told history is not fixed: it will vary from culture to culture and even from historian to historian. Historians, or, more precisely, the perspectives that they espouse, are irreducible constituents of their histories. The stories that they tell are constructed both from the 'facts' as they have perceived them and from the constraints, the directives, the criteria, through which those facts are transmuted into History.

Where the history is one of a particular cultural phenomenon – the history of a genre, let us say – there is a double construction to consider. Cultural phenomena only exist in so far as people 'read' them, ascribe them meaning; they are constituted as *cultural* in the act of reading. And, just as a historian's telling of the story can change, so too can the readings that audiences make of a particular artefact. Accordingly, the artefacts that form the basis for a cultural history are not fixed. They are constructed and reconstructed by their consumers long before they fall into the historian's hands. For this reason – though not only for this reason – cultural historians must be doubly reflective. Like all historians, they have to be aware of the foundations of their own story-telling, open about the essentially reconstructive character of their enterprise. But, more than that, they must also try to encompass the variety of the consumer's reconstructions. Cultural histories are not, therefore, as some art historians seem to suppose, exercises in documenting eternal aesthetic objects.

They are reports of interactions between different 'versions' of the artefacts themselves.

Sometimes this all-too-evident complexity is invoked in order to confound the very possibility of cultural analysis. Since there can be no fixed and final history, it is argued, then any history is as good (or as bad) as any other. This is patently untrue. Though we might not aspire to finality, we can hope to develop a history which will permit us to incorporate as much as possible of the potential variation in 'readings' that an audience might make of a cultural object. That way, there is some chance that the historian's flights of interpretative fancy may be tempered by an obligation to attend to the evident multiplicity of human cultures and subcultures.

In practice — that is, in this book — such multiple cultures must be served by multiple histories. The horror-movie genre is simultaneously both singular and plural, and its history must be told and retold in such a way as to reflect that variation. There is, from one point of view, a single genre and a single genre history: a reservoir of conventions, narratives and iconographic resources. But there are also several genres, open to be understood and reconstructed from a range of vantage points and in a variety of terms. As this study progresses I will seek to juggle with those differences, offering plural perspectives on the genre's development.

This does not mean that there is no order to this work, or that its account of horror-movie history is made purely for its own sake. Certainly I do not claim simply to 'tell it how it is' — how could that be? — but this is also not an aesthetic history, one concerned to make judgements of artistic or moral worth.[1] It is, rather, aimed at understanding the development of the horror movie as a historically specific social and cultural form. In itself that is not unusual. Popular genres in general, and the horror movie in particular, have often attracted that kind of attention. Traditionally, of course, that was because the genre's given designation as 'low culture' meant that it deserved no more, an assumption which — while no longer quite so widespread — is still apparent in some areas of cultural studies. Since the decline of mass-culture theories, however, the model most commonly applied to the horror movie has been broadly psychoanalytic, the genre conceived as a kind of collective dreamworld requiring analysis by methods derived from one or another tradition of psychoanalysis.[2]

Perhaps the most influential recent example of this approach is that of Robin Wood and his colleagues. They develop an analysis based on the proposition that patriarchal capitalism demands certain forms of surplus-repression (of, for example, sexual energy, bisexuality, female sexuality and children's sexuality), and that one way in which this is managed is by projecting that which is repressed outward onto the 'Other'. Horror movies, as collective nightmares, illustrate that process at work; they represent 'the return of the repressed'. This framework – worked through in more detail than this, of course – then leads to specific analyses in terms of these concepts, in terms of the idea that, as Wood puts it, 'the true subject of the horror genre is the struggle for recognition of all that our civilisation *re*presses or *op*presses: its re-emergence dramatized, as in our nightmares, as an object of horror, a matter for terror, the 'happy ending' (when it exists) typically signifying the restoration of repression.'[3]

Whatever one's response to the always-stimulating detail of the 'return of the repressed' argument, like most psychoanalytic perspectives it presents two very general difficulties to a non-adherent. In the first place, it is an inordinately reductive form of analysis, presupposing the overall credibility of a particular perspective and seeking to assimilate the widest possible range of cultural variation to those terms. Of course there is a sense in which all explanation is reductive, at least inasmuch as we try to explain things by mapping them into a pre-existing framework. But the distinctive feature of psychoanalytic reduction, when applied to cultural artefacts, is that the terms of the explanatory theory are also the terms in which the analyst's interpretative readings are constructed. The framework therefore invites 'revelatory reading', uncovering concealed significance. And this, in turn, presents us with a second related difficulty: the approach leads to and requires esoteric readings of the texts it seeks to analyse, readings which definitionally could not be part of any audience's conscious interpretative apparatus.

Naturally, these are only difficulties for those not wholly persuaded by the claims of the psychoanalytic approach, whether in its ambition to uncover the underlying order of cultural artefacts or in its willingness to treat them as a kind of 'collective unconscious'. This is broadly my position, for from a sociological point of view such a perspective fails to conceptualize the genre audience as anything more than a homogeneous assembly of psychoanalytic dupes. Yet a popular genre is significantly constituted by the conceptions of it held by its audience as well as by the texts that instantiate it, and while there may well be intractable difficulties in researching past audiences, that hardly justifies an approach which so minimizes their active contribution to constructing and sustaining genre meanings. And while this is certainly not an argument against all psychoanalytic perspectives, it does suggest that at the very least we need to situate the process of genre-understanding in a rather less totalizing theoretical context.

We can begin to appreciate some of the problems of conceptualizing an active audience by borrowing from Giddens's work on 'structuration'. In seeking to develop a non-reductionist approach to the relation between social action and social structure, he suggests that there are three distinct levels at which human agency can be conceptualized and understood.[4] There is the level of 'discursive consciousness', about which social actors can and do routinely report; there is the level of 'unconscious motivation', not normally available to the individual involved; and, between the two, there is the realm of 'practical consciousness' which 'consists of all the things which actors know tacitly about how to 'go on' in the contexts of social life without being able to give them direct discursive expression'.[5] This general scheme suggests a range of possible approaches to analysing the relations between audiences, reading and texts. An emphasis on discursive consciousness directs our attention to an audience's routinely articulated awareness of genre conventions and attributes — awareness of the screen personae of particular performers, for example, or of the general conventions of story-telling. Concern with the unconscious directs attention elsewhere, to those aspects of the reading process not available to the conscious actor and commonly presumed to be effective through such psychoanalytic mechanisms as repression. And, finally, practical consciousness invokes the vast area of pragmatic understanding of a genre's functioning, ordinarily left entirely unarticulated by the genre audience, but, in principle, intelligible to it. In effect, to study practical consciousness is to consider the audience's implicit conception of the 'language' of the genre. Clearly, then, while this formulation does still leave some conceptual space for analysis in terms of unconscious motives and repression — though perhaps not quite of the kind developed in the 'return of the repressed' thesis — it does so only as one element among others; certainly not as a reductive key to all the rest.

Indeed, whatever form genre analysis might finally take, it can reasonably be argued that its most sensible point of departure lies at the level of practical consciousness. If one seeks, as I do, to sustain a non-reductive view of popular culture, to conceive of it as an 'embedded' feature of social life, as simultaneously both symptom *and* cause, reflection *and* articulation, language of ideological production *and* reproduction, then it is the taken-for-granted and non-esoteric features of the genre-language that are fundamental to that understanding. It goes without saying that horror movies are one aspect of the social construction of the fearful in our society: in their prosaic characteristics, first of all, and in the assembly of conventions that we grasp as part of our practical consciousness, they contribute to the shaping of our 'landscapes of fear'.[6] If we are to comprehend that process — and my interest in the horror movie is informed by a more general interest in the cultural construction of emotion — then we require a kind of social phenomenology of the genre, an account of the fundamental terms within which genre-artefacts are made to make sense by their consumers.

This poses an immediate practical problem. Even if today's audience is accessible to research, yesterday's is not. How, then, can we gain indirect access to the realm of past practical consciousness? In these circumstances any solution is bound to be a second-best one. My strategy in this study is to begin analysis using the kinds of conceptions and terms that would be familiar and intelligible to any genre audience, and then spiral 'outwards' towards second- and third-order constructs and accounts. Naturally this guarantees nothing in itself, but, inasmuch as my reconstructions constantly seek to refer back to a prosaic rather than an esoteric level of interpretative understanding, there is some reason to believe that these multiple versions of horror-movie history will indeed reflect the kinds of terms in which the genre has been routinely understood and used by its audience. What this implies for actual research practice is the concern of the rest of this chapter.

### Analytic Practicalities

Inevitably the first problem is one of definition. I have already suggested that a genre exists in the conceptions of its audience as much as in the artefacts of which it is apparently composed.[7] It is a distinctive reservoir of cultural resources, drawn upon by both film-maker and audience, but transcending them individually. In effect, a genre is a special kind of subculture, a set of conventions of narrative, setting, characterization, motive, imagery, iconography and so on, which exists in the practical consciousness of those fluent in its 'language'. Not everyone is equally fluent. A genre is flexible, open to variable understanding by different users at different times and in different contexts. Thus while most people have ideas about what might generally constitute a horror movie – even those who do not watch them – they might very well disagree about the classification of specific films.

That is hardly surprising. A genre is, after all, a social construction, and as such it is subject to constant negotiation and re-formulation. That means, of course, that a genre's boundaries can never be defined once and for all. They are definitionally blurred, and for that reason any attempt to research a genre cannot hope to provide strict·criteria for identifying its products. Nor should it seek to do so. It is precisely because its 'edges' are diffuse that a genre is able to develop and change. To research genre history, then, it is necessary to include as wide a range of films as possible, while trying not to misrepresent the spectrum of audience conceptions.[8]

In line with this policy, the films which form the data for this study have been chosen on the basis of a catholic definition of the genre, with anything up to 20 per cent of them occupying boundary regions between the mainstream horror movie and other proximate genres – above all, thrillers and science fiction. To preserve some general sense of their consumption by a culturally specific audience, I have included only films, from any source, which were released in Britain between 1931 (the beginning of the 'sound' horror movie) and 1984. Consistent with that point of reference, all dates given relate to the year of British release and not, as is conventional, to the year of production. This yields a list of 990 feature films.[9]

Data relating to these films – including production details, narrative summaries, classifications of character types, sources of monstrous threat, etc. – have been stored in a computerized database. The volume of information was simply too large to be handled in any other way.[10] This is *not* a work of automated content analysis, however. Although the computer facilitated the production of very general 'descriptive statistics' – reported throughout this book where appropriate – its major function was to retrieve information about specific films or groups of films (which could then be subjected to detailed interpretative analysis) and to direct attention to patterns not immediately apparent to the uncomputerized eye. The general terms in which this analysis was conducted are presented at the relevant points in what follows, and were, as the study progressed, altered and refined with continuous reworking of the materials. Naturally this inquiry was not carried on in a theoretical vacuum. Several traditions played a part in forming its terms of analysis, in particular those areas of modern film theory that have been chiefly concerned with narrative. Inasmuch as my methodological strategy is to 'work outwards' from the most prosaic level of understanding and interpretation, however, this study should be seen as an exploratory work which is informed by the theoretical traditions of film semiotics and narrative analysis but certainly not determined or justified by them. For that reason there is no need here to embark on detailed theoretical discussion. Where it is necessary to introduce particular terms, they are appropriately framed at that time.[11]

Preliminary analysis begins, then, in chapter 2, at the most 'common sense' of levels. It is easy enough to imagine a member of the horror movie audience speaking of the genre in terms of its monsters, the source of their threat and power and the ways in which they can be opposed or defeated — categories which are largely those of the films themselves. They are, to borrow a term from Schutz, first-order constructs, concepts used and usable in the everyday context of the genre. Vampires, werewolves, zombies and the rest are part of the conceptual apparatus of any horror movie audience. Science, supernature and the psyche refer unproblematically to 'real' elements of the genre world. In using them to construct a first approximation of the genre's most basic characteristics, therefore, we remain close to the terms in which an audience might reconstruct the horror movie for itself — if set that improbable task.

But that is only preliminary description. It is also necessary to begin to identify the various ordering structures that allow the genre to function as a meaningful system. Several approaches are possible, ranging from the high formalism of some types of narrative analysis through to the diffuse interpretative speculation common in orthodox criticism. Since in this study I am trying to anchor analysis broadly within audience conceptions (while not *absolutely* limiting it to the terms that an audience might employ), my first need is for an account of genre history which goes a little beyond the very simple conceptualization of chapter 2. This is the job of chapters 3 and 4, where I provide a highly condensed historical account organized in terms of the combinations and permutations of three very general distinctions,

distinctions developed by extension from already familiar terms. These chapters are the nearest thing to an 'orthodox' film history in the book. They cover the whole period in some detail.

The aim of this exercise, then, is to take a first 'step back' from the genre's history, framing analysis within categories which, though more abstract than those of chapter 2, still relate to real features of genre development. Unlike chapter 2's terminology, however, these categories do not directly reflect the basic elements of horror-movie narrative — monsters, sources, defenders. Instead, they seek to conceptualize rather more general characteristics of the horror-movie 'threat', essentially for two related reasons. The first is because, as we will see, the 'threat' is *the* central feature of horror movie narrative, the organizing principle around which all else revolves. The other is because if we are ultimately concerned with the different kinds of fears articulated in these movies, then it is in relation to the 'threat' that the most general trends will become apparent.

Three pairs of terms define the parameters of the typology that I shall use. Although they are presented as dichotomous alternatives here, it should be emphasized that the contrasts they reflect are not always absolute. Either pole of each dichotomy represents a broad tendency within the genre, not an exclusive option. Presenting them as paired oppositions is, then, a heuristic convenience; it certainly does not reflect, as it would in some forms of structuralism, a universal bipolar assumption about the basic character of the genre. By the same count, the terms themselves have been chosen because in their everyday use they carry at least some of the desired connotations. But care is necessary: their familiar meanings do not entirely correspond to their usage here. They have been arrived at by working with the historical materials in an attempt to find a set of categories which will stay within appropriate phenomenological limits yet still offer some analytic leverage. In other words, they are designed as practical (and simple) tools, not as profound statements about the 'real meaning' or 'deep structure' of the genre. I shall introduce them here, although they will not fully come into play until chapter 3. The oppositions are:

1 Supernatural/Secular

2 External/Internal

3 Autonomous/Dependent

Let me briefly consider each in turn.

SUPERNATURAL/SECULAR

The contrast between supernatural and secular is the most immediately obvious of the three, if for no other reason than that the horror movie itself often trades explicitly on just such a distinction. My aim in invoking it here is to distinguish between those films in which the *primary* threat originates in some postulated 'supernature' and those in which the threat is essentially a feature of the everyday 'natural' world. Traditional horror movies, with their vampires, witches, werewolves and zombies, fall unproblematically within the 'supernatural', while those focused on invaders from space, prehistoric monsters, creations of mad scientists, and, in most cases, psychotics, are quite clearly 'secular'. Essentially, then, the focus of this distinction is on the degree to which a film's taken-for-granted genre world presumes a separate order of reality as its primary source of monstrous threat. Where such an alternative reality is present, then emphasis falls on the supernatural side of the dichotomy. Where the threat is 'this worldly' (including outer space, which has usually been treated as a continuation of 'this world' in the horror movie), the balance shifts towards the secular end of the scale.

Of course, the genre is not always that simple. Some narratives hinge on an ambiguity about precisely this distinction, while others may seek to create tension by treating a notionally secular threat as if it were an instance of the supernatural. Nevertheless, it is normally not too difficult to distinguish between the two tendencies, even if some films may not fall clearly into one or other category and some may trade on both. But the point is not to label individual films exclusively; it is, rather, to develop classificatory terms which reflect important differences of emphasis within the genre. In this respect, it would be hard to deny the significance of the distinction between supernatural and secular. It is clearly a fundamental division which informs many other features of the genre world − part of the horror movie's basic conceptual apparatus.

EXTERNAL/INTERNAL

While the supernatural/secular distinction relates to ontological assumptions about the realm in which the 'threat' functions, that between external and internal is concerned more with the threat's practical locus of application. Broadly, a threat may be thought of as external or internal with respect to human beings. Obviously, then, this distinction is more complex than that between supernatural and secular, and there are many examples of individual films in which the 'threat' has both external and internal aspects. It is not uncommon, for instance, to find horror movies in which individuals are magically metamorphosed. In this case the magician or witch, the caster of the spell, is external to the victim, while the actual metamorphosis acts upon and within the individual. Similarly with demonic possession movies. The demon invades from outside, as did the space-invaders of the fifties, but the actual locus of its threat is very much internal. It attacks from within, via possession. Or, in a distinctively modern variation, the typical threat, that of psychosis, is internal — generated within human beings — although in other respects the psychotic's relation to his or her victims is much the same as that of any externally threatening monster.

In seeking to distinguish between external and internal, then, I am using a single, somewhat abstract division to capture what is undoubtedly a complicated balance of emphases. It involves making a judgement about the *overall* character of the horror movie threat in an attempt to tap a property of the genre world which is not always straightforwardly reflected in particular cases. What this means in practice will become clearer as the study progresses, for, as we shall see, a shift from externality to internality is central to the long-term development of the genre.

AUTONOMOUS/DEPENDENT

The third distinction is perhaps the simplest of all. In some horror movies the threatening force is simply there, quite independent of humanity, though posing a threat to it. The classic vampire, the space monster, the prehistoric survivor all fall into this autonomous category. They have not been created by human beings either physically, magically or psychically; they simply exist. In contrast, monsters like the mad scientist's abomination, the magically created metamorphant or zombie, or the mutation born of atomic radiation or pollution are all consequences of human actions. They are dependent on human volition, and the threat they pose stands in significant contrast to that presented by more autonomous monsters. In some senses, then, the contrast between dependence and autonomy invokes questions of human responsibility. Are *we* responsible for creating the threatening situation, or does it emerge quite independently of our intentions and actions? Sometimes such questions have featured prominently as motivating elements in horror-movie narratives — particularly where scientific ethics are concerned — and, as we shall see, the significance of this opposition declines in parallel with the collapse of science as a major horror-movie threat.

It is possible to combine these three dichotomies into a general typology, distinguishing eight different combinatorial categories. In table 1.1 I have included examples in each of the cells, though they are by no means exhaustive.

**Table 1.1   Variations of the horror-movie threat**

|  | Supernatural | | Secular | |
|---|---|---|---|---|
|  | *Dependent* | *Autonomous* | *Dependent* | *Autonomous* |
| *External* | magic witchcraft etc. | classic vampires the mummy | medical monsters eco-nasties | space invaders Kong |
| *Internal* | magic zombies possession | some werewolves spirits | some explained psychotics | some parasites disease |

It is this classificatory framework that underlies the otherwise straightforward historical account presented in chapters 3 and 4. In principle, of course, one could classify the whole genre in terms of these abstract categories, expressing the results in a series of eight-part tables. In practice, such a procedure rapidly becomes unwieldy, and, where these terms are used, I shall generally employ only subsets of the full typology.

These, then, are the concepts with which I begin to organize the genre's history in Part I. Part II, comprising chapters 5 and 6, follows with a further escalatory shift, addressing genre history by abstracting its principal narrative conventions. The terms appropriate to that discussion are introduced in the relevant chapters. Then, in Part III, there follows a detailed account of the development of the horror movie's three major sub-genres: those deriving their threat from science, those in which it derives from supernature and those where its source is the psyche. Lastly, and most generally of all, in chapter 10 I shall make some speculative suggestions about the kinds of world presupposed in traditional and modern horror movies.

In effect, then, genre history is retold three times, at each stage from a different though related point of view. That inevitably leads to a kind of repetition, at least in the sense that some of the same films recur at each retelling. Hopefully, however, the three accounts are sufficiently different not to make that a serious problem. In any case, this study's methodology obliges us to spiral upwards from the initial prosaic level of analysis, continually reconstructing horror-movie history as we go. At each turn of the spiral we re-cover some of the same ground, but it is surely only in this way that we can even begin to document the practical consciousness of genre which is so important to its social construction.

Notes

1  Few film histories are purely aesthetic, of course, except those which restrict themselves to recitations of the 'best' films of a particular tradition. Nor do I mean to imply that a broadly aesthetic or evaluative concern is incompatible with perceptive history. David Pirie's rewarding study *A Heritage of Horror* (London, 1973), is ample demonstration of that. Other aesthetically inclined studies from which I have learned include: Carlos Clarens, *Horror Movies* (London, 1968); Charles Derry, *Dark Dreams* (New York and London, 1977); S. S. Prawer, *Caligari's Children* (Oxford, 1980). Readers familiar with these volumes will know that, although I group them together here as broadly 'aesthetic', they actually approach the genre from very different perspectives.

2  See, for example, the essays assembled in Andrew Britton, Richard Lippe, Tony Williams and Robin Wood, *American Nightmare: Essays on the Horror Film* (Toronto, 1979). Another recent discussion partly informed by psychoanalytic concepts — though from a rather different perspective to the above — can be found in James B. Twitchell, *Dreadful Pleasures: An Anatomy of Modern Horror* (New York and Oxford, 1985). Note that both these studies take the horror movie seriously in its own right. Older psychoanalytic approaches were often based on the gross assumption that a taste as perverse as that for horror required special (and hence psychoanalytic) explanation.

3  Robin Wood, 'Introduction' to Britton et al., *American Nightmare: Essays on the Horror Film*, p. 10.

4  See Anthony Giddens, *The Constitution of Society* (Cambridge, 1984), pp. 6–7 and *passim*. See also Anthony Giddens, 'Structuralism and the

Theory of the Subject', in his *Central Problems in Social Theory* (London, 1979).

5 Giddens, *The Constitution of Society*, p. xxiii.

6 The expression is borrowed from Tuan's wide-ranging attempt to chart conceptions of the fearful: Yi-fu Tuan, *Landscapes of Fear* (Oxford, 1979). Though I shall not pursue it here, there is a growing literature concerned with the social and cultural construction of emotion. Some approaches to fear from this perspective can be found in David L. Scruton (ed), *Sociophobics: The Anthropology of Fear* (Boulder and London, 1986).

7 Not surprisingly, mine is a sociologically informed view of genre, broadly an extension of the position first developed in Andrew Tudor, 'Genre: Theory and Mispractice in Film Criticism', *Screen*, 11, 6, 1970, pp. 33–43 (a somewhat different version of which appears in Andrew Tudor, *Theories of Film* (London, 1974), pp. 131–50), and further extended in Andrew Tudor, *Image and Influence* (London, 1974), ch. 8. For a useful general discussion of approaches to genre see Stephen Neale, *Genre* (London, 1980).

8 This is in some contrast to the selective strategy adopted by Will Wright, for example, in his admirably systematic study of the Western, *Sixguns and Society* (Berkeley, 1975). Wright restricts his research to those Westerns achieving a particular level of first-run box-office success, on the grounds that these films are the most popular and thus best represent the genre. Apart from difficulties about using such a measure as an indicator of popularity, the assumption of representativeness seems ill-conceived. If the aim is to chart the variable patterning of the genre, then surely the greatest possible breadth of material is required. And if that is impractical, then more appropriate sampling techniques provide the only legitimate alternative.

9 For obvious reasons I could not rely on the existing histories to assemble this material. Instead I returned to less aesthetically mediated sources, most notable among them the *Monthly Film Bulletin*. It is a matter of some regret to me that the appropriate volume of Phil Hardy's *The Aurum Film Encyclopedia, Horror* (vol. 3 London, 1985), appeared too late to be of much help. It would have considerably accelerated the data-collection process. Similar if smaller scale volumes did prove useful, however, especially Alan Frank, *The Horror Film Handbook* (London, 1982). Naturally I am aware that the eighties have seen a considerable expansion of horror films available on video – some of them only in this format. I have not sought to include such material in this research, though any future extension of the work would clearly need to incorporate video.

10 Analysis began with a system based around a much expanded Sinclair QL (640K) running Psion's Archive database software, and continued – using the same software – on an Opus PCIII. The Archive program proved to be admirably flexible in application to this kind of material.

11 Those entirely unfamiliar with this background could consult Seymour Chatman, *Story and Discourse* (Ithaca and London, 1978), and David

Bordwell, *Narration in the Fiction Film* (London, 1985), both of which cover many of the issues important in relation to film narrative. As far as general film theory is concerned, however, there is no short route to wisdom! The two anthologies edited by Bill Nichols — *Movies and Methods* (Berkeley and London, 1976), and *Movies and Methods, Volume II* (Berkeley and London, 1985) — give some indication of the sheer range of modern film analysis.

# Part I
*Genre History*

# 2

## Facts, Figures and Frightful Fiends

First, some general information. As already indicated, this research is based on 990 films distributed in Britain between 1931 and 1984. Almost 80 per cent of them fall quite unproblematically within the genre. The remaining 20 per cent occupy the genre boundaries in a variety of ways. Some remain predominantly within the bounds of horror-movie conventions, their 'peripheral' status indicating only the presence of another frame of genre reference. This is the case, for example, with many of the science-fiction orientated films of the fifties like *The Thing from Another World* (1952) or *The War of the Worlds* (1953). Other cases are more complex. *Frenzy* (1972), for example, incorporates elements characteristic of orthodox horror-movies of its period — its central threat derives from a sexually predatory psychotic and it features two very graphic sequences of violence — yet it also evokes conventions from the thriller and even from some comic traditions. Furthermore, audiences of the period would have been made aware of it as a 'Hitchcock film', itself enough to generate expectations not entirely coincident with those of the horror-movie.

Despite this variation, it is useful for the moment to treat all 990 films as if they constitute a single body of work. In this way certain very general attributes of the genre become apparent. For example, two-thirds of these films are in colour, and the vast majority of those in black-and-white were made before the sixties. This means that the introduction of obligatory colour falls a little later in the horror-movie than in other, better-financed genres, but it is more or less universal by 1965. Similarly, the typical running time of horror-movies increases over the period, though, once again, a little later than in most other genres. In the thirties average horror-movie length was as low as 71 minutes; by the eighties it had risen to 94. And finally (and last of these gross figures), the USA is easily the genre's dominant production source. Almost 57 per cent of researched films are entirely American or are co-productions involving an American company; as table 2.1 indicates, only Britain stands as a major alternative producer.

**Table 2.1   Production sources of horror movies, 1931–1984**

| Country of origin | Number of films | % of total[a] |
|---|---|---|
| United States | 562 | 56.9 |
| Britain | 248 | 25.1 |
| Italy | 83 | 8.4 |
| France | 38 | 3.9 |
| Spain | 35 | 3.5 |
| Canada | 32 | 3.2 |
| Japan | 25 | 2.5 |

[a] Because of the presence of co-productions, figures reported in the '% of total' column add up to more than 100.

To carry this 'statistical' description any further it is necessary to briefly suggest some of the most general features of horror-movie narrative. Narrative structure will be discussed in some detail later, especially in chapter 5. However, a crude 'core' narrative may appropriately be identified here, if only to provide a background to some of the categories used in the numerical distributions that follow.

By and large, horror-movies follow a three-part narrative pattern familiar from other popular genres: instability is introduced into an apparently stable situation; the threat to instability is resisted; the threat is removed and stability restored.[1] As in the cinema more generally, this pattern has undergone some modification in recent years. Absolute closure (threat removed and stability restored) is no longer obligatory, and the notion of what constitutes a proper ending is not as restrictive as it once was. When *The Birds* (1963) allowed its characters to escape at the end of the film but left their ultimate fate ambiguous and their house surrounded by the (temporarily?) quiescent birds, its 'openness' caused dissatisfaction among audiences accustomed to greater narrative closure. By the seventies, though, similar strategies were sufficiently common to cause little or no comment. Of just over 100 films which exhibit such narrative openness, the vast majority of them (92 out of 104) were produced after 1970. On a less extreme criterion of closure the figures are even larger but the pattern basically the same. Narratives closed in the more limited sense that *this* story is complete, but there still remains some possibility of a continued threat, are also increasingly common in the seventies and eighties − a strategy crudely exemplified in *The Blob* (1959), where the threat is successfully averted, but by resorting to a question mark instead of an end title the implication is left that there is more to come. There are 122 of these 'semi-closed' narratives, 100 of which are post-1970. Taking the two groups together, almost 23 per cent of horror-movies show some degree of narrative openness.

The detail and significance of this shift will be discussed later. For the present it is sufficient to stress the predominantly 'classical' character of horror-movie narratives. Indeed, the nature of the horror-movie's fictional universe is such as to encourage a direct embodiment of the traditional order−disorder−order sequence. The abstract threat to stability and order finds immediate and concrete expression in the monsters around which the movies revolve. Characteristically, the pattern falls into the familiar three phases: an initial period establishing the presence both of the monster and of the stable situation that it threatens; a second and usually lengthy phase in which the monster goes on the rampage and various attempts to deal with it are shown to be ineffectual; a third phase, often quite brief, in which the monster is finally defeated and some level of order is restored.

The nub of the horror-movie, then, is the threatening creature which serves as the major focus for the narrative. Beyond that, both the source of monstrous threat and the nature and character of those who combat it are foregrounded to varying degrees. Accordingly, these three areas − the monster, its source, its pursuers − form the basis for the gross distributions reported in the rest of this chapter. Let me describe each in turn.

MONSTERS

The typical monsters of horror-movies are well established, and the films themselves are usually quite explicit in the labels that they apply to different types of monstrous threat. A rank-order summary appears in table 2.2, though note that this table does not include all the 'monster' categories used in the research: minor categories are omitted or combined. The figures do not add up to 990 since they reflect numbers of cases, not films: some films feature more than one type of monster, and occasionally as many as five or six.

Table 2.2   **Rank order of horror-movie monsters, 1931–1984[a]**

| Monsters | Number of cases | % incidence[a] |
|----------|-----------------|----------------|
| psychotics | 271 | 28 |
| mad scientists | 169 | 17 |
| science creations | 134 | 14 |
| vampires | 101 | 10 |
| mutations | 97 | 10 |
| ghosts | 77 | 8 |
| magicians/witches | 70 | 7 |
| natural nasties | 67 | 7 |
| prehistoric | 57 | 6 |
| space 'men' | 50 | 5 |
| zombies | 48 | 5 |
| demons | 47 | 5 |
| bug-eyed monsters | 43 | 4 |
| satanists | 39 | 4 |
| werewolves | 27 | 3 |
| mummies | 14 | 1 |

[a] Percentage figures have been rounded up or down to the nearest whole number, as they are in all the following rank-order tables.

Table 2.2 gives a gross indication of the distribution of types of monster and hence, as we shall see, of types of threat. Their significance, of course, can only really emerge in detailed analysis and in the context of other features of the genre's development. For instance, the fact that psychotics outweigh all other monsters is partly a consequence of the modern growth of the genre: over 90 per cent of films involving psychotics appear after 1960. Since 730 films fall within this period (74 per cent of all horror-movies), it is clear that the preponderance of psychotics is temporally specific and needs examination within that context. Such reservations necessarily limit the value of a summarizing table of this sort. Nevertheless, this information does provide a very general introduction to the range and distribution of the horror-movie's 'threats to order'.

SOURCES

Horror movies generally offer some 'explanation' for the disruption central to their narratives. In that the vast majority of films focus upon a specifiable monster rather than on a diffuse threat, the form of that explanation is usually cast in terms of the creature's source and/or its characteristic powers. Latterly, it is true, there has been a trend towards narrative strategies which do not provide specific explanations, a development paralleling the move to more open narrative. In such cases I have used a bucket category, somewhat tautologically labelled 'evil'. The overall distributions are summarized in table 2.3; it should be noted that some films invoke more than one explanatory scheme.

The detail of these proffered 'explanations' will be explored in subsequent chapters, particularly in chapters 7, 8 and 9. As far as the figures recorded here are concerned, only one or two points need to be made. First, the 'evil/unexplained' and 'psychiatric' categories are largely embodied in narratives focusing on psychotics: this is the case in 132 of the 136 'psychiatric' cases and 118 of the 132 'evil' cases. Accordingly, the borderline between the two is not always as clear as that between other kinds of explanation, and for most purposes they may be combined to produce a general category, 'the psyche' on a numerical par (25 per cent) with 'science' and 'supernature'. Second, the label 'natural' may be misleading. Only 47 of these cases actually relate to monsters that are 'natural' in that they exist in nature as presently known (e.g. piranhas, bears, sharks, etc.). Of the remaining 57 cases, the largest group is interpreted as 'natural' in a rather more loose sense, so as to include, in particular, prehistoric monsters or

Table 2.3  Rank order of sources of horror-movie threat, 1931–1984

| Source | Number of cases | % incidence |
| --- | --- | --- |
| scientific | 251 | 25 |
| supernatural | 241 | 24 |
| magical | 141 | 14 |
| psychiatric | 136 | 14 |
| evil/unexplained | 132 | 13 |
| natural | 104 | 11 |
| extraterrestrial | 79 | 8 |

overgrown natural creatures such as Kong. Apart from such reservations, however, these figures do give some indication of the general emphasis of the genre's delineation of its sources of threat. Clearly science, supernature and the psyche form the major organizing principles, and, as such, they define the separate sub-genres discussed in Part III.

PURSUERS

Though they are formally essential to the typical horror-movie narrative, pursuers are often relatively insignificant in the actual realization of the films. Indeed, the gap between 'pursuers' and 'victims' has been progressively eroded as the genre has developed. This is particularly true in the post−1970 period, for narratives in which the threat is *not* defeated have no necessary requirement for a specialized monster-catcher. The second and central phase of the classic horror-movie narrative (rampage/pursuit) can function quite effectively as pure rampage, without any distinctive pursuer role. This partly explains the dominance of 'everyperson' in table 2.4, and the special importance of this category in the post-sixties horror movie. That said, it should also be noted that most horror movies do go some way towards blurring the pursuer/victim distinction in both directions: pursuers may become victims, and vice-versa.

Table 2.4   Types of pursuers in the horror movie, 1931−1984

| Pursuer | Number of cases | % incidence |
|---|---|---|
| everyperson | 635 | 64 |
| police | 230 | 23 |
| experts | 134 | 14 |
| scientists | 112 | 11 |
| military | 55 | 6 |

There is little to be added to the information in table 2.4. The most significant features of horror movie pursuers are only apparent in closer analysis of specific developments. For example, the modern decline of a key role for the 'expert' and the 'scientist' is related to a matching decline in the pursuer's likelihood of success. This, too, will be explored in later chapters, particularly chapter 6. Meanwhile these figures stand as testimony to the relative lack of variety in the genre's treatment of those who are formally its 'heroes'.

Nothing has been said so far about style. This is not an accidental omission, for there are stylistic distinctions characteristic of different periods in the genre's development. However, it has not proved possible to establish a suitably discriminatory framework to systematically classify such differences. Though it is quite clear that a broad cinematic 'naturalism' dominates the horror movie, as it does most other genres, it is also notable that in certain periods (the thirties, the late fifties and early sixties) a more stylized idiom is apparent. Gross statistics are even less informative in exploring style, however, and consideration of stylistic change has therefore been left to more detailed discussion.

## Growth and Decline

The simplest metaphor for genre change is that derived from evolution. Genres, and sub-genres within them, develop through a kind of survival of the commercially fittest. Financially successful films encourage further variations on their proven themes, thus generating a broadly cyclical pattern of successes which then decline into variously unsuccessful repetitions of the initial formula. As we shall see, this process works on both a macro and a micro scale: over lengthy periods and in the short term. However, such profit-generated sequencing is overlaid with other less immediately obvious patterns, interrelations that depend upon historically specific conjunctions of commercial, cultural and social factors. In exploring the various 'sub-genres' in Part III, I shall try to elucidate some of these more complex sequences. First, however, it is necessary to establish a broad empirical picture of the genre's growth. A convenient starting point for such an account may be found in figure 2.1.

In figure 2.1 the thick line represents the absolute number of horror movies distributed in Britain in each year, while the thin line represents the proportion of horror movies in the total number. The latter figures have been multiplied by 5 so as to show clearly the point at which the proportion of horror movies starts rising at a higher rate than the total, a process which begins in 1959 and remains a characteristic pattern through to 1984. It will be clear from the graph that the overall picture is one of growth, even though the total of *all* types of film distributed in each year has declined

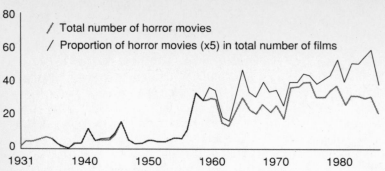

**Figure 2.1     Number and proportion (x5) of horror movies
distributed in Britain**

quite steadily during this period. In the late thirties well over 600 films were put into distribution yearly; by the early eighties the figure had dipped below 300. The yearly number of horror movies, in some contrast, has ranged from 1 (in 1931) up to 41 (in both 1973 and 1974).

These variations apart, the pattern of peaks and troughs in both graphs is largely the same. This suggests a straightforward point of departure for structuring genre history: by focusing upon the periods in which horror movie distribution peaks, we can develop a more detailed picture of those 'phases' in which genre films were most numerous. This does not preclude other bases for sub-classifying the genre's history. Indeed, much of this book tries to compare and combine different views of genre development. For the present, however, simple inspection of figure 2.1 suggest six major periods:[2]

*Phase I: the Classic Period* (1931–1936)

Broadly this runs from 1931 to 1936 during which time 33 horror films appeared. At best, however, the yearly rate was only 1 per cent of total film distribution. This is the period in which, it is commonly claimed, Universal studios 'created' the sound horror movie.

*Phase II: the War Period* (1941–1946)

The two peaks in 1941 and 1946 circumscribe this phase, the latter significantly composed of films produced in the USA during the war years but not arriving in Britain until the end of hostilities. There are 54 films that fall within this period.

## Phase III: the Fifties Boom (1956–1960)

Between 1956 and 1960 there is a sustained upsurge in horror-movie distribution. In 1955 only 7 were distributed, 1.3 per cent of the total, and broadly the same figure as throughout the early fifties. In 1956 that figure doubled to 15 (2.8 per cent), and a year later doubled again to 33 (6.9 per cent). Over the five year period there are 139 horror-movies; there were only 30 in the previous half-decade.

## Phase IV: American Decline (1963–1966)

In 1963, for the first time, the number of horror-movies from American sources drops below 50 per cent of distribution. A year later, out of 31 films (itself the biggest yearly figure for the sixties and 9.5 per cent of total films), 12 are from the USA and 11 from Britain. The US proportion has dropped to 38.7 per cent, and in 1966 reaches a low point of 23.8 per cent – just 5 films. These four years, then, represent a crucial period of change, and cover 100 films in all.

## Phase V: the Seventies Boom (1971–1974)

1971 sees an upsurge on a par with that of the mid-fifties. In 1970 there are 18 horror-movies; in 1971 the figure rises to 38 (8.2 per cent of total) and by 1973 it has risen again to 41 (9.1 per cent), a level sustained in the year following. These four years (159 films) also see the beginning of a recovery in the American share of the market.

## Phase VI: Sustained Growth (1978–1983)[3]

Inspection of figure 2.1 will show that, although absolute numbers drop away from the 1973–4 high point, the proportion of horror-movies in the movie population rises sharply. In 1978 it exceeds 10 per cent for the first time, and passes 12 per cent in 1983. There are 194 films distributed in these six years.

Having isolated these periods as significant 'moments' in the growth of the genre, I shall go on to examine them more closely in chapters 3 and 4 by utilizing the basic classificatory system already introduced in chapter 1.

## Notes

1 For a general discussion of this view of narrative in the context of several film genres see Stephen Neale, *Genre* (London, 1980), pp. 20–30.
2 I do not want to make too much of this division into periods, which is a heuristic convenience as much as anything else. It is certainly not intended to suggest a simple correlation between frequency of production and typicality, though clearly these are years of significant genre expansion.
3 The numerical decline apparent in 1984 is confirmed in the three years following, in which distribution remains at roughly the same level. In 1988, however, there are some signs of an increase, with horror-movies running at about 12 per cent in the first half of the year.

# 3

## Genre History I: 1931–1960

This chapter uses the classificatory scheme introduced in chapter 1 to inform and frame analysis of the first three horror-movie 'peaks'. This is not simply a matter of convenience, for the 1960 dividing point is of some importance. As we shall see, there is a degree of internal consistency to the pre- and post-1960 genres which is underlined by the significant differences discernible between them. In particular, while the pre-1960 horror-movie is dominated by science and, to a slightly lesser degree, by supernatural threats, the years after 1960 witness the rise of the psychotic and the development of a more overt sexual dimension. Of course, these are matters of broad emphasis: the psychotic predates 1960 just as the mad scientist survives into the eighties. But, as we shall see, there are clear differences between these two periods, each – for purposes of this analysis – divided into their three peaks. Let us begin, then, in the 'classic' years.

### The Classic Period: 1931–1936

Perhaps the most distinctive feature of the classic period is stylistic. Of the 33 films that fall within the period only two could be unproblematically described as 'naturalistic' in their visual style. The remainder look variously 'expressionistic'. Along with its contemporary, the gangster movie, the thirties horror-movie was the major beneficiary from the twenties influx of German technicians and from German stylistic influences in general.[1] The studied compositions, elaborate lighting techniques and heavy shadows developed in the German silent cinema found a home in the new Hollywood genres of the thirties. This 'German Style' proved highly effective in suggesting a world in which dimly seen and dimly understood forces constrained, controlled and attacked its unsuspecting inhabitants. The contrast with established conventions of 'naturalistic' lighting and composition could hardly be more pointed. Where routine methods presented audiences with a frame more or less evenly illuminated, the horror-movie often left vast reaches of the image in darkness. Where standard techniques of composition sustained the illusion of 'natural' space and 'proper' perspective, the horror-movie denied its audience such conventional comforts. In short, the *visual* world of the classic horror-movie is, by comparison with the then-established conventions of film imagery, a world internally awry. Today, of course, it is difficult to see the horror-movies of the classic period in those terms. The 'German Style' no longer works directly, but is mediated by our knowledge of these films as belonging firmly to the past. In the mid-thirties, however, part of their undoubted charge must have stemmed from that distinctive and unconventional style.

Of course, style alone is not responsible for creating the world experienced by a genre audience, and in terms of its underlying structure the dominant characteristic of the classic period is the externality of its threat. In the vast majority of cases (24 of the 33 films) the destabilizing force, whether supernatural or secular, is external. Thus within the genre world there is considerable security about the final safety of our minds and bodies. Though we may be threatened with death by all sorts of violent means, these threats do not come from within. There is no paranoia here about the fundamental stability of humanity itself, and, perhaps not surprisingly, no cases in which the threat is not successfully averted. This is not to say that human beings bear no responsibility; the other distinctive characteristic of the period is its emphasis on dependence rather than autonomy. Though the locus of the threat may not be within us, it is usually dependent on human actions.

The scale of this imbalance may be seen in table 3.1 (figures in brackets represent percentages of the total).

Table 3.1  Sources of threat in horror movies of the classic period, 1931–1936

|          | Dependent | Autonomous | Total |
|----------|-----------|------------|-------|
| External | 17 (55%)  | 7 (23%)    | 24 (78%) |
| Internal | 5 (16%)   | 2 (6%)     | 7 (22%) |
| Total    | 22 (71%)  | 9 (29%)    | 31 (100%) |

As the table shows, the external/dependent type overwhelms all else, and I shall begin by considering some of the films that fall within this category. I shall follow that with discussion of the external/autonomous group and conclude by considering all the internal cases together.

EXTERNAL/DEPENDENT (55 PER CENT)

The most common films here, of course, are mad-scientist movies, and certainly the best-known articulations of such themes are those rooted in the Frankenstein story: *Frankenstein* (1932) and *The Bride of Frankenstein* (1935). *Frankenstein* typifies many elements subsequently fundamental to mad scientist/monstrous creation movies:

1 The scientist who is obsessed with, and consumed by, his work, and who seeks and seems to have mastered the 'secret of life itself'.

2 His creation who, by accident or design (in *Frankenstein* as a consequence of the unknowing implantation of a 'criminal brain'), turns out to be monstrous and malevolent.

3 A visibly crippled assistant or aged retainer (to varying degrees a contrast to the 'perfection' envisaged in creating life) who is often instrumental in initiating the creature's rampage.

4 The younger male and female characters who constitute the film's 'threatened innocents', often (as in *Frankenstein*) paid only desultory attention in the actual realization of the film.

5 The laboratory setting, frequently contained within an isolated castle or mansion, and filled with elaborate pseudo-scientific apparatus.

6 A surrounding environment (Hollywood nineteenth-century mid-European), which provides both representatives of existing bourgeois authority (police chiefs, judges, physicians) and a population of potential victims who finally rise, *en masse*, against the threat.

Both *Frankenstein* and *The Bride of Frankenstein* follow this basic pattern, though the latter displaces the true 'mad scientist' role onto Dr Pretorious, and turns Frankenstein and his wife into the romantic leads. Whatever the variations, however, it is significant that the *formal* locus of identification, the 'good' characters, are lent rather less narrative and emotional credibility than are the notional villains of the piece. In both films this extends as far as the creature itself, wringing pathos from its more childlike actions. In this, Karloff's, version of it, the Frankenstein monster is given its most sympathetic portrayal.

Other mad-scientist movies are similar, though they do not carry the overt appeal for sympathy quite as far as *Frankenstein*. *Dr X* (1932), for example, boasts some of the most elaborate 'scientific' sets of the period, betraying a mixture of design influences from both German cinema and art deco. The film revolves around a series of murders, apparently involving cannibalism, which prove to be a consequence of experiments in the creation of synthetic flesh. The research is conducted by a dedicated group of scientists, working in a large mansion (though set in the American present rather than the mid-European past of *Frankenstein*) complete with an aged retainer. The obligatory romantic interest is provided by the principal scientist's daughter and, not uncommon in the thirties and forties, an investigating reporter. As always with such movies, *Dr X* exploits the tension between what may be properly done in the name of science and the impact of obsessive research on those involved in it. As the film's mysterious retainer observes: 'The human mind will only stand so much – we're all a bit strange up here.' It is that 'strangeness', bred of science, which is at the heart of so many of these movies; a fear that human values will be sacrificed in the untrammelled search for knowledge.

Most such classic-period films follow this general pattern, though there are some mad-scientist movies in which the dangers of science itself are largely unremarked. In *The Raven* (1935), for example, Bela Lugosi plays a surgeon whose actions are informed as much by inherent evil as by an obsessive concern with knowledge, while in *The Invisible Ray* (1936), Karloff's scientist is driven insane by the substance ('Radium X') that he discovers. In both cases the direct threat of science is covert in comparison with *Frankenstein*, although it is never entirely absent.

All the external/dependent cases in which the threat is secular revolve around mad-scientist themes, even if some (*The Devil Doll* (1936), *The Vampire Bat* (1933), *Murders in the Rue Morgue* (1932)) inflect their science with other genre conventions. Most of the remaining external/dependent cases – those in which the threat is supernatural – revolve around a kind of mad scientist equivalent: the magician. Unlike scientists, however, most horror-movie magicians of this period are unremittingly evil. While some ambiguity is permitted with science (science is presumed to have 'good' qualities, even if it does subvert the moral awareness of its exponents), almost none is apparent in the treatment of magically created threats. Thus, the mummy itself in *The Mummy* (1932) and the presumed Satanist of *The Black Cat* (1934) are represented as having no redeeming features.

EXTERNAL/AUTONOMOUS (23 PER CENT)

After the external/dependent all other categories are numerically minor, and will be treated only briefly here. The external/autonomous is composed mainly of vampire movies along with two secular cases: *King Kong* (1933) and its sequel, *Son of Kong* (1934). The orthodox pattern of the vampire movie was set in 1931 by *Dracula*, and its basic elements are simpler even than those found in mad-scientist movies: the vampire who terrorizes the surrounding countryside, whether Transylvania, Yorkshire, London or, later, the USA; the 'young innocents' who are caught up as potential victims, particularly the females; the expert, classically Professor Van Helsing, who is the only character capable of defeating the threat; and, of course, all the familiar apparatus of movie vampire-lore. *Dracula's Daughter* (1936) roughly follows this model; so does *Mark of the Vampire* (1935), except that it closes its narrative by the improbable expedient of exposing the seemingly supernatural as a cunningly constructed plot designed to solve a crime. *Condemned to Live* (1935), however, differs in being centred on a basically sympathetic character who is unaware of his own vampirism. Unusually for a vampire movie, he finally commits suicide in company with his faithful servant.

The three mainstream cases also exhibit the sexual overtones so common in vampire movies, with a hint of lesbianism appearing for the first time in *Dracula's Daughter*, where the female vampire's taste for young women combines with the conventionally sexualized image of the sucking and biting vampire. It is tempting to suggest that the fears central to many such horror-movies are metaphorical representations of deep-seated concerns about sexuality; and, more particularly, that 'supernature' itself is an expression of dimly understood desires which we experience as seemingly 'external' forces. Certainly, this does make some sense in the external/autonomous films: even the giant ape's celebrated passion for Fay Wray in *King Kong* could not be described as sexually neutral. However, sexuality is not yet foregrounded in the genre, as it will be in subsequent periods, and it would be over-exercising interpretative license to make this more than a passing suggestion at this stage. The matter will be discussed at greater length in chapter 8.

INTERNAL (22 PER CENT)

There are few films in the 'internal' category, and not all of them present a threat that is unambiguously internal. Consider *White Zombie* (1932), for example. It incorporates several features apparent in the mad-scientist tradition − an isolated castle (in Haiti), the young couple, mysterious servants − as well as a voodoo zombie-master. Rejoicing in the delightful name of 'Murder Legendre', he turns the film's heroine into a zombie (herein lies the internality of the threat) at the request of a rich plantation owner who desires her for himself. In fact, Legendre has his own purposes (the plantation owner also becomes his victim), though apart from his satisfaction at exercising power for its own sake they are never entirely clear. That there is an underlying sexual element to his domination, however, can hardly be doubted. In turning Madeline into a zombie he makes her entirely compliant to his will, although nowhere does the film fully draw out the implications of that absolute power.

*White Zombie* is a mixed type, combining a conventional external source (manipulated supernature) with an internal locus of threat. The fact that the heroine herself becomes the victim emphasizes the element of internality (not present, for example, in the later *Revolt of the Zombies* (1936)), though with nothing like the force found in the zombie movies of later periods. Similar considerations apply to most films focusing upon forced metamorphoses: the degree of internality of the threat varies in line with different narrative strategies. In *The Werewolf of London* (1935), for instance, much emphasis is placed upon the accidentally infected werewolf's anguish at his state, and on his attempts to eliminate the consequent threat to others. This characteristic internality (characteristic, that is, in the werewolf tradition) generates certain rhetorical possibilities which play upon our sympathy for the plight of the creature, a strategy also found in films like *Dr Jekyll and Mr Hyde* (1932), where the focus of our concerns is as much the metamorphant's anguish as it is the rampage of his monstrous *alter ego*. In contrast to later developments, emphasis on internality in the early horror-movie is often combined with a sympathetic treatment of the 'infected' character. Even madmen like Ivan Igor in *The Mystery of the Wax Museum* (1933) are accorded some sympathy because of the circumstances of their insanity.

In summary, then, the classic period is overwhelmingly dominated by external threats derived from the actions of human beings. In most cases disorder is rooted in an obsessive search for knowledge, particularly through the medium of medical science, though in a small number of films science, like magic, is simply a way of achieving power. Here, the magician or scientist has not been corrupted in the search for knowledge; he is simply presumed to be evil. In both types, however, the fundamental character of the movie world is clear enough. Knowledge, above all scientific knowledge, is dangerous: even in moral and apparently responsible hands it can lead to disaster.

In the minority of films in which the threat is supernatural, the basic ordering relations are more ambiguous. Though some part of the fears articulated in these films may well rest on a presumed belief in the 'reality' of these alternative supernatural domains, there is also some reason to think that supernatural threats metaphorically externalize other features of human experience – in particular, that the power of human sexuality plays a role analogous to that of 'the lust for knowledge' in classic mad-scientist movies. Lastly, the period's very few examples of internality operate mainly to evoke our sympathy for the monster, whose responsibility is thus limited.

## The War Years: 1941–1946

The war period is *the* period of American B-pictures, the period when Universal – always the dominant influence in the early years of the genre – was joined by 'Poverty Row' studios like Republic and Monogram. Never heavily resourced, the genre in these years is dominated by the cheap quickie: second-feature vehicles for established horror-movie performers like Karloff and Lugosi. Partly because of the obvious financial limitations, the German Style is less apparent in the forties. Though there do remain some cases of 'expressionist' visuals the newly dominant style is straightforwardly naturalistic. Thus, although many of the thematic emphases of the classic period continue into the forties, they are no longer expressed in a style evoking mystery and inexplicable threat. Perhaps only in the films produced by Val Lewton at RKO does the distinctive use of light and shade play its once-familiar role.

In most other respects, though, the war period simply extends the patterns already established in the thirties, in some cases to desperate limits. In such films as *Frankenstein Meets the Wolf Man* and *House of Frankenstein* (both 1946), characters made familiar during the previous decade are thrown together in a pot-pourri of borrowed story-lines, bent genre conventions, and familiar horror-movie performers. *House of Frankenstein* is worth describing in full, if only because it so well represents the period's characteristic tendency towards lunatic excess. It gives us Karloff as an archetypical mad scientist, newly escaped from languishing in prison for trying to transplant the brain of a man into a dog. Fleeing in company with a convicted killer (J. Carrol Naish), he encounters Count Dracula, staked; removing the stake he engages the grateful vampire (John Carradine) as an instrument of revenge against those who had him imprisoned (among others, George Zucco and Lionel Atwill). Dracula perishes in sunlight, while Karloff and company (now including a gypsy dancer) travel on, finally arriving at Frankenstein's ruined laboratory. Discovering both the Wolf Man (Lon Chaney) and the Frankenstein monster (Glenn Strange) frozen in an ice cavern, Karloff sets about resuscitating them, with the inevitable consequence that werewolf and monster embark upon the expected rampage. The dancer (by now in love with the werewolf's human manifestation) is obliged to kill the wolf, and all is resolved when mad scientist and Frankenstein monster are pursued into a local bog by the furious Transylvanian peasantry.

Though no other forties film reaches quite these heights of absurdity – *House of Dracula* makes a valiant effort but, though produced by Universal in 1945, I shall not consider it here since it did not arrive in Britain until the fifties – *House of Frankenstein* is symptomatic of the period's lack of inspiration. Both invention and finance had flagged, and many forties horror movies were undoubtedly seen by audiences as second-rate programme-fillers. This was not a period of genre innovation; therefore it is hardly surprising that the overall pattern is broadly consistent with that of the thirties. Externality still dominates: though the gross figures suggest some rise in the number of films posing an internal threat, this needs to be seriously qualified. A significant number of apparent cases of internality are on the extreme margins of the genre. There are eight such films, and table 3.2 is to be read with that qualification in mind.

Table 3.2   Sources of threat in horror movies of the war years, 1941−1946

|          | *Dependent* | *Autonomous* | Total |
|----------|-------------|--------------|-------|
| *External* | 25 (45%) | 12 (22%) | 37 (67%) |
| *Internal* | 5 (9%) | 13 (24%) | 18 (33%) |
| Total | 30 (54%) | 25 (46%) | 55 (100%) |

As before, I shall briefly consider the most numerous subgroupings suggested by table 3.2: external/dependent, external/autonomous, and internal.

EXTERNAL/DEPENDENT (45 PER CENT)

Predictably, the majority of external/dependent cases are secular in emphasis (18), and most of those are mad-scientist movies of one sort or another. However, they rarely match the narrative and thematic complexity of the thirties originals and almost never aspire to the German-influenced visual style of the earlier period. Even the one overt variation on the Frankenstein story (discounting wild amalgams like *House of Frankenstein)* drifts towards formula repetition. *The Ghost of Frankenstein* (1942) takes up where *Son of Frankenstein* (1939) left off, though without the latter film's strikingly Germanic sets and, indeed, without Karloff in the role that he played in all the thirties versions. *Ghost of Frankenstein* does retain many of the standard ingredients − elaborate laboratory sets, threatened innocents, a crippled servant − but it never fully exploits the tension between the positive and corrupting features of science foregrounded in earlier versions. There is still some attempt to generate sympathy for the monster, particularly in relation to the little girl who befriends it, but without the more resonant narrative context of the earlier films.

Most mad-scientist movies of the war period are, like *Ghost of Frankenstein*, simplifications of the classic model. They remain medical in emphasis, often concerned somehow to bridge the evolutionary gap between ape and human. No less than five of them involve ape− human transformations or transplants: *The Ape* (1941), *Dr Renault's Secret* (1946), *Jungle Captive* (1946 − in this case an ape-woman), *The Monster and the Girl* (1941) and *The Monster Walks* (1941). Others, typified by *The Devil Bat* (1941), concern themselves with monstrous creations of varying plausibility (here, giant bats), while one small group begins to develop slightly different variations on the traditional mad scientist story. *The Electric Man* (1941), for example, has Lon Chaney as a survivor of an electric train crash who is able to absorb electricity. The subject of experimentation, he becomes super-human, even soaking up the charge from an electric chair. *The Devil Commands* (1941) involves its scientist (Karloff again) in attempts to communicate with the dead; *The Man With Two Lives* (1942) has a murderer's soul in the body of a man who is operated upon to restore life; and *The Mad Ghoul* (1946) revolves around a newly discovered poison gas which creates a state of death-in-life. Of this latter the *Monthly Film Bulletin* observed: 'scarcely a film to be recommended to those seeking pleasant relaxation after six years of total war'.[2] Given their straightforward naturalism and their often somewhat morbid concerns, much the same might be said of any of this period's mad-scientist movies.

Most of the remaining external/dependent cases are supernatural, involving some appeal to magic or witchcraft. Elements of this are found in *The Seventh Victim* (1944), *The Soul of a Monster* (1945) and *The Woman Who Came Back* (1946), but apart from some ambiguity about the nature of the supernatural forces involved (later to become an important source of tension in witchcraft films) and a tendency to feature women as central characters, there is no real pattern apparent within this group. There are also three descendents of the classically established 'Mummy' cycle in this period: *The Mummy's Hand* (1941), *The Mummy's Tomb* (1942) and *The Mummy's Curse* (1946). All retain some features of their thirties forerunner, but, like *The Ghost of Frankenstein*, they are somewhat formulaic repetitions. Though still displaying a degree of visual stylization, they mostly share the commercially enforced 'naturalism' of this under-resourced period.

The sense of mystery classically conveyed through visual style all but disappeared from supernatural movies of the war years, either by choice or from financial necessity. Their supernature is far more prosaic than that of the previous decade, and at its least plausible it teeters on the edge of the totally absurd. *The Mummy's Curse*, with its pedestrian narration and ill-fated attempt at 'poetic' speech ('the hours of darkness do not linger' several times serves as an invocation to haste), must surely have provoked more laughter than thrills, and it is significant that the forties also see an increase in comedy/horror movies such as *The Boogie Man Will Get You* (1943) and *You'll Find Out* (1941).

EXTERNAL/AUTONOMOUS (22 PER CENT)

The vampire, once the dominant incarnation of external/autonomous supernature, is in retreat by the war years, which offer only three cases, all rather implausible variations upon the familiar themes. John Carradine's near-parody of Dracula in *House of Frankenstein* needs no further comment here. Of the other two vampire movies, one, *The Vampire's Ghost* (1946), transfers the basic narrative to a West African setting, while the other, *The Return of the Vampire* (1946), ingeniously has its vampire released when a German bomb exposes its London grave and an unsuspecting workman removes the stake. In none of these films is there any real sense of the powerful, external and covertly sexual malevolence commonly found in the classic period. The forties vampire has become yet another formula monster.

It is hardly surprising, then, that the vampire gives way to the ghost as the most significant threat in the external/autonomous category. Just as the mad-scientist movies of the period show an increasing concern with life after death and the restoration of life, so, too, ghosts rise to new prominence. They are found right across the range, from big-studio exercises in haunted-house atmospherics like *The Uninvited* (1944) to poverty row productions like PRC's *Strangler of the Swamp* (1946), taking in films as diverse as *Dead of Night* (1945), *Curse of the Cat People* (1944) and *The Unknown* (1946) along the way. Beyond their shared concern with ghosts, however, and therefore in several cases with haunted houses, these films have little in common. Viewed in context they do suggest a significant increase in interest in the life/death borderline, and accordingly in supernatural threats that seek to cross it — perhaps unsurprising in the wake of a world war.

Finally, there are only two films in this category in which the threat is fundamentally secular, and only one of them needs to be mentioned here. *Man and his Mate* (1943) stands at the beginning of a tradition which moves away from the horrific and towards films overtly directed at children. This prehistoric monster sub-genre, partly based on the early success of *King Kong*, was to expand in the fifties and sixties.

INTERNAL (33 PER CENT)

I have already suggested that the figures for 'internal' are potentially misleading. Overall, the pattern of internal threats is broadly similar to that of the classic period, its most interesting component revolving around metamorphoses of one sort or another. Apart from secondary roles in combination movies (there is a werewolf servant in *Return of the Vampire*, for instance), werewolves turn up in their own right in *Cry of the Werewolf* (1945) — where the werewolf is female for the first time — and in *The Wolf Man* (1942), which extends the classic model and establishes a number of conventions important in subsequent werewolf films. The period also includes a version of *Dr Jekyll and Mr Hyde* (1941), a big-budget production from MGM which is distinctive only in its attempt to graft crude Freudian ideas onto the traditional story.

Today the best-remembered films in the internal category are those produced by Val Lewton at RKO: *Cat People, The Leopard Man* and *I Walked with a Zombie*, all of which reached Britain in 1943. The reason for their fame is interesting. Many aesthetic histories single out these and other Lewton productions as the most significant horror movies of the period, thus revealing a perspective on the horror movie which places particular value upon lack of explicit nastiness, expressionistically inclined lighting and what might be termed 'literary' qualities. Seen in historical context, however, it is clear that the importance of the Lewton films was, and is, exaggerated because of these aesthetic commitments. Though they are skilful and effective movies, and though *Cat People*, in particular, retains the crucially important affinity between sexuality and supernature, they hardly represent a dominating and influential genre development. If anything they run counter to the main trends of the genre's subsequent years.

Little needs to be said by way of summary since the war period is not startlingly innovative. The primary threat given expression in these movies remains external, dependent and secular: it is that engendered by science, though generally shorn of the personalized corrupting potential found in the classic period. Science, like magic, is a likely source of monstrous threats, now not so much a consequence of attempts to *create* life as of attempts to recombine or modify existing forms. In this respect the war years evince a simplification of the concept of science fundamental to the classic period, though there are a few indications that a more generalized image of scientific practice is emerging. Supernatural threats also follow the classically established pattern, but with one significant change. Though treatment and style are resoundingly matter of fact in most films, ghosts and haunted houses enjoy a minor vogue.

## The Fifties Boom: 1956—1960

The fifties are widely recognized as the era when the idea of 'outer space' entered western popular culture. The horror movie is no exception to this development, and the boom of 1956 to 1960 includes 18 per cent of horror films based around invasion from space. Significantly, it is also a period in which supernature is minimally significant. The classic monsters of the thirties are almost entirely absent, and were it not for the renewal of that tradition wrought by the British production company, Hammer Films, in the late fifties, they would have no place at all. In this sense at least, this period is the most 'secular' in horror-movie history, and the characteristic style of many of these movies is the most flatly naturalistic to be encountered in the genre.

In both the classic period and the war years, autonomy/dependence and external/internal were the primary dimensions of variation. In the fifties this changes. The films of the fifties boom are divided almost equally between dependence and autonomy, and it is now the supernatural/secular division that encompasses most variation. There are no less than 117 (82 per cent) fifties boom films that propose secular sources for their threats, with only 25 invoking supernature. So instead of organizing discussion in terms of external/internal and autonomous/dependent, as was the case in the last two sections, it is now more helpful to use the supernatural/secular opposition as a major parameter. Combined with external/internal this gives rise to the following table.

Table 3.3  **Sources of threat in horror movies of the fifties boom,
1956—1960**

|  | *Supernatural* | *Secular* | Total |
|---|---|---|---|
| *External* | 21 (15%) | 88 (62%) | 109 (77%) |
| *Internal* | 4 (3%) | 29 (20%) | 33 (23%) |
| Total | 25 (18%) | 117 (82%) | 142 (100%) |

The overwhelming importance of the secular, on a scale far in excess of anything seen in the previous two decades, is immediately apparent from table 3.3. Though secular threats were more frequent than supernatural in both the earlier phases, they were only marginally so.

In the classic period the relevant figures are 58 per cent secular to 42 per cent supernatural; in the war period 56 per cent to 44 per cent; and in the fifties boom 82 per cent to 18 per cent. This expansion is primarily a consequence of the prominence of 'science' in the films of the fifties boom, and it is with this central aspect that I shall begin in considering the external/secular category. For clarity of presentation I shall sub-divide this group into dependent and autonomous, and then discuss the internal/secular and the supernatural at much less length.

EXTERNAL/SECULAR (62 PER CENT)

## Dependent

Of the 88 external/secular cases, 47 also conceptualise their threat as dependent upon human intervention. As ever, the major articulation of the external/secular/dependent threat is the 'mad scientist', though the Frankenstein model (with its overtones of blasphemy and mental anguish) is almost entirely absent. Frankenstein himself, however, does reappear during the fifties boom in a new and subsequently influential guise. In 1957 a small British production company which had experienced some success two years earlier with a SF/horror film, *The Quatermass Experiment*, released *The Curse of Frankenstein*. As popular with audiences as it was subject to hysterical condemnation by critics (C. A. Lejeune of *The Observer* 'apologised' to American audiences on Britain's behalf), *The Curse of Frankenstein* began a new period in the history of the horror movie, though its real significance was not to be apparent until well into the sixties.

  *The Curse of Frankenstein* is more fully discussed in chapter 7. For the present it is necessary only to observe that the Baron (played here, and on several other occasions, by Peter Cushing) is more ruthlessly obsessed than many of his predecessors, and that gruesome detail presented in strong primary colours is strikingly apparent. This explicitness, in the absence of any portentous and justificatory moralizing, provoked much of the controversy attendant upon both this film and Hammer's version of *Dracula* which followed it. As one review characteristically observed, *The Curse of Frankenstein* exhibits 'a preoccupation with disgusting – not horrific – charnelry'. Ignoring the implicit evaluation, there is no doubt that one of *The Curse of Frankenstein's* innovatory features was its graphic display of 'gory' detail. Combined with effective direction, design and acting, their willingness to push visual horror one step further made Hammer's newly emergent style massively successful. Theirs was to prove the first major genre innovation since the thirties.

Hammer followed up a year later with *The Revenge of Frankenstein*, its bigger budget permitting more elaborate laboratory designs and more carefully orchestrated effects. There is, for instance, a very striking scene in which the Baron demonstrates the capabilities of a brain, a pair of eyes and a hand stored in individual tanks: the eyes watch a bunsen burner move toward the hand, and the hand moves in response. It was such attention to detail ('sordid detail' as some insisted) that distinguished the new Hammer idiom. However, theirs was not yet the dominant vision of the horror-movie mad scientist, and other nominal Frankenstein movies are more typical of the fifties. In *Teenage Frankenstein*, for instance, or *Frankenstein 1970* (both 1958) the frame of reference derives from mad-scientist movies of the war years along with the science-fiction concerns of so many fifties horror movies. *Teenage Frankenstein* (its original title better suggests its partly humorous intent: *I Was a Teenage Frankenstein*) tells a messily absurd story of a modern-day Frankenstein who sets out to construct a teenager. It is not easy to take the film seriously (in notable contrast to Hammer's films, which could hardly be read other than seriously), a feature reinforced by such splendid lines as 'I know you've got a civil tongue in your head because I sewed it there myself.' Compared to this, it's hardly surprising that *The Curse of Frankenstein* seemed so startling to fifties audiences.

Though such B-picture pastiche is an element in many mad-scientist movies of the fifties boom, it is not their dominant characteristic. Several are straightforward extensions of trends already apparent 10 years earlier, though usually now set in the present rather than in an imaginary nineteenth-century Europe. In *The Unearthly* (1959), the mad scientist seeks the secret of eternal life, producing a cellar full of failures along the way. A similar concern to prolong life is found in *The Man Who Could Cheat Death* (1959) and *The Man Who Turned to Stone* (1957), while in *The Creature with the Atom Brain* (1956) and *Womaneater* (1958) the aim is to resurrect the dead. All these mad medicos have clear enough roots in earlier periods, though there are detailed differences in the kinds of 'science' they use. In *The Man Who Turned to Stone*, for instance, scientists prolong their lives by absorbing 'bioelectrical energy' from their victims, while in *The*

*Creature With the Atom Brain*, radiation is used to raise the dead. This concern with radiation is a major feature, and many movies invoke some kind of nuclear threat.

Perhaps the classic mad scientist of these years, however, is André in *The Fly* (1958). Though he is obsessed with his work, the work itself is not morally problematic in the conventional way of mad-scientist movies. Instead, this threat arises by accident. His research is into matter transference, and when a fly accidentally enters the apparatus, it produces a man with a fly's head and arm, and a fly symmetrically endowed with human features. In minor respects, then, *The Fly* invokes a partly internal threat. However, it is not this, but ambiguity about the scientist's culpability which is the film's most interesting feature. Though science and the scientist are the single most prominent source of threat in the fifties boom, they are often more sympathetically treated than hitherto, and in *The Fly* much of the film's undoubted power stems from our capacity to identify with André's plight.[3]

In line with this apparently changing view of science, a significant number of films loosen the direct link between science, scientists and the threat that they produce. In *Beginning of the End* (1960), for example, giant locusts are a consequence of *accidental* exposure to atomically irradiated plants. They are finally eliminated with the aid of the scientist whose work occasioned the accident in the first place. A similar stretching of the causal sequence is apparent in both *The Killer Shrews* (1959) and *Tarantula* (1956), where greatly enlarged natural creatures also constitute the major threat, while an even more elaborate sequence of accidents produces the fiend of *The Fiend Without a Face* (1959). A scientist experimenting with 'materialized thought' inadvertently creates a monster nourished by energy from a local atomic plant.

Such films as these, and others like *First Man into Space* (1959) and *The Amazing Colossal Man* (1958), both of which centre on science-based accidents, weaken the element of dependence traditional to scientific threats. In some ways they assimilate traditional horror-movie conceptions of mad science to a specifically fifties emphasis on external, secular, *autonomous* threats.

## Autonomous

This, perhaps more than anything else, is the unique contribution of the period: a body of films in which the threat is firmly beyond our control, but still entirely secular. There are 41 such films (as compared to two each in the classic and war periods) and their most dramatic expression is in movies centred on invasion from space. A few are quite strongly internal in their emphasis, but for the most part a straightforward, malevolent externality is the order of the day.

Many such films involve invasion with a view to 'conquering the earth', though some simply use space travel as yet another source of rampaging monsters. Thus, in *Twenty Million Miles to Earth* (1957) the monster is a fast-growing lizard-like creature accidentally brought to earth in a returning space shot; in *The Monster from Green Hell* (1957) experimental wasps sent out in a rocket are returned much enlarged; and in *First Man Into Space* (1959) the pilot himself comes back as a vampiric killer. Such narratives always follow the generic pattern for simple monster movies, usually with some combination of scientific know-how and military strength finally stopping the rampage. It is rare to find a space monster undefeated — though the large red jelly of *The Blob* (1959) is only frozen into submission, its fate left open by the jokily suggestive question mark which ends the film.

More subtly motivated invaders are treated similarly, though the supposition of intentionality on the part of an invading force clearly opens up wider narrative possibilities. Monsters simply rampage; invaders can be much more devious than that. Their most common strategy is some form of mental control of human beings, the external sign of which is dehumanization. Where the dehumanization itself becomes the major source of narrative drive (as it is, for example, in *Invasion of the Body Snatchers* (1956)) the threat is more properly conceptualized as internal. Most fifties films do not go that far, however, suggesting that the invader's control is spreading through dehumanization, but without making that the central emphasis. This is the case with, among others, *Quatermass II* (1957), *It Conquered the World* (1956) and *The Brain Eaters* (1959). Other invaders may work under cover (as in *Not of this Earth* (1957) which is one of the few films of the period to leave its narrative unresolved), or they may pretend to be friendly before launching an all-out attack, as is the case in *The Mysterians* (1959). Yet others remain unintelligible except in their apparent desire for domination, such as the great obelisks of *The Monolith Monsters* (1958), the mysterious object in *The Beast with a Million Eyes* (1956) and the creatures in the cloud of *The Trollenberg Terror* (1958). Whatever the specific variation, however, the films all share a concern with the threat posed by invasion itself rather than with simple attack by rampaging monsters. In other words, the fear articulated here is focused upon a threat to our 'way of life' as much as to our persons. Monsters may kill us; invaders want to take over. This is a significantly new development, trading as it does on a social as well as a personal fear, and it has persuaded many observers to suggest a link between these films and the 'communist conspiracy' ethos of the period.[4]

The remainder of the external/secular/autonomous cases are variously straightforward monster movies. There is a distinct subgroup in which the threat is somehow occasioned by atomic energy: the creatures of *Godzilla* (1957), *Rodan* (1958) and *Gigantis the Fire Monster* (1960) are all awakened or resurrected as a consequence of nuclear explosions. (It is not insignificant that these are all Japanese films; many Japanese horror movies share a concern with nuclear power.) Otherwise, threats can emerge from almost any source: prehistoric monsters (*The Lost World* (1960), *The Land Unknown* (1958), *The Deadly Mantis* (1957)); mutations (*Attack of the Crab Monsters* (1957), *The Black Scorpion* (1958)); or just plain overgrown nasties like the magnified delights of *The Spider* (1959) or *The Giant Gila Monster* (1960). Invariably they follow the familiar threat—rampage—combat sequence until the monster is finally destroyed.

INTERNAL/SECULAR (20 PER CENT)

There are half a dozen cases of 'invasion from space' which focus on the occupation or simulation of human beings. In the classic example, *Invasion of the Body Snatchers* (1956), the invaders replicate humans, replacing the originals with emotionless copies. It is an interesting reflection of perceived pressures for closure in narratives of this period that the film's original ending − the 'pods' taking over everywhere and our hero unable to convince anyone that the threat is real − was changed before distribution. In the distributed version the authorities accept his story and begin to act against the invasion, a resolution in line with all other examples of this type, where victory over the invader is invariably assured. Thus, the body occupiers of *Invisible Invaders* (1960) are vanquished using high frequency sound; the brain in *The Brain from Planet Arous* (1959) is dispatched with an axe; and the monsters of *I Married a Monster from Outer Space* (1959) are repulsed with the aid of hunting dogs. In most cases invaders are represented as entirely deserving their fate, though one film − *Night of the Blood Beast* (1959) − intimates that its otherwise standard invader is actually seeking to save the world from self-imposed nuclear annihilation.

The second major internal/secular subgroup focuses upon metamorphosis. Virtually all these films posit scientifically caused metamorphoses, including a werewolf created by radiation experiments (*The Werewolf* (1956)), and a pair of metamorphants who suffer side-effects of medical treatment: *The Alligator People* (1959) and *The Wasp Woman* (1960). Other variations, edging nearer to the supernatural, invoke hypnosis, regressing their subjects to a primitive state, as in *I Was a Teenage Werewolf* (1957), or even into a prehistoric monster in *The She-Creature* (1956). Lastly, and perhaps inevitably, the Jekyll/Hyde theme is taken up by Hammer in *The Two Faces of Dr Jekyll* (1960), telling the familiar story in their characteristic style. Otherwise, and apart from the 'scientification' of traditionally supernatural monsters (especially the werewolf, which also turns up in *The Daughter of Dr Jekyll* (1957)), metamorphant movies show no particular pattern or distinctive innovation.

Much the same observation might be made of those internal/secular films that depict insanity, whether in the trappings of melodrama as in *The Fall of the House of Usher* (1960), or in 'old dark house' settings like *House on Haunted Hill* (1960). The latter was one of the first horror movies to use an extra-cinematic marketing gimmick: a plastic skeleton that rattled across the auditorium on a wire. 'Emergo', as the system was called, was not a strikingly successful shock effect, though as a publicity enterprise it clearly had its virtues. But for the most part, the madmen of the fifties boom are straightforward extensions of the melodramatic figures of earlier years. The two crucial exceptions to that generalization, however, *Peeping Tom* and *Psycho* (both 1960), proved to be forerunners of the horror movie sub-genre that was to dominate much of the next three decades. Both films will be more fully considered in chapter 9; here I shall mention only two of their distinctive attributes. First, their psychotic killers are represented in such a way as to emphasize the psychological roots of their disorders. This is not simply a question of the films offering overt psychological explanations, though they both do so with different degrees of conviction. It is, rather, a feature of their treatment of internality, a sense of these men's psychosis as *potentially* present within any of us. This connects in both films to a second important feature. The psychosis that afflicts the two characters is, overtly and metaphorically, linked to sex. Both are shown taking gratification from voyeurism, and their principal killings are laden with sexual connotations. *Psycho* and *Peeping Tom*, then, introduce a loose equation between sexuality, repression and psychosis, and in so doing lay the foundations for a new kind of movie monster.

SUPERNATURAL (18 PER CENT)

There are very few supernatural threats in the fifties boom and the vast majority of them are external in emphasis. The single largest group features vampires, including the first two Hammer vampire movies, *Dracula* (1958) and *The Brides of Dracula* (1960). Both films are set in Hammer's newly refurbished vision of the classic Transylvanian castle, and *Dracula* (considered in more detail in chapter 8) partly returns to Bram Stoker for its inspiration. A considerable commercial success, it exhibits an even richer visual style than was apparent in *The Curse of Frankenstein*. The same attention to gory detail, the same emphasis on reds and blues, the same carefully constructed decor, make *Dracula* look just as innovatory as its immediate predecessor. Its influence – particularly Christopher Lee's suave, ruthless and sensual Count – was to be very strong in the vampire movies of the next decade.

Most of the other vampire movies of this period are amalgams or extensions of other prevailing themes. Thus, *Curse of the Undead* (1959) finds its vampire in a Western township; *The Fantastic Disappearing Man* (1958) places him in the body of a fugitive from behind the Iron Curtain; while *Blood is my Heritage* (1958) gives us a schoolgirl vampire magically created by her chemistry mistress. In effect, these films are the final despairing efforts of the failing American tradition.

Other than vampire movies there is little of interest within the supernatural category. There are several films posing threats by witchcraft or magic, the most notable of which is *Night of the Demon* (1958). This film, made by Jacques Tourneur in the 'threat by suggestion' style familiar from his forties work for Val Lewton, was amended by its producers to include explicit shots of the demon itself. Whatever the aesthetic impact on the film (the orthodox consensus is that these sequences fail), this addition is symptomatic of the late fifties trend toward graphically presented horrific detail. Unsurprisingly, this is also apparent in the Hammer 1959 version of *The Mummy*, which rehashes the familiar story, but beyond that most of the period's supernatural movies simply rework old traditions, ranging from voodoo to feline metamorphosis, and from possessive spirits to, in one case, a vengeance-seeking ghostly tree-stump!

The boom years, then, are appropriately summarized by the external/secular label. Whether generated by science, by radiation, by invasion from space or by plain monstrous accident, the threats of the fifties come from 'beyond' to assail us in our everyday lives. The dominant style of the period is naturalistic, at times almost documentary. The fears articulated here, compared to those of earlier periods, are firmly this-worldly, an expression, perhaps, of collective concerns with invasion, communism and the atomic bomb. Nevertheless, there are signs of change as the decade ends. On the one hand, the newly enriched Gothic cinema just beginning to emerge in Hammer Films, in Roger Corman's Poe cycle, and in the work of their Italian imitators, was once more to shift the horror movie away from the everyday and secular. On the other hand, the psychotic excesses (and commercial successes) of *Psycho* and *Peeping Tom* were to redirect one stream of the genre very strongly into the everyday and into the dangers posed by our unpredictable psyches. In effect, from collective fears about threatening forces somewhere 'out there', the horror movie was moving towards a twin conception of malevolent super- and psychic-nature. It is that development which forms the major topic for chapter 4's history.

## Notes

1 There are a number of reasons for the flow of German film-makers into the USA in the twenties and thirties, not least a deliberate attempt on the part of the expanding American industry to undermine its most powerful European competitor by buying up its talent.
2 *Monthly Film Bulletin*, 13, 1 (1946), p. 17.
3 There is a fuller discussion of *The Fly* and of this ambiguity in chapter 7.
4 One of the most interesting discussions of this much-invoked theme is to be found in Peter Biskind, *Seeing is Believing* (London, 1984), which explores the idea in relation to a wide range of Hollywood films.

# 4

## *Genre History II: 1961—1984*

While the horror movies of the first three decades revolve around the twin poles of science and supernature, and their monsters threaten us largely, though not entirely, from 'outside', the second three decades bring the genre's central threat much closer to us. In these years the horror movie begins to articulate a radically different type of anxiety. The threat posed by post-1960 horror movies can be seen as expressing a profound insecurity about ourselves, and accordingly the monsters of the period are increasingly represented as part of an everyday contemporary landscape. That is why of all horror movie creatures it is the psychotic that is pre-eminent. We have long since ceased to derive open amusement from the insane (as did the curious visitors to Bedlam and other early institutions), and we no longer accept the quasi-mystical accounts of madness that serve to insulate and protect people from their fears of insanity in so many societies. In a word — and this is a gross simplification — our characteristic view of insanity has been secularized, returned to us. The conceptual revolution associated with Freud's name, if not with the detail of his work, opens up a whole new realm of fear: fear of ourselves and of the ill-understood and dangerous forces that lurk within us.

It is important to recognize that this is a matter of emphasis; the modern genre is not exhausted by psycho-movies. Nevertheless, the underlying argument of this chapter does suggest a change in the fundamental constitution of the horror movie, a shift which has an impact throughout the genre, not just on horror-movie psychosis. In chapter 10 I shall consider the significance of this change in more detail. Here I shall simply try to document both the changing and the stable elements, following a similar plan to that of chapter 3. That is, I shall take each of the three phases in turn — American Decline

1963–1966, Seventies Boom 1971–1974, Sustained Growth 1978–
1983 – and consider the most significant sub-groups of films within
each. First, though, a word of warning. To give a detailed history of
the modern genre is an enormous task, and this chapter, like the
history it recounts, is both long and tangled.

## American Decline: 1963–1966

In chapter 3 I suggested that the end of the fifties saw the beginning
of a return to the supernatural as an important source of horror
movie threats. This trend continues during the years of American
decline, although secular threats, at 66 per cent of the total, do still
dominate. Most variation in this period can be ordered in terms of
the supernatural/secular and external/internal distinctions. Accordingly, the basic categories for this section's analysis are the same as
those applied to the fifties boom.

Table 4.1  Sources of threat in horror movies of the period of American
decline, 1963–1966

|  | Supernatural | Secular | Total |
|---|---|---|---|
| *External* | 29 (28%) | 32 (32%) | 61 (60%) |
| *Internal* | 6 (6%) | 35 (34%) | 41 (40%) |
| Total | 35 (34%) | 67 (66%) | 102 (100%) |

The most immediately striking feature of this table is that in 34 per
cent of films the internal/secular constitutes the primary focus, and it
is with these that I shall begin, followed by briefer analyses of the
external/secular and the supernatural.

### INTERNAL/SECULAR (34 PER CENT)

The single largest group of films within this category (more than half
of them) focuses upon madness, whether real or contrived. Although
*Psycho*'s success may have been the precipitating factor, it is notable
that these movies are not uniform copies of Hitchcock's film. They
take their inspiration from a variety of sources both within and
beyond the genre. Grand Guignol, the 'old dark house' tradition,
investigative thrillers and psychological trickery of the type made

famous in *Les Diaboliques* all combine in the characteristic psycho-movies of this period. As befits what is, essentially, a time of transition, no single line of development absolutely dominates the horror movie's representation of insanity in the mid-sixties. The genre appears to 'test out' a variety of possibilities without finally settling into one clear pattern. I shall describe some of the more common variations.

Although those Hammer movies with carefully contrived one word titles — *Paranoiac* (1963), *Maniac* (1963), *Fanatic (1965), Hysteria* (1965) — may recall Hitchcock's film in this aspect, and although that fact may well have framed the expectations of their audiences, the films themselves bear only the broadest resemblance to *Psycho*. Three of them (written by Jimmy Sangster and shot in monochrome) are elaborate psychological thrillers with 'surprise' twists at their ends: their plots hinge on persuading a central character to believe a cunningly constructed fiction. In this respect they owe more to *Les Diaboliques* than to *Psycho*, and they follow the pattern successfully set by Hammer's first expedition into this territory: *Taste of Fear* (1961).

The fourth of the set, *Fanatic*, is rather different in that it is in colour and lacks the elaborate plotting of the other three. If *Paranoiac* and the rest require our involvement in terms of the arcane complexities of their narratives, *Fanatic* engages us more at the level of our concern for the well-being of its central victim. Patricia, arriving at a lonely country house to meet the mother of her deceased fiancé, finds herself steadily forced to submit to the older woman's insane will. The mother is played to the hilt by Tallulah Bankhead, not the first former Hollywood leading lady to find a role as a repressed and aging psychotic in sixties horror movies. Though the insane in these Grand Guignol enterprises are not always entirely what they seem, it is a significant feature of the period that Bette Davis (*Hush...Hush Sweet Charlotte* and *The Nanny* (both 1965)) and Joan Crawford (*Straight-Jacket* (1964)) were able to further extend the 'crazed' images they so successfully articulated in *Whatever Happened to Baby Jane?* (1962). Though overlaid with other characteristics (not least because the Davis and Crawford vehicles depend upon the same contrived plotting and surprise twists as the Hammer psychological thrillers), there is an element of *Psycho*'s Mrs Bates (Norman's mother) in this concern with aging female psychopaths. In both *Fanatic* and *The Psychopath* (1966), for instance, the primary threat lies in the destructive psychosis of a possessive mother, and more generally in these movies there is often some sense of family-based potential for insanity. Psychosis, as it does in *Psycho*, grows from the past mistakes and excesses of intimate family history.

This is also apparent in some of the 'old dark house' variations, in many of which the skeletons in the family cupboard prove to be alive, well, and quite off their heads. Whether it be a twin brother concealed since childhood or the crazed father of a long-forgotten illegitimate child, the family settings of *Trauma*, *The Haunted and the Hunted*, *Horror*, *The Black Torment* and *The Castle of Terror* (all 1964) are breeding-grounds for murderous insanity. To some extent these killers are secular versions of the ghosts and vampires of an earlier horror-movie age, the mysterious forces of supernature replaced by the equally mysterious forces of the psyche. They are a curious amalgam of horror-movie forms, these transitional movies, with their classic castles or manor-houses and their deliberately misleading invocations of a supernature which is finally shown to be fraudulent. Like the Hammer psychological thrillers, they begin to develop the genre in new directions while still harking back to more traditional frames of reference.

This insecurity of reference is a characteristic of many sixties psycho-movies, though most are not as distinctive as those so far considered. All offer variations on familiar genre themes. Some extend the investigative thriller in more graphically horrific directions, as is the case, for instance, with two films directed by the Italian Mario Bava, *The Evil Eye* (1965) and *Blood and Black Lace* (1966). Others take disfigurement (*The Face of Terror* (1964)), rejection in love (*Wheel of Fire* (1964)), or just plain evil madness (*Terrified* (1964) and *Chamber of Horrors* (1966)) as the source of their psychotic threat, operating as traditional horror movies in all but their psychological embellishments. The exception to this generalization is *Repulsion* (1965), which documents a young woman's collapse into homicidal psychosis. Although it shares something of the post-*Psycho* spirit, *Repulsion*'s refusal to employ an elaborate or melodramatic narrative distinguishes it from most of its contemporaries. As he would more than once, its director (Roman Polanski) brought an innovative sensibility to a genre subject.

The one significant group of internal/secular films that does not revolve around psychosis are those SF-influenced variations on metamorphosis or possession themes. There is, for example, a telling development of the alien-invasion-by-replication idea in *The Day*

*Mars Invaded Earth* (1963), which, true to the period's penchant for twist endings, finally reveals that the invading Martians have replaced all the film's central characters, a downbeat denouement also to be found in *Unearthly Stranger* (1963). There is a sequel to *Village of the Damned* — *Children of the Damned* (1963) — which charts a similar invasion by impregnation, while *The Crawling Hand* (1964) uses an accident with a space-shot to allow a malevolent alien intelligence to possess a human being. Most of these films, of course, are straightforward extensions of their fifties predecessors, adding nothing new, and forming a kind of coda to the SF/horror movies of those years. As we shall see, such throw-backs also survive in the external/secular category.

EXTERNAL/SECULAR (32 PER CENT)

As ever, the external/secular group has its fair share of mad scientists, broadly divisible into creators of traditional medical monsters, and scientists involved in more 'modern', non-medical experimentation. On the traditional side, the Baron himself reappears in yet another Hammer adaptation, *The Evil of Frankenstein* (1964). The film retains some features of the established Frankenstein narrative (the monster even approximates the Karloff image), though, as with all the Hammer versions, the Baron's obsession is more evil than redeemable. The 'price of science' subtext, once part of the genre's foreground, becomes less prominent as the Hammer cycle progresses. Similar limitations apply to other mad-medico movies of the period. These villains traverse the range from doctors who kill in order to restore beauty to disfigured lovers/daughters/wives, as in *The Demon Doctor, Drops of Blood* and *Seddock* (all 1963), through to surgeons concerned to keep disembodied heads and other appendages alive, as in *Vengeance* (1963) — one of several versions of Siodmak's story *Donovan's Brain* — and *The Head* (1959). Most of these scientists attract no sympathy — they are not pitiful victims of scientific progress, but, rather, evil abusers of scientific knowledge. Among the traditional mad-scientist movies, only *Terror is a Man* (1965) encourages empathy with its scientist.

Even *The Curse of the Fly* (1965) diverges from its predecessors in eliminating sympathy for the scientist, as well as incorporating a range of elements from elsewhere in the genre. However, other more 'accidental' monster-creators are sympathetically treated, at least in

so far as it is often the scientist himself who has the misfortune to become the monster. In *Hand of Death* (1963), *The Evil Force* (1965) and *The Projected Man* (1966), scientists pay the ultimate price of research, not because they are evil or mad, but because there are risks involved in science itself. Perhaps the most interesting of such films is *The Man With the X-Ray Eyes* (1963), in which scientific obsession surfaces in a much more sympathetic context than usual. Dr Xavier, experimenting upon himself, develops X-ray vision, and the film charts his doomed attempts to grapple with it. Motivated by his sense of medical responsibility (his newly acquired vision could be a priceless diagnostic tool) he finds himself in a world implacably opposed to any such possibility. He is finally reduced to performing in a carnival, his scientific commitment sacrificed to ignorance and greed.

The other role for science in this period's horror movies is to create danger as an unintended consequence of other activities. The dangers themselves largely follow the patterns set in the fifties, in several cases invoking radiation as a significant factor. Godzilla reappears twice, in *King Kong versus Godzilla* (1963) and *Godzilla vs the Thing* (1965), and in both cases radioactivity and atomic weapon testing are partly to blame. In *The Horror of Party Beach* (1964) radioactive waste dumped in the ocean produces a motley crew of monsters who attack a teenage beach-party. The police turn to a scientist who, true to fifties form, finds that simple application of sodium will destroy the nasties. *The Horror of Party Beach*, of course, is the *reductio ad absurdum* of that SF/horror-movie story in which a scientifically occasioned threat is eliminated by the intervention of responsible science. This form, common enough in the fifties, is in decline by the mid-sixties. One of the last serious examples is *Island of Terror* (1966), in which cancer researchers accidentally create a silicon-based life form which feeds voraciously on the calcium in bone. In a nice inversion of the normal pattern, the creatures are eliminated by poisoning the cattle on which they are feeding with radioactive isotopes. Shot in rural locations and in naturalistic colour, *Island of Terror* is the final flourish of a basically fifties idiom.

The only remaining group of external/secular films, also developed from fifties roots, focuses upon invasion from space. Some follow the familiar pattern of rescue by scientific ingenuity and/or military might — *The Atomic Submarine* (1963) or *Mutiny in Outer Space* (1965) — but that kind of optimism is clearly beginning to fail. Thus, in *The*

*Day of the Triffids* (1963) the final solution is discovered accidentally
– the lumbering plants are allergic to sea water. As in *War of the
Worlds* a decade earlier, a religious gloss is given to the fact of
humanity's final relief, though as with the earlier film that gloss
seems so extraneous as to be laughably implausible to any audience.
The true distinctiveness of *The Day of the Triffids* lies in the in-
capacity of established authority to deal with the threat. That is also
to be seen in *The Earth Dies Screaming* (1965), where humanity is all
but destroyed, and, more interestingly, with another sort of 'invader'
in *The Birds* (1963). Hitchcock's film, like all his contributions to the
genre, was both highly individual and subsequently very influential.
The prospect of 'invasion' by unexplained, malevolent nature was to
prove a significant element in the horror movies of the seventies and
eighties, and in this sub-genre *The Birds* is seminal.

SUPERNATURAL (34 PER CENT)

Since there are so few examples of the internal/supernatural, I shall
consider all the supernatural cases together. As one might expect of a
genre in transition, there is no dominant pattern. While it is true that
the largest discernible subgroup of supernatural films shares a concern with witchcraft and magic, when examined in detail these films
prove to be diverse in other respects. Several – *Crypt of Horror*,
*Devils of Darkness*, *Witchcraft* (all 1965), *The Revenge of the Blood
Beast* and *The Skull* (both 1966) – revolve around the reincarnation
of, reappearance of or possession by a long-dead witch or magician,
but beyond that general similarity they differ in details of setting,
style and narrative. Others are even less specific about the nature of
the magical threat, including, notably, five films directed by Roger
Corman: *Tales of Terror* (1963), *The Masque of the Red Death*, *The
Terror*, *The Tomb of Ligeia* (all 1964) and *The Haunted Palace*
(1966). Nominally based on Poe (and, in the case of *The Haunted
Palace*, Lovecraft as well), the Corman movies do share a distinctive
style. Much influenced by Daniel Haller's ingeniously rich set design
and Floyd Crosby's fluent camerawork, the 'Corman style' is, in
effect if not in origin, a heightened extension of that first seen in
Hammer's Gothic remakes.

   Indeed, it is to this Hammer-inspired style that one must look to
find any real communality among the supernatural movies of the
mid-sixties. It is conventional to single out particular authors as the

distinguishing feature of sixties horror: Italians such as Riccardo Freda (*The Terror of Dr Hitchcock* (1963)) and Mario Bava (*Night is the Phantom* (1965)); Terence Fisher, long the dominant director at Hammer, still developing the orthodox vampire canon, with Christopher Lee in *Dracula – Prince of Darkness* (1966); Corman himself; and John Gilling with two very influential 1966 movies, *The Plague of the Zombies* and *The Reptile*. I have no wish to underestimate the importance of these film-makers for the horror movie. But the very fact that authorship seems to be the most plausible organizing principle precisely reflects the lack of generic patterning in the period's supernatural movies. The most one can say of them is that many share a strong and colourful visual style rooted in the innovatory Hammer films of the late fifties. This lends some – notably the work of the directors singled out above – an intensity that had been missing from supernatural horror movies since the classic period. In this respect, at least, the emergent style is a colour equivalent to the monochrome extravagances of 'expressionism', and it serves to lend new credibility to the power of supernature in the sixties horror movie. Just as the 'German Style' suggested unseen forces lurking in the shadows, so this developing 'Colour Gothic' style suggests a world of heightened and constraining experience.

None of this is to suggest that all supernatural movies of the period follow the Hammer/Corman/Italian pattern; merely that it is the single most significant feature in what is clearly a time of transition and experiment. There are also traditionally styled films, particularly where monochrome is preferred to colour. *The Haunting* (1964), for example, originates in the classic fear-by-suggestion tradition (its director, Robert Wise, had worked with Lewton at RKO) and, apart from its 'scope aspect-ratio[1] and its lesbian overtones, it could have appeared at any time in the previous two decades. Similarly with such 'ghost' films as *The Tell-Tale Heart* (1963) or, at an even more B-picture level, *Tormented* (1964), both of which seem untouched by the post-Hammer trend towards direct presentation of the horrific.

To some extent the internal incoherence of the supernatural sub-genre reflects a general tendency in sixties horror movies. If there are any clear trends to be distinguished here, they are to be found in the rapid expansion of horror-movie interest in insanity, and in the consolidation of a heightened and highly coloured visual style as a newly effective means of suggesting supernatural forces. Apart from this, the period of American Decline illustrates exactly that: the distinctively American horror-movie forms (the traditional mad scientist; the space invader) are either changed or rendered insignificant. The newly discovered European horror cinema, particularly the British and Italian, goes from strength to strength, remaining a powerful force until the end of the decade. There are also some broad hints as to likely future developments, most notably in the nascent sexualizing of the genre. That, however, is best discussed in relation to the Seventies Boom, when a relaxation in censorship and a massive expansion of supernatural horror movies pushes it into the foreground.

## The Seventies Boom: 1971–1974

These are years of unprecedented expansion and consolidation. There is expansion, in that the sheer volume of horror movies reaches new heights: nearly 40 films per year during the boom, and an average of 34 over the seventies. There is consolidation, in that many trends only beginning in the sixties are fully established by the mid-seventies. Perhaps unsurprisingly, then, the supernatural/secular and external/internal distinctions remain the most significant for general classificatory purposes, just as they were in the sixties.

Table 4.2   Sources of threat in horror movies of the seventies boom, 1971–1974

|          | Supernatural | Secular   | Total       |
|----------|--------------|-----------|-------------|
| External | 55 (33%)     | 35 (21%)  | 90 (54%)    |
| Internal | 19 (12%)     | 57 (34%)  | 76 (46%)    |
| Total    | 74 (45%)     | 92 (55%)  | 166 (100%)  |

Comparison with table 4.1 shows that major growth has taken place in the two supernatural categories, with the 'external' rising from 28 per cent to 33 per cent and the 'internal' from 6 per cent to 12 per cent – an overall rise of some 11 per cent. Nevertheless, the secular remains dominant (though reduced from 66 per cent to 55 per cent), and I shall begin, as I did in the last section, by considering the single largest group of films, the internal/secular, and following that with the external/secular and the supernatural.

INTERNAL/SECULAR (34 PER CENT)

All but half a dozen of these films are concerned with madness, which in most of them is 'caused' in some discernible way. Indeed, the move from the sixties to the seventies shows an increase in films in which the threat is dependent rather than autonomous (from 48 per cent to 56 per cent), a general pattern reflected in the period's psycho-movies. In earlier horror movies, most 'mad' characters were glossed as simply evil, their madness (if it was even given the name) an autonomous feature of a constantly malevolent world. After 1960, however, and most particularly in the seventies, madness becomes psychosis: a secular, dependent and internally articulated threat. Of course, many of the 'explanations' of psychosis offered in these films are no more sophisticated than the psychoanalyst's account tagged onto the end of *Psycho* − pop-Freud at best. What is important is not the explanations themselves but the fact that these films conceptualize insanity as caused at all, and that they increasingly do so in terms of a specific cluster of ideas.

These ideas do not make much sense as a coherent psychological theory, but − and this will be amplified in chapter 9 − they do invite us to understand horror movie psychosis from a definite vantage point. They constantly allude to a loosely interlinked array of themes: family- or parent-derived repression (classically mother/son); perverse sexuality; male-upon-female voyeurism; a link between violent killing and sexual gratification; and, especially in the eighties, a predator − prey relation between male psychotics and female victims. Generally no one film exhibits all these characteristics. After all, though they define the conceptual arena within which psychosis is narratively constructed, they do not form an ideal-typical model for all horror movie psychotics. Nevertheless, even the most rudimentary examination of seventies psycho-movies confirms this as the 'psychological' ground in which they are rooted.

At least a dozen of them firmly locate psychosis in a family context. In some cases the causal link is crudely physical. *The Beast in the Cellar* (1971), for example, creates its psychotic by the simple expedient of incarceration. Two women, horrified at their father's fate in the 1914 − 1918 war, brick their brother into the cellar to prevent him fighting in World War II. He is reduced to a murderous madman. More commonly, however, there is a clearer psychosexual context for these disturbed family relations. In *Hands of the Ripper*

(1971) the psychotic is Jack the Ripper's daughter, childhood witness to her father's stabbing of her mother. As many have, the film exploits the tension between psychiatric and supernatural explanations, but, whatever its final disposition on that question, it does establish a connection between her father's post-murder embrace and her subsequent responses to being embraced and kissed. Any such stimulus turns her into a violent killer, 'possessed' by her father's consciousness. In *Demons of the Mind* (1972) the second generation's sanity is prejudiced by the father's cruelty and mother's consequent suicide; in *The Fiend* (1972) the son of a family of religious fanatics murders prostitutes in an attempt to ensure their ultimate salvation; in *Blood Brides* (1973) the central psychotic feels compelled to kill the women he marries because, as it finally emerges, he has repressed the memory of murdering his mother and stepfather on their wedding night; in *Night Hair Child* (1973) a 12-year-old boy makes sexual advances to his father's new wife, having already murdered his mother; and in *Night of Bloody Horror* (1974) a mother, living with the corpses of her dead child and suicidal husband, insistently slaughters her grown-up son's girlfriends.

This recitation of family horrors could be continued, but it would become pointless repetition. What most such films share is a clear diagnosis of the origins of psychosis in a psychosexual and familial context, an emphasis reinforced by the period's growing permissiveness in matters of on-screen sex and nudity. Indeed, these are the years in which the so-called 'sexploitation' horror movie emerges for the first time with films like *Anybody Anyway*, *Blood Mania* and *Private Parts* (all 1973), though the latter (directed by Paul Bartel) is perhaps more perversely comic than pornographic. There are also some vaguely Sadeian psycho-movies, variously touching upon deviant sexuality, and set in repressive institutions: a girl's boarding school in *The House that Screamed* (1972), an orphanage in the charge of sadists in *Blood and Lace* (1973), an asylum in *House of Madness* (1974). Most singular of all is *House of Whipcord* (1974), in which a young woman is kidnapped, tried and punished by a retired judge and his mistress, a former prison governess. Imprisoned with several other young women in their private jail, she is subjected to progressively sadistic treatment finally leading to her death.

Though *House of Whipcord* is hardly typical, it is nearer to the seventies norm than are the few 'traditional' psycho-movies. The highly contrived 'psychological thriller' does just survive in the shape of *Fear in the Night* (1972), this time not only written but also

directed by Jimmy Sangster for Hammer, and in *The Night She Arose from the Tomb* (1972) and *Scream* (1974). However, these films seem more like the last gasps of a now-outdated form than fresh examples of a thriving sub-genre, their traditional virtues sacrificed to growing commercial pressures for innovation. Similar desperation is apparent in the period's few attempts to portray the full-blooded madmen of melodrama, and there is a distinct tendency to fortify such stories with self-consciously camp black humour. *The Abominable Dr Phibes* (1971) and *Theatre of Blood* (1973) are good examples, featuring Vincent Price making even his Poe performances for Corman look understated!

Few internal/secular films are not straightforwardly concerned with psychosis. There are two versions of the Jekyll and Hyde story, one of them—characteristically for the period—putting a new interpretation on the familiar theme of self-inflicted metamorphosis. The film's title, *Dr Jekyll and Sister Hyde* (1971), is enough to suggest the character of that innovation. There are also a few odd developments of the familiar invasion theme, *The Andromeda Strain* (1971) and *The Omega Man* (1972) focusing upon disease, while *The Bubble* (1973) and *Horror Express* (1974) postulate rather unusual space-invaders. Lastly, there are two films that ought be mentioned if only because they are precursors of subsequent trends. One of them, *Fright* (1971), has a teenage girl trapped by a psychotic in the house in which she is baby-sitting. This 'terrorizing' narrative, in which young isolated women are preyed upon by marauding psychotics, is hugely important in the horror movies of the late seventies and eighties. The other, *Death Line* (1973), is significant in the drift towards increasingly graphic portrayal of blood and gore. I have already observed that Hammer had several times pushed back the boundaries of acceptability in this respect, a process that had continued in fits and starts throughout the sixties. *Death Line*, with its detailed depiction of the decomposing detritus of enforced cannibalism, suggested a new dimension to horror-movie physicality. As we shall see, such dwelt-upon detail is also to be found in other seventies films and is even more significant in the 'splatter movies' of the eighties.

EXTERNAL/SECULAR (21 PER CENT)

Although the single largest group of external/secular movies is still those featuring mad scientists and their medical creations, these display neither the range nor the depth of narrative invention once familiar. The mad scientist of the seventies boom is but a pale shadow of his or her former self. Perhaps the simplest way to appreciate that is to consider the half a dozen films of the period which invoke the Frankenstein tradition by name. One of them, *Frankenstein and the Monster from Hell* (1974), is from Hammer, directed by the man responsible for the studio's major forays in this area, Terence Fisher, and featuring Peter Cushing in his well-established persona as the Baron. Even with these credentials, however, it is apparent that the film has lost touch with the kinds of subtext variations which had encouraged Frankenstein's longevity in the genre. By now the Baron has become merely harsh and brutal (a process first set in train by Hammer in 1957), a stereotypical authoritarian, and such conviction as there is to this version of the story depends on the graphic violence both of the monster's rampage and of the lunatic asylum inmates who finally tear it apart.

Even more emphasis on violent detail is to be found in an Italian production, *Lady Frankenstein* (1972), which, typically for the period, pays close attention to sex. The rampaging creature displays an improbable ability to happen upon sexually engaged couples, while the title lady herself (the Baron's daughter) creates a second monster by transplanting her lover's brain into a young and handsome body. Unfortunately for her, their love-making turns out to have murderous repercussions. I mention these details not from prurient fascination, but because they suggest the degree to which some seventies boom films contrive their narratives so as to incorporate sexual activity. At a B-picture level this reduces to periodic undressing sequences, as in *Frankenstein on Campus* (1971), but in many cases explicitly presented sex is a prominent feature.

The remaining Frankensteinian mad scientists illustrate slightly different aspects of the period's movies, while still suggesting the relative decline of the sub-genre. *Frankenstein: The True Story* (1974), originally a lengthy American TV version, does notionally return to the science/blasphemy themes of early mad scientist movies, and even to Mary Shelley. Significantly, however, the version for British cinema distribution is cut in such a way as to reduce the intelligibility and importance of these 'classical' elements. By 1974 the centre-of-gravity of mad-scientist movies has long since moved away from the ethical issues raised by obsessive devotion to science.

In that respect, of course, the seventies films complete a trend already clear in the previous decade, and also to the fore in the last two of these six Frankenstein movies. *Blood of Frankenstein* (1974), rather like *House of Frankenstein* some 30 years earlier, packs in a whole array of movie monsters to variously comic effect, while *Jesse James Meets Frankenstein's Daughter* (1974), which was actually made in 1965, is, as its title might suggest, not entirely serious. Like *The Incredible Two-Headed Transplant* (1971), these films find a mixture of intentional and unintentional humour in the conventions of B-picture mad science, a potential more carefully and hilariously exploited in *The Thing With Two Heads* (1974) and, in the year following the boom period, *Young Frankenstein* (1975).

The overwhelming impression left by the mad medico movies of the seventies is that the threat of science is no longer enough. By resorting to ever more gory detail, to sex, to comedy, these films seek alternative means of retaining audience involvement. Consequently, many of them operate even nearer to the B-picture base-line than they did in the forties: *The Mad Doctor of Blood Island*, *Blood Devils* (both 1971) and *Superbeast* (1973), all shot in Philippines jungle locations, are effectively colour updates of their forties ancestors. There are one or two 'new' developments, but they shift the major focus away from the traditional mad scientist. Thus, *The Creeping Flesh* (1973) amalgamates 'science' themes with elements typical of seventies supernatural movies, while *The Only Way Out is Dead* (1971) builds a broadly conventional thriller around the then much-discussed potential of transplant surgery. But these are exceptions. For most of the seventies, mad science is minimally significant.

The opposite is true, however, of 'mad' – or, at least, angry – nature. Whether inexplicably, by individual encouragement or by scientific accident, 'natural nasties' are on the increase. Indeed, over the whole decade, nearly 10 pen cent of films feature some such threat. Those of the boom years are fairly typical, except that they predate *Jaws* and therefore show little in the way of piscatorial horrors. Ranging through rats (*Willard* (1971) and *Ben* (1973)), snakes (*Stanley* (1973)), ants (*Phase IV* (1974)), bats (*Chosen Survivors* (1974)) and assorted reptiles (*Frogs* (1972)), these films are narratively very simple. They fall broadly into two groups. In one (*Willard*, *Ben*, *Stanley*) a lonely isolate befriends a creature, thus providing himself with some power over a generally antagonistic world. In the other – more common over the whole seventies period – an unanticipated consequence of human activity is the antagonism of normally indifferent nature. Thus, the giant rabbits of *Night of the*

*Lepus* (1973) are a result of attempts to control rabbit breeding, much like the irradiated giant ants, mantids and spiders of the fifties. More distinctly modern, however, is the anti-pollution gloss given to the otherwise traditional narrative of *Frogs*. Though no formal explanation is offered, it is clear from the movie's context that pollution is the 'cause' of nature's revolt, a pollution which is in turn a corollary of industrial greed and exploitation.

This 'eco-doom' framework subsequently becomes very common in movies postulating a natural threat, though it never entirely dominates the sub-genre. Throughout the seventies and early eighties films also continue to document inexplicable attacks from nature, some (exemplified here by *Trog* (1971) and *Bigfoot* (1972)) revolving around encounters with evolutionary leftovers. In effect, the familiar invaders of the fifties and sixties are transmuted into the 'natural nasties' of the seventies. Invasion no longer comes from space (or from whatever that metaphorical 'out there' represented) but from our immediate natural environment. Thus, real space invaders, like traditional mad medicos, become something of a joke: witness *Dracula versus Frankenstein* (1971), *Yog − Monster from Space* (1973) or *Son of Blob* (1974). Our external/secular threats are no longer as external as once they were, for it is nature, the very essence of our own world, that is rising against us, and in these natural apocalypses human beings are routinely found guilty.

SUPERNATURAL (45 PER CENT)

Although the seventies see a significant rise in the number of internal/ supernatural cases, I shall still group all the supernatural films together. Essentially this is because the bulk of the rise is accounted for by one subtype: films focusing upon threats by possession. The *locus classicus* here is *The Exorcist* (1974), though its direct demonic possession is actually quite rare in the boom period, and was never as common as popular memory might suggest. Nevertheless, *The Exorcist* was extremely influential both in promoting the horror movie into big-budget-mass audience entertainment and in changing the boundaries of horror-movie permissiveness. The former will not concern me here, other than to observe that for much of their history horror movies have played to 'specialized' audiences. Only occasionally (the early Universal films, perhaps; also *Psycho* and *Halloween*) has a horror movie transcended its specialisation and attained real mass success. *The Exorcist* did so, as had *Rosemary's Baby* (1969) before it and as would *The Omen* (1976) two years later.[2]

I shall not try to explain such popularity here — in any case, there is no single explanation — but I will consider *The Exorcist* in more detail later. What should be noted, however, is the degree to which this film put the seal of approval on a violent and graphically detailed style of horror presentation. Though in its early sequences, *The Exorcist* does operate by suggestion and allusion, in its 'rampage section' shock effects are central. By and large this is achieved by showing hitherto unseen horrors: the head revolving on the girl's shoulders; her plunging a bloody crucifix into her vagina; verbal obscenity on an unprecedented scale; the famous green bile that coils from her mouth. All this, and more, is given unremitting close-up attention, with the spectator permitted little or no relief. *The Exorcist*'s success with this approach had two general effects on subsequent genre developments. First, and obviously, it encouraged direct imitations, and the rest of the decade saw a number of *Exorcist* lookalikes. More far-reaching than that, however, it legitimated the broad trend of post-fifties horror movies towards a style of 'heightened realism' specializing in highly coloured representation of sickening physical detail. *The Exorcist* alone was not responsible for this; the style clearly predates Friedkin's film. But *The Exorcist*'s massive success did lend it impetus, and over the next 10 years this style came to permeate almost all areas of the horror-movie mainstream.

Few of the other internal/supernatural movies of the boom period are quite as extravagantly horrific as *The Exorcist*, though they do share that film's strong sense of internality. The very idea of possession, whether by demonic invasion, reincarnation, or witchcraft, is a particularly distinctive threat since it postulates a highly personal attack upon our being. The fact that our bodies may be inhabited, and even physically changed, generates rhetorical possibilities previously only minimally exploited. Thus, though they do not even begin to match *The Exorcist* in tension-creation and narrative drive, films like *The Possession of Joel Delaney* (1972), *Night of the Devils* (1973) and *Crucible of Terror* (1972) do share in the former film's distinctive thrust. Like many seventies horror movies, they play upon insecurity about the sanctity of our selves.

In the early part of the decade, however, this particular version of horror-movie paranoia is found in only a substantial minority of cases. The single largest group of supernatural movies of these years (almost half of them) focuses upon vampirism of some kind, a proportion unmatched in any other period, and examination of the full range suggests a shift away from the traditional format. Only *Count Dracula* (1973) and *Dracula* (1974) approximate to the pattern of the Stoker source, most of the rest falling into two distinct groups. In one, emphasis is on the sexual dimension of vampirism, and, perhaps more significantly, inasmuch as a concern with explicit sex is not restricted to vampire movies, on female (often lesbian) vampires. Le Fanu's story 'Carmilla' had already been plundered for the female vampire of *Blood and Roses* (1962) and, more significant in the modern development of the theme, for Hammer's *The Vampire Lovers* (1970). The combination of a voluptuous and often naked vampire (in *The Vampire Lovers* played with considerable erotic aggression by Ingrid Pitt) with highly charged sexual encounters between female vampire and female victim evidently gave new commercial life to the seventies vampire movie. Unsurprisingly, Hammer followed up rapidly with *Countess Dracula* (again with Ingrid Pitt), *Lust for a Vampire* and *Twins of Evil* (all 1971).

These three share Hammer's characteristically enriched colour and the explicit violence common to so many seventies horror movies. They are also unrelenting in their insistence upon sexual display, not merely in frequent female nudity but also in blurring the boundary between their predator's sexual and vampiric predilections. They are nothing if not explicit, and parade a somewhat blatant taste in sexual symbolism. As the reincarnated Mircalla of *Twins of Evil* seduces and vampirizes Count Karnstein, she pointedly fondles a phallic candle, while elsewhere in the same film one of the title twins sucks her blood from a victim's ample breast. Blood, indeed, is more in evidence here than ever before. The countess of *Countess Dracula* (one of several films inspired by the newly popularized story of Countess Bathory, who allegedly preserved her youth via the blood of thousands of young women[3]) bathes in it, while in one of the more celebrated images from *Lust for a Vampire*, Mircalla's naked upper torso is appropriately drenched.

These and other films featuring voracious female vampires − *Sex and the Vampire* (1971), *Shadow of the Werewolf* (1973) and *The Devil's Plaything* (1974) − constitute one of the most striking developments of the seventies boom. Though there had always been a sexual dimension to the vampire movie, and though there had always been female vampires, this is the first period in which the two are conflated and placed at the heart of the vampire narrative. It is tempting to see in this remarkable development growing fears about predatory female sexuality. These were, after all, the years in which 'women's lib' (as it was abusively labelled in the popular press) was much publicized and much maligned. Why should this not find devious expression in the vampire movie? I shall return to that question in chapter 8, however, for the moment confining myself to more prosaic observations. It seems likely that horror-filmmakers, freed from the constraints of earlier censorship, saw an opportunity to attract and titillate the genre's predominantly male audience by indulging their fantasy desires to voyeuristically contemplate aggressive, perverse (i.e. for this audience, lesbian) and visually explicit sex. The seventies are years in which sex features increasingly prominently in all areas of the genre. Given the commercial motor of genre evolution, it only needs one success with a particular sexual variant to provide the impetus for a whole series.

The second significant development in the seventies vampire movie is much more straightforward. Classically, movie vampires have always occupied a kind of *elsewhen* — commonly given expression in their nineteenth century Transylvanian locations, but sustained even in notionally modern settings by features of style and design. In the seventies, for the first time, the traditional male vampire is most often found in modern urban locations. Hammer — throughout the sixties the dominant force in vampire movies — made an attempt at this updating process in *Dracula A. D.1972* (1972) and *The Satanic Rites of Dracula* (1974), the latter ingeniously turning the Count into a London property speculator. But the centre of gravity for this innovation lay not in Britain but in the USA, in a striking series of movies including *Count Yorga, Vampire*, *The Return of Count Yorga*, *House of Dark Shadows* (all 1971), *Blacula* (1973) and *Grave of the Vampire* (1974). These films do not eliminate the traditional apparatus of movie vampire-lore — Yorga even has something approximating a castle in contemporary California — they merely adapt it to its new setting. Shot in a largely naturalistic style (though with carefully chosen colours — *Count Yorga, Vampire*, for instance, is dominated by shades of red) these films returned some of its traditional power to the modern vampire movie.

This shift in setting had another, more diffuse, effect. The divorce of the classic vampire narrative from its period context partly undermines its 'other-worldly' character. Vampirism is no longer a matter of peasant superstition or mid-European folk memory. These vampires stalk their prey in downtown Los Angeles or London's West End; they have become part of our everyday environment, no longer safely insulated in mythic history. This penetration of the everyday world by malevolent supernature is a significant feature of seventies supernatural movies, and one which extends right through the decade and into the eighties. Of course, there are still 'period' supernatural horror movies. But even they show some increase in the level of their evil protagonists' ferocity, and it is not unreasonable to suggest that these years see a general rise in the intensity with which the horror movie's supernatural threat is articulated.

These changes — more graphic violence, explicit sex, female malevolence, invasion of the everyday by supernature — can be found in most of the period's supernatural movies, including those of the one remaining major subgroup: witchcraft movies. Witches or satanists feature in 23 films (sometimes in combination with other forms of supernatural threat), both in period and modern settings. Often the films show malevolent spirits summoned up, who then destroy all semblance of orderly life around them: this is the case, for example, in *Cry of the Banshee* (1971), *Disciple of Death* (1972) and *The Demons* (1974). Others focus upon witch cults or covens, whether in a small American town (*The Brotherhood of Satan* (1972)), seventeenth-century rural England (*Blood on Satan's Claw* (1971)), or — though this is very much a deviant variation — a pagan nature cult on an island off the west coast of Scotland (*The Wicker Man* (1974)). Whatever their differences, however, they share a presupposition that supernatural forces may be channelled into the secular world, where they can and will destroy everybody with whom they come into contact. Indeed, as with many of the period's movies, there is a growing tendency to 'resolve' these narratives by the apparent victory of the forces of evil, or, — if not quite at that extreme — to leave good less than triumphant. Once such forces are permitted entry to the everyday world they are not easily excluded; for, in its seventies version at least, supernature is all too often more powerful than any 'expert' ranged against it.

If one word can summarize the general developments of the early seventies, it would be *paranoia*. Of course, there is a sense in which the horror movie itself is a paranoid form: it is founded on the supposition that we are constantly under threat from many directions. However, the seventies see an extension of that fear, partly conveyed in the typical narratives of the period, and partly conveyed through style and a tendency to dwell upon more overtly horrific detail. These films hit harder than their predecessors, and the threats that they present are less easily defeated — if they can be defeated at all. A straightforward list of typical seventies traits suggests the general direction of the trend: psychosis as a consequence of the psycho-sexual dynamics of the family; invasion from antagonistic and polluted nature; the relative insignificance of science; the exceptional malevolence of supernature often directed at the innocent self; predatory female sexuality; and invasion of the modern everyday by vampires, witches and demons.

The horror movie world-view suggested by these developments is one in which typical threats have increased in intensity and become more focused. *We*, in our familiar domestic and everyday settings, are the unwitting prey of graphically presented horrors created by *our* failings (psychic, physical or moral) or by invasion from a seemingly malevolent natural world. Victory is no longer assured, and seventies *homo horrificus* has become a paranoid victim.

### Sustained Growth: 1978–1983

In the late seventies and early eighties we begin to see the fate of some of the trends apparent in the seventies boom. In particular, the relative decline of the mad scientist is confirmed. Where science does now have an impact (in only 14 per cent of films) it is via mutations created as a consequence of unanticipated pollution, radiation or accident, or via similarly unpredictable effects upon natural creatures. But these are minority themes. The two major sources of horror-movie threat remain psychosis and supernature, and of the two, psychosis dominates. During the period of sustained growth, psychotics figure in 38 per cent of films, passing the 50 per cent mark in the early eighties: no less than 73 films over the six years. Unsurprisingly, then, it is the internal/secular category that is most prominent in table 4.3.

Table 4.3  Sources of threat in horror movies of the period of sustained growth, 1978–1983

|  | *Supernatural* | *Secular* | Total |
|---|---|---|---|
| *External* | 46 (24%) | 41 (21%) | 87 (45%) |
| *Internal* | 17 (8%) | 91 (47%) | 108 (55%) |
| Total | 63 (32%) | 132 (68%) | 195 (100%) |

The 47 per cent of internal/secular cases is easily the highest figure ever recorded in this category, and only rarely has any single category so dominated a period. The only comparable instances are the external/dependent of both the classic and war periods, at 55 per cent and 45 per cent respectively, and, at 62 per cent, the external/ secular films of the fifties boom. I shall begin, therefore, with the internal/secular, moving on to consider the external/secular and, finally, the supernatural.

INTERNAL/SECULAR (47 PER CENT)

Most of these films are psycho-movies, an expansion precipitated by the box-office success of *Halloween* (1979). In the year of *Halloween*'s British release, there were only six movies featuring psychotics, 22 per cent of total output. One year later that figure had risen to 42 per cent (14 films), and in 1981 to 51 per cent (17 films). Overall, some 80 per cent of the period's psychotics appear after *Halloween*, a fact which, combined with the movie's obvious influence on the character of subsequent psycho-movie narrative, makes it one of the most important horror movies in the modern genre. This is not to deny the significance of another highly successful psycho-movie of the early eighties: *Friday the 13th* (1980). In practice, however, *Friday the 13th* is no more than a crude template for the creation of formula *Halloween* clones. It abstracts generic elements from *Halloween*, recombining them in a form that can be made effective with only minimal resources of labour, skill and materials.[4]

*Halloween*'s basic elements are simple enough, though in narrative strategy and style it is rather more subtle. I will discuss the film at greater length in chapter 9; for the moment, the barest outline will do. At its heart is a near superhuman, male, masked killer who preys upon young people, mostly females. Inevitably this carries some sexual overtones, at least in that the three women he actually kills (one during the film's 'preface', set 15 years in the past) have all either just engaged in sex or are setting out with the intention of doing so. However, no clear connection is spelled out, and for much of the film *Halloween*'s psychotic serves as an apparently unmotivated homicidal threat. He stalks and then terrorizes three young women, the last of whom survives. The essence of our involvement, then, is of the 'where is he?', 'when will he strike next?', 'will she get away?' type, and the movie works as a series of tension-building sequences culminating in moments of intense shock and economically portrayed violence. Unlike some of its successors, however, *Halloween* does not dwell unduly upon the detail of cut flesh or spilled guts.

What *Friday the 13th* takes from this model is its basic idea of a seemingly invincible psychotic terrorizing an isolated group of young people. In this, the first of a series, the killer turns out to be a woman seeking revenge because her son died in an earlier summer camp swimming accident, though in the next two sequels (*Friday the 13th Part II* (1981) and *Friday the 13th Part III* (1983)) the psychotic is her inexplicably resurrected son Jason himself. All three films use *Halloween*'s mixture of tension-building, frenzied killing of isolated victims and an increasingly predictable quota of female nudity and love-making, though marshalled together in an altogether cruder fashion than in *Halloween*. Nevertheless, the fundamental situation is that of the terrorizing psychotic, and all the films climax with the pursuit of the solitary surviving female. The threat articulated here, then, is that of an omnipotent human predator, seen at its most intense (though not exclusively) in situations of male-upon-female pursuit. It is rare to find this subtext of male predator and female prey foregrounded, however, so the potential identification of sexual and physical violence remains largely submerged. It is there, of course, and in some films – *Nightmares in a Damaged Brain* (1983), *Don't Go in the House* (1981) or *Don't Answer the Phone!* (1980) – it is of overt narrative significance. But given the reputation of this period's psycho-movies, it is worth noting that the sexual dimension is less integral to these films than it was to many of their sixties and seventies predecessors. The earlier trends that find expression here lie not so much in the area of the psychosexual as in further development of the terrorising narrative and in the increasingly gory detail with which these films present their many murderous episodes.

Any list of movies utilizing the basic narrative strategy of *Halloween* or *Friday the 13th* would be very long, including at least *Prom Night* (1980), *Terror Train* (1980), *The Burning* (1981), *Happy Birthday to Me* (1981), *My Bloody Valentine* (1981), *Rosemary's Killer* (1982), *Hell Night* (1982), *Halloween II* (1982), *X-Ray* (1982), *Campsite Massacre* (1983) and *The Slumber Party Massacre* (1983). All place their juvenile leads in jeopardy from a violent, all-powerful, often masked killer; all bloodily eliminate most of their major characters, finally focusing on one terrorized victim; and many leave the outcome in some way ambiguous, even if they don't actually concede total victory to tic the psychotic. *The Slumber Party Massacre*, note, is unique in having its psychotic killed by three surviving females acting in consort, a twist which underlines the role of victim normally assigned to women in these films.

This 'youth in jeopardy' story is the major innovation of eighties psycho-movies; most other significant features are simple extensions of earlier trends. The pervasive presence of extremely bloody detail (both in the acts of violence themselves and in the camera's often studied exploration of the consequent human remains) is hardly new, even if it does reach new heights. The genre's conventions of acceptability in this respect had been almost continuously extending since the late fifties. Though eighties viscera may seem shocking to a genre-outsider – an effect apparent in many contributions to the British 'moral panic' about video-nasties – it seems rather less significant to the longer-term observer.[5]

More interesting, perhaps, is the period's continuing concern with the familial character of psychosis. The range covered by such films is much as it was in the Seventies Boom. There are, for instance, those offspring who have 'gone wrong' and so have been incarcerated in various attics, cellars and secret rooms. Thus, *Humongous* (1983) has a monster son in the cellar, the result of a rape and an isolated upbringing, while *Silent Scream* (1980) has a mad sister in the attic, driven to insanity by her lover's desertion. Both films, interestingly, combine these traditional situations with the newer emphasis on terrorized college students.

Other movies are more specific about the repressive and the psychosis inducing features of their families. *Unhinged* (1983), for example, has a mad son forced by his man-hating mother to assume a female identity; to complete the symmetry, the mother's hatred of men dates from her husband's exposure as a child-molester. Both *Savage Weekend* (1979) and *New Year's Evil* (1982) feature husbands driven mad by their wife's neglect or ambition, while *Psycho II* (1983) resorts to the conceit of identifying Norman Bates's real mother and having him slaughter her.

All these, and several more, invoke the familiar psychosexual and family repression themes. The only really distinctive development is to push the idea of psychosis one step further, edging towards a conception of the psychotic family rather than the psychotic individual. The major source for this trait of eighties psycho-movies is *The Texas Chain Saw Massacre* (1976) with its 'family' of insane, cannibalistic killers. Although not common, this focus upon a crazed, sometimes surrogate, family group — usually isolated somewhere in the social and geographical backwoods — has an innovative rhetorical potential. Though neither *The Hills Have Eyes* (1978) nor *Just Before Dawn* (1982) develop it at any great length, the moral relativism of judgements of insanity can easily be made a constitutive feature of such narratives. If it were to be developed further it would significantly refocus the psycho-movie.

Most remaining eighties psycho-movies are orthodox variations on traditional forms, if rather more naturalistically bloody than their predecessors. Many make the familiar link between sexual repression and psychotic violence, though few with quite the blatant insistence of *Dressed to Kill*'s (1980) torrid opening scenes. As for the rest of the internal/secular cases, so swamped are they by the sheer numbers of psychotics that it is difficult to discern any clear patterns. However, two groups that can be distinguished actually relate quite closely to the psycho-movies. In one the primary threat derives from a central character's psycho-kinetic powers. *The Fury* (1978), *The Medusa Touch* (1978), *Patrick* (1979), *Tourist Trap* (1981) and *Scanners* (1981) all use this kind of narrative device to set up a situation broadly similar to that of the threatening psychotic, though invoking rather different causal presuppositions. *Scanners* also belongs to a second group of distant relations of the psycho-movie. Ultimately descended from the hugely influential *Night of the Living Dead* (1970), this group includes *The Crazies* (1978), *Zombies* (1980), *Zombie Flesh-Eaters* (1980) and *Zombie Creeping Flesh* (1982), all of which postulate the spread of a dehumanizing 'disease' and present an apocalyptic vision of total social collapse. In effect, they create a world of mass psychosis in which we are doomed to decline into a subhuman state. Unsurprisingly, given their thoroughly apocalyptic tone, they all end with the implication that the 'disease' will continue to spread unchecked.

The only other coherent group of films in the internal/secular category centres on space invasion. Compared to psychotics, however, space invaders are minimally significant in this period — there are only six such films. Most follow the traditional pattern, and the two most successful — *Invasion of the Body Snatchers* (1979) and *The Thing* (1982) — are remakes of well-known fifties movies, though the latter is less a remake than a return to the earlier film's source from a distinctly eighties perspective. The fifties version (*The Thing from*

*Another World* (1952)) was definitely external in the threat that it
posed, while the eighties 'thing' occupies or takes on the form of its
victims. The 'invasion' of these films, then, as it is also in *Laserblast*
(1979) and *Xtro* (1983), is emphatically *internal*, and – once more
unlike the optimistic invasion movies of the fifties – these invaders
are ultimately undefeated.

EXTERNAL/SECULAR (21 PER CENT)

The once-pervasive mad scientist has almost entirely disappeared
by the eighties – there are perhaps a dozen such characters, and
hardly any of them follow the established Frankenstein model.
Accordingly, the threat posed in the vast majority of the external/
secular films is not the deliberate creation of an obsessed scientist. It
is, as one might expect given seventies trends, typically 'nature'
which threatens humanity. Two groups of films can be distinguished,
accounting for more than half of the external/secular category between
them. In one group there is some apparent cause for nature's assault,
usually either industrial pollution or an unanticipated consequence of
human (scientific) activity. In the other group, the threat is unexplained, the monstrous attack occurring for no reason ever elucidated
in the films.

Among the former there is, at least, a distant relationship to the
mad-scientist tradition in that several of these films' nasty creatures
are indirect consequences of scientific experiments. Thus, in both
*Piranha* (1978) and *Piranha II Flying Killers* (1982) the fishy threat
ultimately derives from government-funded research into the
development of 'natural' weapons, and in *Alligator* (1982) a private
research laboratory dumps animal corpses used in hormone experiments into the sewers where they are eaten by an alligator. The
hapless reptile grows into a giant, finally erupting through the pave-
ment into a terrified city. In *The Lucifer Project* (1978), government
research on aggression leads, via pollution, to rampaging barracuda
and aggressive humans, while in *Monster* (1980), an experiment with
DNA-treated salmon gives rise to an apocalyptic invasion by
humanoid sea creatures. Borrowing its nastier elements from all over
the eighties genre, *Monster* has its humanoids pursue and rape the
local women, and, in the film's postscript one of the impregnated
victims gives birth to a new creature – *Alien*-like, through her
abdomen.

Other forms of pollution include the fifties prototype, radioactive mutation, producing – as it did in the fifties – giant ants in *Empire of the Ants* (1978). Insects also feature in *Kingdom of the Spiders* (1978), where tarantulas begin to work co-operatively because of ecological pressures: agricultural developments have deprived them of their natural prey. In an obvious echo of *The Birds*, the embattled humans emerge to find the spiders gone but the town encased in webs. Such 'open' endings are very common in these eco-threat movies, if only by the simple narrative device of yet another creature emerging in the film's final shot. This is the case in *Prophecy* (1979), for instance, where mercury poisoning from a local mill produces a giant mutant bear.

It will be clear by now that eco-threat movies are simple in construction, and that they exhibit little in the way of the bloody and sexually explicit features common elsewhere in the eighties genre. This is also true of the more 'autonomous' versions of the natural threat theme, although the *Jaws* derivatives – *Jaws 2* (1978), *Shark* (1982) and *Jaws 3-D* (1983) – generally display some bloody remains. Nevertheless, by eighties standards most films featuring natural nasties are gentle affairs, a fact reflected in the relative lack of BBFC X or 18 certificates among these movies. Bees (*The Swarm* and *The Savage Bees* (both 1978)), bats (*Nightwing* (1980)) and dogs (*Dogs* (1979)) fulfil the proper narrative role for a horror-movie threat, but, with the exception of a few films like *The Boogens* (1981) and *Monster*, where the creatures are 'unnatural' and nasty, we are spared the detail of their havoc. In effect, most eighties eco-nasties are descendants of the tradition given classic expression in *The Birds*, though not many of them aspire to that film's concern with exploring the specifically human foibles and stresses laid bare by the threat. Only *Cujo* (1983), which centres on a mother and young son trapped by a rabid dog, begins to invoke the period's otherwise-familiar concern with the family under stress. For the most part, eighties eco-threat movies appear to have developed in relative isolation from the rest of the genre.

The remainder of this category's films, generally products of established traditions but not in any number or with any distinctively innovative qualities, exhibit no particular order or significance. Even the film that proved to be one of the more commercially successful of the period – *Alien* (1979) – provoked few imitations other than the improbably titled *Inseminoid* (1981). Based on a typical fifties story (derived from *It! The Terror from Beyond Space* and *The Thing from Another World*), *Alien* is overlaid with elements from several different areas of the modern genre. Skilfully assembled into a highly effective terrorizing narrative (including a finally isolated female victim), *Alien* joins *Invasion of the Body Snatchers* and *The Thing* as one of the few modern expressions of the SF/horror tradition. But compared to the multitude of eco-nasties, they occupy only the very fringe of the external/secular group.

SUPERNATURAL (32 PER CENT)

Vampires, the leitmotif of supernature in the seventies boom, show signs of severe anaemia by the early eighties. Much of their seventies expansion depended on the sexual potential of vampirism, and it is a sign of the relative decline of overt sexuality in eighties horror movies that the vampire, too, seems to be in retreat.[6] Even the period's most 'serious' vampire movies − *Nosferatu the Vampyre* and *Dracula* (both 1979) − resort to extra-generic frames of reference, the one taking its inspiration from the European art movie and Murnau's silent classic, while the other retains many 'theatrical' features of the successful stage play on which it was based. Neither relates in any very clear way to the mainstream of the supernatural horror movie, an observation which could equally be applied to almost all of this period's vampires. It is the familiar story of flagging invention requiring a desperate search for outside inspiration.

Thus these years bring to the vampire movie comedy and pastiche in *Blood Relations* and *Love at First Bite* (both 1979); pornography (though heavily cut in Britain) in the exquisitely titled *Dracula Sucks* (1980); glossy pretentiousness on a grand scale in *The Hunger* (1983); and what the *Monthly Film Bulletin* informatively described as 'the first soft-porn-vampire-disco-rock movie' in *Nocturna* (1979). Only *The Blood Spattered Bride* (1980), a Spanish version of Le Fanu's 'Carmilla', resembles the distinctive vampire movies of the early seventies − which is hardly surprising since the film was actually made in 1972. The very unevenness of this mixture underlines the fact that the vigour and invention of seventies vampire movies was unique to that period. By the early eighties it is almost entirely dissipated. The single exception is *Martin* (1978), George Romero's ingenious updating of the vampire story set in contemporary Pittsburgh. I shall pay closer attention to *Martin* in chapter 8's discussion of the vampire sub-genre. For the present, however, it is necessary to look elsewhere for the characteristic eighties approach to supernature.

As far as the external/supernatural is concerned there are two important subtypes. One group postulates varying degrees of demonic intercession in the world's affairs and is rooted in *The Omen*'s 1976 success. Indeed, it includes both sequels to that earlier account of Satanic manipulation: *Damien Omen II* (1978) and *The Final Conflict* (1981). The other subtype is best represented by yet another major box-office success: *The Amityville Horror* (1979). In this group the principal threat is more specific than Damien's apocalyptic goal of world domination, focused as it is upon families or, more rarely, whole communities. *The Amityville Horror*'s genre pedigree derives from the 'haunted house' movie, but with distinctively modern additions. Thus, the house — once the residence of a Satanist — does not merely haunt the newly arrived family (noises, mysterious events, etc.), but also begins to 'possess' the family's father, turning him into a potentially homicidal maniac: a psychotic created by supernature. This adds an internal/secular element to the movie, a feature extended even further in *Amityville II: The Possession* (1982) and found to some degree in relation to many of this period's otherwise external threats. This blurring of the boundaries between external/internal and supernatural/secular leads to the kind of cross-fertilization between sub-genres which is crucial to several eighties developments.

Other instances of family- or community-directed supernatural threats include *Poltergeist* (1982), *The Fog* (1980), *Ghost Story* (1982), *The Bogey Man* (1981), *Something Wicked This Way Comes* (1983), *Halloween III: Season of the Witch* (1983) and, always assuming that it really does involve supernature, *The Shining* (1980). However, prominent though their trans-individual emphasis may be, it is important to resist the temptation to collapse all these films into an undifferentiated category of 'family horror'. Though there are supernatural movies in which the family itself somehow produces the threat, as is generally the case with psychotics and mutant children, a rather larger proportion use the family (or community) as a convenient and powerful focus for audience identification. The tension-generating mechanisms of these films do not depend exclusively on threats to individuals, but also on involving us as proxy members of larger, positively valued collectivities. The 'family', therefore, is not conceptualized homogeneously throughout the genre.

I have already observed that one distinctive group of supernatural movies involves demonic intercession. In their most apocalyptic versions – *Holocaust 2000* (1978) as well as *The Omen* sequence – such stories have the Antichrist born into a human family and working towards the final destruction of humanity. Other 'demon' movies are a trifle less extreme in their ambitions. For example, the title character of *The Redeemer* (1978) and the conjured demon of *Revenge of the Dead* (1978) both function to punish sin, while *The Entity* (1982) and *Incubus* (1983) yoke together elements of the psychotic and the demonic into all-powerful supernatural rapists. And, of course, there are still some post-*Exorcist* cases of possession, though now – in the likes of both *Nurse Sherri* (1980) and *Possession* (1982), if not the rather more original *The Manitou* (1978) – they approach the lower depths of unflattering imitation.

A more significant reworking of the possession theme – and certainly far more successful – is *The Evil Dead* (1982), the bearer of a singular reputation in Britain because of its much-prosecuted status in video form. Though packed with knowing genre references, *The Evil Dead* also functions as a gory assemblage of eighties conventions. Borrowing the modern psycho-movie's vision of terrorized youth in a remote rural area, the film has them possessed, raped, slaughtered, and generally surrounded by viscera, putrefaction, malevolent demons, and gore. A battery of wild effects and ferocious shocks make *The Evil Dead* one of the more effective supernatural 'splatter movies', and its narrative control is singular in an area of the genre much given to waywardness in story and character development. More typical in this latter respect are the films of the Italian director Lucio Fulci: *The Beyond* (1981), *City of the Living Dead* (1982) and The *House by the Cemetery* (1983). No less detailed than *The Evil Dead* in their insistent exploration of decaying flesh and spilled organs, they are narratively almost incoherent – perhaps the price to be paid for the eighties taste in gross special effects.

Though there are a number of other supernatural horror movies in this period (including several omnibus films like *Creepshow* (1982) and *Twilight Zone, the Movie* (1983), as well as highly original works such as *The Shout* (1978) and *Q – The Winged Serpent* (1983)), only one small group seems sufficiently distinctive and successful to demand mention here. These are films in the classic internal/supernatural mode of metamorphosis, most notably *An American Werewolf in London* and *The Howling* (both 1981), along with *Cat People* (1982). Compared to *The Evil Dead* or the Fulci studies in visceral exhibitionism, they occupy the 'respectable' end of the eighties market. Though not lacking in lurid shock effects — Rick Baker's werewolf make-up for the first two makes their human– animal transformations singularly compelling — they operate more firmly within the conventions of Hollywood realism than their cheaper neighbours. In the case of *Cat People* and *The Howling*, interestingly, the release and/or repression of sexual desire is a signi- ficant narrative element — a central one in the former. Sexual release has, of course, always featured as a potential subtext in metamorphant movies, but has only rarely surfaced explicitly, and is certainly not common elsewhere in eighties horror.

In overall character, the years of 'sustained growth' show the strongest assault on the everyday found in any period of the genre's history. Whether the threat derives from psychosis, from polluted or mutated nature, from invading 'diseases', from space, from inexpli- cable malevolence or from a supernature populated by demons or by overpowering forces, the point of application is very much here and now. In this respect eighties horror movies extend and elaborate the paranoia of their seventies predecessors. The typical threats of these years invade our houses, our communities, our institutions and our bodies. Often such resistance as we can muster is insufficient, and at the limit we are faced with apocalyptic destruction of all human life. Of course, there are still films in which the threat is finally overcome. But in comparison with earlier periods they are not common, and all too often the 'victory' that they depict could hardly be construed as a positive declaration of humanity's capacity to resist its own destruction.

Along with this broad pessimism goes a growing willingness to present the often nauseous detail of the monstrous rampage. Gone are the stylized compositions and designs of earlier years, the dis- tanced worlds of Transylvania or Victorian England. The horror movie of the eighties, with its relentless physicality and its everyday settings, seems far removed from the niceties of the 1931 *Dracula*. Quite how far removed is something to be considered in the next two chapters.

Notes

1 Here and elsewhere in this book, 'scope (derived from the trade name CinemaScope) refers to anamorphically produced wide screen images. Their most common aspect ration — width to height of the image on

screen — is 2.35:1, but there was some variation prior to that standard emerging in the late fifties. In horror movies anamorphic wide screen processes have never been common, and most horror movies after the fifties achieve their wide screen effect (nominal aspect ratio of 1.85:1, though in British cinemas it is more often 1.75:1) by the cheaper and optically inferior method of masking a standard image in the projector.

2 Easily accessible rank order lists of box-office successes appear in Phil Hardy (ed.), *The Aurum Film Encylopedia, Horror*, vol.3 (London, 1985), Appendix 1, and David Pirie (ed.), *Anatomy of the Movies* (London, 1981), p. 264.

3 See David Pirie, *The Vampire Cinema* (London, 1977), pp. 17—18, for an account of the Countess Bathory story.

4 *Friday the 13th* thus generates the modern genre's record number of sequels: *Friday the 13th Part II* (1981); *Friday the 13th Part III* (1983); *Friday the 13th — The Final Chapter* (1984); *Friday the 13th — A New Beginning* (1985); *Friday the 13th Part VI — Jason Lives* (1988). Part VII is expected.

5 Those unfamiliar with these fascinating events of 1982—1983 could usefully consult Martin Barker (ed.), *The Video Nasties*, (London, 1984).

6 Late in the decade there are signs of a resurgence in the vampire movie, especially in *Near Dark* (1988).

# Part II
*Narrative Resources*

# 5
# Narratives

Ask people about a movie and, almost invariably, they'll tell you its story. This doesn't mean that audiences are somehow unaware of the significance of acting, of cinematography, of a film's thematic organization or direction. Rather, our routine concern with plot reflects the fact that, in most forms of popular cinema, narrative is the primary channel through which aesthetic experience is filtered. It is in the popular cinema's capacity to tell stories that we ground our basic vocabulary of response, whatever complexities of interpretation we might subsequently mount upon a film.

Narrative, then, has to be a central focus for any socially sensitive approach to a popular genre; doubly so, perhaps, where one seeks to 'build outwards' from a core of routinized audience perceptions. I have already paid some attention to story, both in identifying basic elements of the horror movie (in chapter 2) and in the detailed 'history' of chapters 3 and 4. However, other than to observe that horror movies typically depend upon a very direct embodiment of the classic order–disorder–order sequence, I have not given much consideration to horror-movie narrative as a topic in itself. Though it is true that all horror movies are variations on the 'seek and destroy' pattern – a monstrous threat is introduced into a stable situation; the monster rampages in the face of attempts to combat it; the monster is (perhaps) destroyed and order (perhaps) restored – this general and abstract genre-model can be realized in a variety of ways and located in a range of possible settings. As this chapter progresses I shall describe successively three fundamental horror movie-narratives. First, however, I want to make some general observations about the structure of meaning within which these different narrative possibilities are realized.

There are several ways of describing this genre-context, more or less elaborate according to the heuristic purposes to be served. For the moment I am interested only in providing a schematic account of the basic parameters of the genre world as a general framework within which my three narrative types may then be located. For these purposes one of the more economical strategies is to formulate a table of oppositions of the kind once popular in cultural studies of a Levi-Straussian bent. Inasmuch as horror-movie narratives routinely posit an ordered 'known' world under threat from an 'unknown' of some kind, the fundamental terms for such a schema — *known* versus *unknown* — are clear enough. The detail of what counts as known or unknown varies from case to case, of course, although as in most popular genres severe limits are placed on the potential range of that variation. Moreover, the evident simplicity of the horror movie (as compared with, say, the Western) means that its basic oppositional framework can be satisfactorily expressed in relatively few categories.

The general list of oppositions that follows is derived from the analysis reported in chapters 2, 3 and 4, and forms a *minimum* set of categories necessary to describe the topography of known and un-known in the horror movie. It is possible to develop a more elaborate framework by further sub-classification; certainly such strategies have been common enough in 'structural' analysis. However, since my aims here are nothing like as grand as those espoused in many structuralist studies, and since I do not share their characteristic assumptions about the ontological significance of oppositional struc-ture, I have no need to embark upon such an ambitious project. The simple set of contrasts of table 5.1 is sufficient for my purposes.

How, then, does narrative operate within this context of basic oppositions? Essentially, different kinds of horror-movie narratives work upon different subsets of oppositions, developing their motivat-ing threat with reference to one or two contrasts 'selected' from the array available. Of course, all horror movies pose some kind of threat to order and, invariably, to life and limb; I shall take that to be narratively constant. The structure of oppositions serves as a more precise formulation of the kinds of narrative space in which this order–disorder–order sequence is played out. Typically, a horror movie will exploit the tensions implicit in a particular contrast, confronting known with unknown, and — at least in closed versions — finally returning the threatening impulse to its proper domain. In

Table 5.1  Basic oppositions[1] in horror-movie narratives

| *Known* | *Unknown* |
| --- | --- |
| life | death |
| the secular everyday | the supernatural |
| normal physical matter | abnormal physical matter |
| human normality (earth) | alien abnormality (space) |
| the conscious self | the unconscious self |
| 'normal' sexuality | 'abnormal' sexuality |
| social order | social disorder |
| sanity | insanity |
| health | disease |
| culture | nature |
| | |
| (Good) | (Bad) |

the course of this narrative progression, known and unknown normally come to be associated with a particular framework of moral judgements which, unlike those found in, for example, the gangster movie, routinely stand in a stable and unambiguous relation to the genre's basic structure. It has only been very late in horror-movie history that 'good' and 'bad' have been anything but conventionally located.

Let me now introduce the three main narrative sub-types in broad order of their temporal significance: first, what I shall call the Knowledge Narrative; second, the Invasion Narrative; and, finally, the Metamorphosis Narrative.[2] Though instances of all three can be found at every stage of the genre's development, knowledge and invasion narratives are dominant up to the sixties, while invasion and metamorphosis narratives take precedence thereafter. I shall begin, then, with the knowledge narrative.

## The Knowledge Narrative

The subset of oppositions within which the knowledge narrative is most commonly grounded is that contrasting life with death, secular everyday with supernature, and normal physical matter with abnormal physical matter. The narrative itself functions by proposing the existence of a body of knowledge capable of mediating between these domains of known and unknown. In the hands of, most frequently, a scientist, knowledge gives rise to a threat to the ordered world of the known, whether as a matter of deliberate intent or as an unanticipated consequence of 'meddling' in things that one should not. This leads to a period of rampage, during which attempts are made to resist the threat with a combination of expertise (sometimes based on exactly the same kind of knowledge as that originally causing the disorder) and coercion. In the much more common, closed version, resistance ultimately succeeds in once more insulating known from unknown and the monster is returned to its proper domain.

The general pattern of the closed knowledge narrative is illustrated diagrammatically in figure. 5.1.

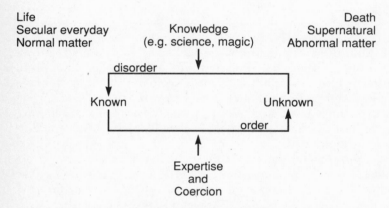

**Figure 5.1   The closed knowledge narrative**

Forms of this narrative − particularly those relating to scientific knowledge − dominate the pre-sixties period. They figure in never less than a third of horror movies during these years, and the proportion is not infrequently as high as 50 per cent. After 1960, however, they decline, more or less in line with the decreasing significance of science in the modern horror movie; by the eighties, knowledge narratives feature in, at a generous estimate, only 15 per cent of films.

Classically, of course, this is the world of the mad scientist, most familiar to us in the many variations on the Frankenstein story. Indeed, the basic framework of all knowledge narratives, here seen in its life/death variant, is neatly introduced in the spoken preface to Universal's 1932 *Frankenstein*: 'We are about to unfold the story of Frankenstein, a man of science, who sought to create a man after his own image, without reckoning upon God. It is one of the strangest tales ever told. It deals with the two great mysteries of creation: life and death.' The triangle of man, science and moral presumption thus established, *Frankenstein* goes on to develop what will become the classic pattern for the knowledge narrative. Let me consider it, therefore, in a little more detail.

The movie's opening section establishes the characters of Henry Frankenstein and his crippled assistant Fritz, both first encountered stealing a freshly buried corpse. The stylized sets and lighting of the film's early scenes, both in the graveyard and in the laboratory, are in stark contrast to the 'naturalistic' normality of the settings in which we are introduced to Elizabeth, Frankenstein's fiancée, his friend Victor and Dr Waldman, his former teacher. Characteristically for the period, the orderly world of the known is stylistically counterposed to the disordered and threatening domain of the unknown, an opposition through which we are steadily made aware of impending disaster. The climax to these opening intimations of disorder − a punctuation point marking the transition to the period of monstrous rampage − comes with the creation of life in the creature and Frankenstein's staring intensity at the scene's end as he mutters hysterically, 'It's alive!'

The rampage phase, occupying much of the rest of the film, follows after a brief interlude in which a degree of sympathy is established for Frankenstein. Some such digression is found in all versions of the knowledge narrative that favour ambiguity in moral representation of the scientist − narratively essential, of course, if we are to have any basis for empathic identification with this central figure. Typically this involves our recognizing that although knowledge inevitably is dangerous, the man of knowledge himself (it invariably is a man) may yet prove to be acceptably motivated. In *Frankenstein* this is principally conveyed in the scene in which Henry, obviously inspired rather than simply crazed, explains his views to Waldman. 'Where should we be if nobody tried to find out what lies beyond? Have you never wanted to look beyond the clouds and stars, to know what causes trees to bud and what changes darkness into light? But if you talk like that people call you crazy...'. The thematic tension between aspiration and reality is underlined by the fact that this scene is precipitately interrupted by our first full sight of the creature, an image which must have had a remarkable impact on period audiences as yet unfamiliar with Karloff's extraordinary make-up, movements and gestures.

Occasioned both by Fritz's mistreatment of the creature and the fact that a 'criminal brain' has been accidentally implanted — another way of minimizing Frankenstein's moral liability — the full rampage now follows. It begins in the context of Waldman's attempt to resist the monster by expertise. He drugs it, effectively saving Frankenstein's life, but then succumbs first to the temptations of knowledge and then to the creature itself when it proves to be cumulatively resistant to the drugs. From this point on — as so often in such movies — the coercive solution becomes the only possibility. As the narrative develops to its climax, the celebratory activities of Elizabeth and Frankenstein's wedding day are interrupted by the creature's assault of Elizabeth and by the father carrying his dead child into the midst of the festivities. The brightly lit normality of village and house gives way to the darkness in which the creature is finally tracked down. Hurling its creator from the top of a windmill, it is burned to death in a climactic sequence of frenzied mob violence. The threat now safely returned to the unknown, normality and order can be restored, and in our last sight of Henry he is being tended by the faithful Elizabeth.

*Frankenstein* exemplifies a narrative strategy fundamental to all knowledge narratives, though here found in its most elaborate form. As the genre moved into the forties it became less common to emphasize the scientist-as-victim, and many later mad scientists suffered far more ignominious fates than Henry. Thus, in *Behind the Door* (1940), *The Ape* and *Before I Hang* (both 1941), Karloff's mad scientists, though still in some sense victims of the search for knowledge, are less conventionally redeemable than Henry Frankenstein, and are consequently eliminated. As the knowledge narrative was simplified, therefore, and as the horror movies of the forties grew shorter and cheaper, the locus of formal identification shifted away from the mad scientist and towards the ubiquitous 'juvenile leads'. Unlike the anguished Henry (although perhaps kin to Victor and Elizabeth), these characters serve only a narrative-enabling function: they are of no significance beyond their formal positions as potential victims or monster-catchers. In these unadorned versions of the knowledge narrative, knowledge itself is only the formal source of the disordering impulse (embodied, as always, in flamboyant laboratory *mise-en-scène*), and the films thus become event-oriented to a quite remarkable degree. While their overall structure does remain that so clearly laid out in *Frankenstein*, they are progressively denuded of all references to the morally defensible aspirations of science.

The pattern is very similar in those few films that revolve around knowledge of supernature rather than of science. Indeed, it has often been observed that horror movie science has much in common with magic, at least in its proponents' apparent ability to achieve instantaneous miracles. Magical knowledge, however, has not conventionally attracted the same positive moral evaluation as horror-movie science, and it is therefore rare to find a magician accorded the kind of sympathy given to the early Frankenstein. Magical knowledge can be positively valued, of course, and in a few films, such as *The Devil Rides Out* (1967), it may also be seen as a corrupting influence on those who, like some mad scientists, hunger for knowledge itself. Generally, however, magical powers are invoked simply as a means of creating a variety of supernatural threats, of breaching the barriers protecting the known secular everyday from the unknown domain of supernature.

In any case, magical variants of the knowledge narrative are not numerous. In the pre-sixties period less than 1 per cent of horror movies invoke such knowledge as a serious narrative device, and even within the larger post-sixties proportion of 14 per cent, few are concerned with magic in the context of an unmodified knowledge narrative. As we shall see later in this chapter, a somewhat abbreviated version of a magical knowledge narrative is sometimes employed as the precipitating factor for a metamorphosis, but in these cases it is the metamorphosis form that proves dominant. Only in a bare handful of movies − *Night of the Demon* (1958), *Night of the Eagle* (1962), *The Dunwich Horror* (1970) − do we find a direct magical analogue to the familiar mad-scientist story.

Nevertheless, these supernatural variations are significant in developing the scepticism characteristically expressed by disbelieving rationalists when faced with the scientist's or magician's claims. While that has always been part of the battery of devices used to ensure the mad scientist's isolation (as Waldman observes of Henry Frankenstein's work, 'His researches in the field of chemical galvanism and electro-biology were far in advance of our theories here at the University'), it is only in cases of magical manipulation that such doubt becomes critical in generating tension and involvement.[3] Will he/she believe in the supernatural soon enough to combat it? Thus, Holden in *Night of the Demon* and Taylor in *Night of the Eagle*, both academic researchers and, therefore, candidate 'experts', are initially unable to fulfil that role because of their rationalist disbelief. Only when the rampage phase is in full swing do they finally accept the reality of the threat. Unsurprisingly, then, the primary focus of supernatural knowledge narratives is often upon the (expert) combatants rather than on the magician, and the resolution may depend more on individual expertise than on coercion. Holden defeats *Night of the Demon*'s magician by out-manœuvring him on his own magical ground, returning the runic inscription just before the curse takes effect.

This emphasis on individual expertise also features in the third principal variation of the knowledge narrative: those movies, mostly of the fifties, which invoke a rather different order of scientific knowledge. Prior to the fifties the most common science-based threat derived from medical knowledge, usually leading to the construction or resurrection of some monstrous creature. However, in the fifties and sixties a less medically orientated science came to figure more prominently. The key concept here was 'radiation', and the key opposition not that between life and death (though there are cases where radiation was employed to overcome death, as in *Creature With the Atom Brain* (1956)), but that between normal and abnormal physical matter.

Most of these movies lean on the common fifties currency of atomic energy, some generating their nuclear threat via unanticipated effects, some postulating a more intentional connection between scientist and disorder. On the whole, however, the out-and-out evil scientist is rare; many of the radiation-based threats are, strictly speaking, accidental. Whether they are mutations of natural creatures like giant ants in *Them!* (1954), overgrown molluscs in *The Monster that Challenged the World* (1957) or giant locusts in *The Beginning of the End* (1960), radiation-awakened prehistoric monsters such as *Godzilla* (1957), or even direct embodiments of radioactivity like the nuclear horrors of *The Magnetic Monster* (1953), *Fiend Without a Face* (1959) or *The H-Man* (1960), their basic narrative form is familiar enough. Investigation of the 'abnormal' world of atomic structure causes or occasions the threat; there follows a rampage period during which scientific and coercive expertise combine; finally, in the closed version at least, the forces of order are triumphant and the threat eliminated.

Take for instance *X the Unknown* (1956), in which, typically for this sub-type, the opening pre-rampage phase is very brief. After all, if there is no central 'mad scientist' and no 'scientific temptation' subtext, then there is little need for extended character development or elaborate scene-setting. Accordingly, *X the Unknown* introduces its threat immediately: an unexplained explosion in an isolated military-training area produces radiation burns on its victims. An expert scientist is summoned to help, and it emerges that an unknown 'thing' from beneath the earth's surface has been attracted by the presence of the atomic energy on which it feeds. After a rampage, including a greatly enlarging meal at a nuclear-research station, scientist and military tempt it with radioactive bait and wipe it out by an energy overdose.

The very simplicity of *X the Unknown* reflects the basic character of all such narratives. Knowledge is now central only in so far as a kind of counter-factual can be established: were it not for scientific work on atomic energy the threat would not exist. Thus while no individual mad scientist is responsible, it is still the temptations of science itself which are the fount of disorder. By investigating that which we should not — by splitting the atom, the fundamental constituent of matter — science occasions the monstrous attack. Typically, however, the focus of identification is now on the experts who combat the monster, a combination of scientists skilled in this dangerous branch of science, and coercive specialists commonly represented by the military. In this new context, then, there is a kind of ambiguity about science. Though most of these later versions of the knowledge narrative tacitly presume that we would be better off without nuclear knowledge, they also articulate our dependence on both science and scientists. Note that this is not the relatively optimistic ambiguity of the Frankenstein story, where, although science is dangerous, it can also represent a positive aspiration. Here there is a more resigned recognition of our reliance on those expert authorities who protect us from threats over which we have no control.

To a considerable degree, then, the progression of the knowledge narrative from the thirties to the fifties sees some marked changes of emphasis. In particular, though scientific knowledge is still narratively essential, it diminishes in its threatening significance. In the seventies and eighties that diminution accelerates, and the threat of knowledge becomes so indirect that it all but disappears. In a film like *Monster* (1980), though the assumption is that an experiment in genetics has adversely effected undersea evolution, the scientific background plays little part in the narrative. The only role for knowledge here is as a subsidiary precipitant, and *Monster* ends up as a curious mixture of invasion and metamorphosis forms. Even the candidate 'expert' — a marine biologist — is not in a position to marshal her scientific capacities in effective resistance to the mutant humanoids, and, as with so many horror movies of this period, *Monster*'s narrative is never finally closed. The film ends with the birth of a new mutant.

It should be clear by now that the knowledge narrative belongs firmly to the first phase of horror-movie history. Its contingent tendency towards narrative closure, its presumption that major threats are a direct and controllable consequence of human actions and, above all, the very specificity of its threat, all contrast strikingly with the characteristic narrative forms of the seventies and eighties. Only with the introduction of nuclear science in the fifties did the knowledge narrative begin to edge towards a more open, indirect and diffuse formulation, and in so doing it lost many of the features that once made it so distinctive. To understand the significance of that decline, however, it is first necessary to explore the genre's other two narrative forms.

## The Invasion Narrative

The invasion narrative is the simplest and, in some respects, the most pervasive of horror-movie narratives. In one version or another it is to be found throughout the genre's history, a consequence of both its accessible simplicity and its capacity for flexible adaptation to a wide variety of contexts. Its subset of informing oppositions is concomitantly extensive, including, minimally, the contrasts between life and death, the secular everyday and the supernatural, human normality and alien abnormality, and culture and nature, as well as intimations of 'normal' versus 'abnormal' sexuality and health versus disease. Unlike the knowledge narrative, no precipitant is required; the unknown simply invades the known, for reasons which may or may not be forthcoming but which are, in any case, an autonomous feature of the threat itself. At its most simple, the invasion narrative is all rampage: the monster appears out of the blue, goes on the rampage, is faced with the customary combination of expertise and coercion and, perhaps, is finally returned to the unknown. In more elaborate versions, time may be spent in developing the pre-rampage phase, usually in terms of a steady rise in anticipatory tension, and in some of the most complex variations of all, invasion and metamorphosis narratives amalgamate to form what is almost a new narrative type.

Whatever these variations, however, the basic pattern of the invasion narrative is simple to represent.

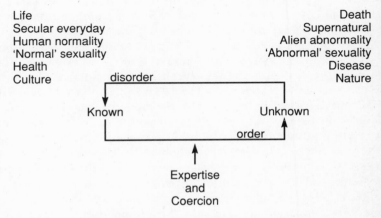

**Figure 5.2    The closed invasion narrative**

Figure 5.2 represents the closed version. Unlike knowledge narratives, open versions of invasion narratives are quite numerous in certain periods of the genre's history — most notably from the seventies onward, and I shall return to them toward the end of this section. During the early years, however, it is the closed version that predominates.

In the thirties and forties the most common form of invasion narrative revolves around invasion from supernature, especially by vampires. Now it might be argued that vampire movies represent not so much invasion from supernature as a kind of co-presence of the secular everyday and the supernatural: vampires are *in* this world even if not entirely of it. However, this is to be over-literal in interpreting the label 'invasion'. The essence of an invasion narrative is that the threat crosses the oppositional boundary unbidden, whether it is that between secular and supernatural, earth and space or life and death. Most invasion narratives specifically mark that crossing in some way, thus dramatizing the domain-distinction between alien threat and normality. Many vampire movies, for example — including Universal's first *Dracula* in 1931 — have recourse to the image of long fingers emerging from the vampire's coffin, its lid slowly rising — the creature symbolically and actually penetrating the secular world. Later, such images become more aggressive, with whole corpses thrusting their way out of their graves; but even as early as the 1946 *Return of the Vampire* there is a quite startling shot of a vampire's hand erupting from beneath the soil.

In their main outline, vampire movies follow the standard pattern for the invasion narrative, with — prior to the changes wrought by American urban vampires in the seventies — substantial emphasis on the vampire-catcher's expertise. The 1931 *Dracula* introduces much of the arcane knowledge necessary to the properly equipped vampire-hunter: crucifixes, wolfbane, mirrors, wooden stakes, sunlight and the rest of the esoteric apparatus. In the person of Van Helsing it also introduces the best known incarnation of the expert bourgeois individualist, whose role is to convince the world of the seriousness of the threat — 'The superstition of yesterday can become the scientific reality of today' — and then act to destroy it. Like many of its successors, however, the first *Dracula* also presupposes a rather more elaborate oppositional structure than is captured in the simple distinction between supernatural and secular. The sexual overtones of vampirism, for instance, imply a contrast between 'normal' and 'abnormal' sexuality, while the sustained animal references — including, in *Dracula*, wolves, rats, bats, spiders and some creatures that look suspiciously like armadillos (as well as Dracula's now-famous observation upon the night's animal noises: 'Listen to the children of the night; what music they make...') — all serve to identify the vampire with a particular kind of malevolent nature. The life/death opposition also plays a significant role, sometimes even to the degree of inviting our sympathy for the poor vampire, doomed to eternal life. To again quote Lugosi's Count: 'To die, to be really dead; that must be glorious.'

In all these respects, then, vampire movies weave a complex web of invention around the basic invasion narrative. In some cases the main narrative line evolves towards the metamorphosis type, usually by emphasizing the perilous transformation of the human victim into a vampire. There is an element of that in the first *Dracula*'s conception of Lucy, though quite restrained compared to later movie adaptations of the Stoker novel — Hammer's 1958 *Dracula*, for example, offers a more full-blooded account of her transformation. And in some later variations, the demonic invasion of *The Exorcist* (1974) for instance, metamorphosis becomes the principal narrative focus while supernatural invasion serves only as its major precipitant. In the end this blurs the distinction between the two narrative types, a slippage which, as we shall see, has become a significant feature of the modern horror movie.

Before considering that development, however, it should be noted that vampires are not the only invading monsters of the thirties and forties. A few films, such as *The Uninvited* (1944) or a couple of the stories told in the omnibus movie *Dead of Night* (1945), propose supernatural invasion by ghosts, and a slightly larger group — the most famous of which is *King Kong* (1933) — allows a 'natural' creature (albeit prehistoric) to breach the culture/nature boundary. These prehistoric-monster movies are often the simplest of invasion narratives, at least in their tendency to focus upon the monster's depredations at the expense of all else; but for all their action-filled potential, giant apes, lizards and birds did not even begin to challenge the classical dominance of the vampire. That kind of monstrous invasion had to wait until the fifties, and the discovery of 'space', before it fully came into its own.

Invasion narratives figure in 20 per cent to 25 per cent of horror movies in the genre's first two decades, while in the fifties the figure exceeds 50 per cent. The most common opposition on which such films are founded is, of course, that between human normality and alien abnormality, more specifically represented in the contrast between human beings and space invaders. These SF-inclined horror movies fall broadly into two groups. In one, the more numerous, invasion is no more than an occasion for physical rampage, with bug-eyed monsters of all shapes and sizes wreaking various kinds of apocalyptic havoc in the face of the combined might of science and the military. The list of such films is enormous, ranging from *The Thing from Another World* (1952) to *Attack of the 50-Foot Woman* (1959), and taking in movies as diverse as *The Quatermass Experiment* (1955), *Quatermass II* (1957), *The War of the Worlds* (1953), *Twenty Million Miles to Earth* (1957) and *Invasion of the Hell*

*Creatures* (1957). The second, less common group is not so much devoted to documenting physical rampage as it is concerned about the alien threat to human *social* normality. These invaders want to take over the world, not simply destroy it. A significant innovation here postulates invasion of our very being, leading to alien imitations of human originals. *Invasion of the Body Snatchers* (1956) is perhaps the best remembered of such films, but others — *The Day Mars Invaded Earth* (1963), for example, or *Invisible Invaders* (1960) and *Not of this Earth* (1957) — also feature invasion by simulacra whose goal is to infiltrate and thus eliminate human normality. Occasionally, as in both *The Day Mars Invaded Earth* and *Not of this Earth*, the stories remain open-ended, the aliens neither repelled nor eliminated.

For the most part, however, closed versions of invasion narratives are *de rigueur* up to the seventies, and the importance of the expert concomitantly is stressed. Whether the monster is a vampire, a rampaging fungus or a space-borne reptile, expertise is required to resist it. Though there is some room for non-expert characters, if only in the purely narrative-enabling roles of monster-fodder or people to whom things must be explained, major emphasis is on the confrontation between monstrous threat and specialized combatants. The exceptions to this pattern are those films with open narratives: they have no successful expert defences and, in many of them, an 'everyperson' figure fights a losing battle. Declining efficacy on the part of the monster-catching expert is a prominent feature of the genre's later years, and while there are still many closed invasion narratives (witness *Jaws* (1975), *Squirm* (1976), *The Car* (1977), *Alien* (1979), *The Fog* (1980), *Poltergeist* (1982), and *Cujo* (1983)), the seventies and eighties do see a striking growth of the open type. The principal oppositional context for this expansion revolves around combinations of secular versus supernatural and nature versus culture, and the general pattern is diagrammatically represented in figure 5.3.

The simplest way of 'opening up' invasion narratives is a kind of postscript technique: in the film's final moments, often its last shot, the invasion is seen to begin all over again. Thus, in vampire movies like *Count Yorga, Vampire* (1970) or *The Return of Count Yorga* (1971), the final image reveals that one of the film's principal characters has now become a vampire. Similarly with 'natural' invaders like the one in *Alligator* (1982), where the movie ends by showing us another unwanted baby alligator flushed into the sewers;

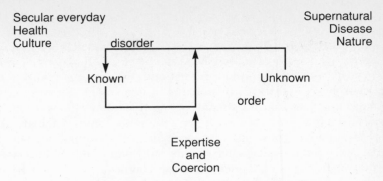

**Figure 5.3    The open invasion narrative**

or with the unseen beach-dwelling creature of *Blood Beach* (1981),
where we are left with the growing realization that others still live
beneath the sand. In some ways such postscripts are little more than
narrative gimmicks. We are given the conventional satisfactions of
narrative closure, while the *formal* possibility of a continuing threat
is tantalizingly held before us. This superficial lack of closure does
not seriously disrupt the generic order−disorder−order sequence,
and our emotional investment in that process is broadly sustained.
Narrative emphasis remains with the successful, if temporary,
reimposition of order.

This is not the case, however, in a second group of open invasion
narratives, where the disruptive effect is more far-reaching. In these
movies the impulse to disorder is never even temporarily overcome,
and the characteristic narrative sequence translates order into disorder
and stops at that. At best, the films' protagonists are forced to
retreat in the face of the undefeated threat, as in, for example, *The
Amityville Horror* (1980); at worst, they are destroyed and we are
left with the prospect of a continuing cycle of disaster. It is this more
apocalyptic form of invasion that has become common in recent
metamorphosis/invasion amalgams like *Zombies* (1980), and in some
invasion narratives focused upon natural attacks, such as *Frogs* (1972).
Apart from the fact that it reflects a more general change in the
genre's narrative conventions, this development also lends many
modern horror movies a somewhat pessimistic edge. If the fears here
represented are undefeated, then the cultures within which such
narratives make sense must surely be less secure than they once were.

## The Metamorphosis Narrative

If the invasion narrative is the simplest of horror-movie forms — and few narrative structures are simpler than one based around a monster that comes out of the blue and straight onto the rampage — then the metamorphosis narrative is potentially the most complex. Its structuring context includes many of the basic oppositions, though historically the most significant have been the contrasts between conscious and unconscious self, normal and abnormal sexuality, social order and disorder, sanity and insanity and health and disease. In the modern period, moreover, these contrasts have often been overlaid in narrative patterns that more or less equate the emergence of the threatening unconscious self with abnormal sexuality, social disorder, insanity and disease, thus generating a kind of psychiatrically overdetermined horror-movie world. Add to that the metamorphosis narrative's undoubted potential for combining with the other basic narrative forms (the precipitants of metamorphosis narratives are often knowledge or invasion narratives in their own right) and you have a blueprint for what has become if not the most frequent, then certainly the most distinctive horror movie narrative of the modern period. Its closed version is given diagrammatic expression in figure 5.4.

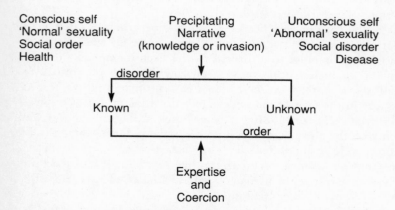

**Figure 5.4  The closed metamorphosis narrative**

Broadly, and leaving variation in the precipitant to one side, this overall structure is implemented in two basic forms. In the first and more common — the 'individual' type — a human metamorphoses into a monster and henceforth functions much as would an anthropomorphic threat in an orthodox knowledge or invasion narrative. Indeed, the line may be blurred between a knowledge narrative in which, say, the scientist creates a threatening medical monstrosity, and a metamorphosis variation on the same theme. A judgement as to which form predominates, if either, would involve assessing the film's discursive detail. Where weight of emphasis lies with the scientist, then inevitably requirements of the knowledge narrative will be paramount. Where the metamorphosis itself is central, then knowledge would be reduced to the status of major precipitant and the principal locus of narrative involvement will rest with the metamorphant. Such ambiguity is characteristic of, for example, different versions of the familiar Jekyll and Hyde story, doubly so in that there the metamorphant is also the man of knowledge.

The second and 'collective' form of the metamorphosis narrative is distinctive in character and restricted in period. Here, though metamorphants may well slaughter and maim with the best of them, it is the metamorphosis itself which is the primary threat. Collectively, *we* have become potential victims, to be transformed into zombies, gibbering maniacs or diseased wrecks. For whatever reason — it need not be made entirely clear for the proper functioning of the narrative — human physical and social orders are faced with direct transformation into their disordered opposites. In the most apocalyptic versions of the form there is no narrative closure. No combination of expertise and coercion can halt the growing threat of metamorphosis, and all humanity is helpless in the face of spreading 'infection'. Yet however vast its scale, the heart of this narrative lies in the emphatically *internal* quality of its threat. It is not simply that we may be destroyed, as we might have been by a score of traditional movie monsters. It is also that we will be fundamentally altered in the process; that our humanity itself is at risk. In the best-known recent variations on this theme — *Night of the Living Dead* (1970) and its numerous spawn — we are all fated to become lumbering, cannibalistic zombies, indiscriminately preying upon former friends and family. In one of the more memorable images from Romero's film, a young girl is seen happily gnawing on her father's half-eaten arm.

In the early years of the genre, however, it is the individual version of metamorphosis that predominates, partly through the Jekyll and Hyde story (major-studio adaptations were made in 1932 and 1941, both under the title *Dr Jekyll and Mr Hyde*) and, perhaps more significantly, in the person of the movie werewolf. The basic narrative pattern for werewolf movies was set in two films: *The Werewolf of London* (1935) and *The Wolf Man* (1942). The former is framed in familiar knowledge-narrative terms. Botanist Dr Glendon is bitten and infected by a werewolf in the course of his researches in Tibet, having single-mindedly continued into the forbidden valley despite contrary advice. An aged priest warns him that 'there are some things it is better not to bother with,' though, true to the characteristic ambiguity of thirties knowledge narratives, he also adds: 'you are foolish — but without fools there would be no wisdom.' The price of Glendon's thirst for knowledge, then, is metamorphosis into a werewolf: 'neither man nor wolf, but a satanic creature with the worst qualities of both'. In their regular invocation of 'dual personality' (in *The Wolf Man* lycanthropy is actually described as a form of schizophrenia), these early werewolf stories bear a more than passing resemblance to the Jekyll and Hyde model, a similarity further confirmed in the moral and emotional anguish to which their protagonists are routinely subjected. Like Dr Jekyll, both Glendon and Talbot (in *The Wolf Man*) are horrified at the actual and likely behaviour of their metamorphosed selves; unlike most horror-movie creatures, their actions are constantly informed by conscience.

Therein, of course, lies the distinctiveness of the traditional metamorphosis narrative. The monster and the principal character with whom we are invited to identify are one and the same, and our concern is as much for the werewolf as for its victims. Thus most of *The Wolf Man*'s narrative drive depends on our being involved in Talbot's progressive awareness of his fate and his desperate attempts to protect the movie's heroine from his own likely actions — 'the werewolf instinctively seeks to kill the thing it loves best', Dr Yogami tells us in *The Werewolf of London*. Accordingly, the classic metamorphosis narrative is rather more subjectively focused than is normal in horror movies; its narrative point of view is firmly grounded in the metamorphant's own perspective. Indeed, *The Wolf Man*'s actual scenes of lupine depredation seem almost perfunctory compared to those which narrate Talbot's inner turmoil, and the film's overall mood is gloomy rather than visceral or frightening.

Werewolf movies, classical and modern, clearly function within the general opposition between supernatural and secular, but are often overlaid and sometimes overwhelmed by other structuring contrasts. As in so many metamorphosis narratives, the unconscious lurks somewhere in the background even where the formal cause of metamorphosis would appear to be supernatural. Thus, in *The Wolf Man*, which undoubtedly set the generic scene for many subsequent werewolf movies, there is a curious mixture of psychology and supernaturalism. As Sir John Talbot observes of lycanthropy, 'like most legends it must have some basis in fact — it's probably an ancient explanation of the dual personality in most of us'; later in the film, he notes 'a variety of schizophrenia...the good and evil in every man's soul; in this case evil takes the shape of an animal'. Though such explicit rationalizations are rather less common later, and though precipitants of lycanthropy move beyond simple infection into both scientific experiment (*The Werewolf* (1956) and *I was a Teenage Werewolf* (1957)) and inheritance (*The Curse of the Werewolf* (1961)), these and other individual metamorphosis narratives always retain the basic features of the classic period. As time goes by, of course, the idea of the unconscious 'Hyde' persona is more explicitly related to the release of uncontrollable sexual drives. A theme which is always present in the various adaptations of *Dr Jekyll and Mr Hyde* and in the early identification of female sexuality with feline metamorphosis in the likes of *Cat People* (1943), the opposition between an unknown domain of voracious sexuality and that of 'normal' heterosexual love, is foregrounded in metamorphosis narratives of the seventies and eighties. To take just three modern versions of traditional metamorphosis stories: *Doctor Jekyll and Sister Hyde* (1971), *The Howling* (1981) and *Cat People* (1982) are all quite open in glossing the disordering impulse in sexual terms, while still retaining sympathy for protagonists who are put under impossible stress by the recurrent onset of metamorphosis.

In this, of course, such movies reflect the general significance of overt sexuality in the modern genre, a feature peculiarly suited to a narrative form focused upon human metamorphoses from 'normal' to 'abnormal' states. There is a similar sexual emphasis in the movies that follow *Psycho* (1960) and *Peeping Tom* (1960) in portraying the periodic metamorphoses of seemingly sane young men into compulsive killers, the eruption of the unconscious self into the world of normal human relationships. Sharing the traditional tension-generating mechanisms of the metamorphosis narrative (when will he change next? who will be the victim?), these psycho-movies also place the monster fully at narrative centre. I shall not systematically describe the many detailed variations of the psychotic metamorphosis film, leaving that task to chapter 9's analysis of the whole sub-genre. It is sufficient here to observe that of the 33 per cent of post-1960 horror movies involving psychotics, the few sixties examples of metamorphosis narratives (including *Homicidal* (1961), *Repulsion* (1965), *The Psychopath* (1966), and *Twisted Nerve* (1969)) are succeeded by very many more in the seventies and eighties. From *Hands of the Ripper* (1971) to *Dressed to Kill* (1980), from *The Fiend* (1972) to *The Shining* (1980), from *Deranged* (1976) to *Nightmares in a Damaged Brain* (1983), we are given protagonists overwhelmed by the disordering impulses of their own psyches. Note that these are not the virtually anonymous psychotic killers of the likes of *Halloween* (1979) or *Friday the 13th* (1980), where the typical story-form is more of an invasion narrative. As with almost all metamorphosis narratives, those involving psychosis place considerable characterizing emphasis on the psychotic monster. The nature of the *Halloween* killer's insanity is fundamentally irrelevant to the operation of the movie; he is, as its final moments concede, 'the boogie man'. The form of the metamorphosis killer's psychosis, however, is crucial to the movie's narrative and to the nature of our involvement in it.

There remains one further variation on the individual metamorphosis narrative which has been of some significance since the early seventies. Bracketed by the huge success of *The Exorcist* in 1974 and the controversy surrounding *The Evil Dead* in 1982, the decade saw a steady stream of possession movies in which occupying demons metamorphose their victims. Generally such films employ different combinations of narrative types, usually beginning as some kind of invasion narrative and then introducing elements of metamorphosis. In this sense, if in no other, they resemble those few fifties invasion/metamorphosis amalgams which postulated space creatures invading human minds. Unlike demonic possession films, however, those fifties movies were often somewhat collectivist in emphasis, their invaders seeking finally to overwhelm the whole of humanity.

Though relatively infrequent in the fifties, it is this focus upon collective metamorphosis that is particularly notable in the horror movie's modern period. The mass spread of metamorphosis by infection was always a rhetorical possibility in the werewolf movie, and even in *The Werewolf of London* Yogami threatens an 'epidemic that will turn London into a shambles'. For most of horror-movie history, however, it has only been in those films focused on zombies that more than a hint of collective metamorphosis has been found, and only really in their post–1970 development has this form reached its zenith. Early instances of the zombie, such as *White Zombie* (1932), *King of the Zombies* (1941), and *I Walked With a Zombie* (1943), though making some play with personal metamorphosis, featured their zombies largely as weapons of magical knowledge and power. Whether zombies were created by mad scientists (*Teenage Zombies* (1960)), space invaders (*The Earth Dies Screaming* (1965)) or, most commonly, voodoo (*The Plague of the Zombies* (1966)), most pre-1970 zombie movies used metamorphosis as a kind of subtext to other narrative forms. It was only in the wake of George Romero's startlingly innovative *Night of the Living Dead* (1970) that the distinctively modern zombie movie emerged, its narrative distinguished by the relentless attack of the abnormally metamorphosed upon the surviving representatives of normal human life.

This form, of course, is much simpler than many traditional metamorphosis narratives, its epidemic pattern escalating dramatic action to the exclusion of the more meditative possibilities of classic werewolf movies. Characteristically, such films begin with an isolated case (in *Night of the Living Dead* a zombie is encountered in a graveyard) and then build rapidly towards a situation in which embattled humanity struggles against a growing army of marauding creatures. In the more elaborate developments of the pattern, including *Night of the Living Dead* itself, *Shivers* (1976), *Rabid* and *Blue Sunshine* (both 1977), *The Crazies* (1978) and *Zombies* (1980), in which narrative precipitants range from parasites through drugs to disease, those caught up in the struggle are given quite complex characterization and are framed within distinctive social contexts. Consequently, whatever restrictions are imposed by sheer pace of events, these films do provide some basis for audience identification and involvement. In contrast, the rather less elaborate and often bloodier variations (*The Living Dead at the Manchester Morgue* (1975), say, or Lucio Fulci's films like *Zombie Flesh-Eaters* (1980) or *City of the Living Dead* (1982)) permit little development of either character or context. The escalating spread of destruction stands as sufficient in itself.

Whatever these differences, most modern movies that involve collective metamorphosis do share two principal features. Though they might allow us to know the fate of their major protagonists, they leave open the ultimate fate of humanity. Like those nature invasion movies that propose an eco-apocalypse, their narratives remain open in so far as the threat continues unabated: the 'disease' will spread. There is no safe return to order, and the typical narrative structure is that of figure 5.5.

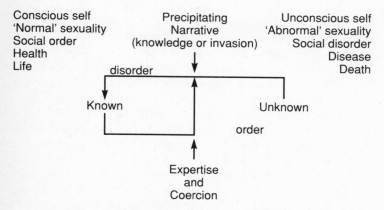

**Figure 5.5    The open metamorphosis narrative**

Second, although a significant part of the threat in these films is death at the hands of metamorphosed monsters, a major narrative strategy is to play upon our involvement with characters who are subsequently metamorphosed. The dehumanizing threat is therefore as important as traditional expectations of violence and destruction. Taken together, these features of modern metamorphosis narratives suggest a genre universe which, in comparison with earlier periods, has become profoundly insecure, a pattern also encountered in other aspects of the genre's recent history. Perhaps, then, there is a fundamental division in the development of the horror movie?

### Security and Paranoia

From whatever angle we approach the overall development of the genre, we encounter a distinct shift in emphasis somewhere in the sixties. So wide are the ramifications of this change that it is tempting to conclude that there are indeed two distinctive horror-movie worlds, each incorporating characteristic narratives, settings, styles, and motifs. Of course, to make such a hard-and-fast distinction is to elevate a broad trend into a mutually exclusive division, and it is therefore important to note that almost all types of horror movie can be found in most periods of the genre. Yet there clearly are analytic differences to be discovered, seen most dramatically at either extreme of the genre's history but also apparent in the overall pattern of pre- and post-sixties horror movies. This is sufficient to encourage a provisional but more systematic attempt at typifying these two horror-movie worlds.[4]

The fundamental distinguishing feature of the genre's first world is its relative security. Of course, given that the narrative basis of all horror movies requires that order is subjected to threatening and disorderly impulses, this is very much a comparative question. Yet it is certainly the case that the large majority of pre-sixties horror movies presume a world which is ultimately subject to successful human intervention. This can be seen very clearly in the key role played by expertise in both knowledge and invasion narratives of the period. The coercive and/or knowledgeable expert is vital to the process of restoring order in these invariably closed narratives, while it is often the intentional activity of scientists which actually occasions the basic threat. In these films, then, human beings possess significant volition, while authorities and institutions generally remain credible protectors of social order. There is rarely any sense that the monster will survive and prosper long enough to overwhelm the movie's principal protagonists, let alone the whole of humanity, and our anticipatory involvement in both dramatic event and character always presumes secure narrative resolution.

The horror movie's second world is far more insecure than this, so much so as to reasonably invite the label 'paranoid'. Here, both the nature and course of the threat are out of human control, and in extreme metamorphosis cases, disorder often emerges from *within* humans to potentially disrupt the whole ordered world. Expertise is no longer effective; indeed, experts and representatives of institutional order are often impotent in the face of impending apocalypse. Threats emerge without warning from the disordered psyche or from disease, possessing us and destroying our very humanity. Lacking control of our inner selves, we have no means of resisting, and there is a certain inevitability to humanity's final defeat. Even the environment has become malevolent − polluted nature as a dark mirror of our own physical and psychological pollution.

Each of these 'worlds' accords primacy to a distinctive subset of contextual oppositions. In the world of 'secure horror', traditional contrasts hold sway: life/death, secular/supernatural, normal/abnormal physical matter and human/alien. The divisions they represent are clearly marked, and, therefore, the line of defence against the unknown easily distinguished. In the contrasting world of 'paranoid horror' the principal oppositions are more internal in their emphasis, whether internal to human beings themselves or to their cultures and social systems. Conscious/unconscious, normal/abnormal sexuality, social order/social disorder, sanity/insanity and health/disease all generate threats of a rather different kind. By their very nature they insinuate the unknown into the known in ways not normally found in more traditional reaches of the genre. Even a horror-movie character as orthodox as the vampire becomes far more 'this-worldly' in its more paranoid modern representation. Like psychotics, modern vampires can pass as ordinary occupants of the everyday secular world, no longer patently obvious trespassers from some Gothic domain of supernature.

'Security' and 'paranoia', then, are the key reference points for the two horror-movie worlds. Though there have always been instances both of *secure* and of *paranoid* horror, historically the one has succeeded the other as the genre's dominant form, a process which begins in the sixties and comes to fruition in the seventies and eighties. It is this cumulative change − seen so far in relation to narrative structure and in the 'historical' accounts of chapters 3 and 4 − which frames the genre's more specific shifts of detail and inflection, and it is to documenting some of those changes that chapter 6 will turn.


Notes

1 Note that the scope of reference of these contrasting pairs varies from period to period. What might count as 'normal' sexuality, for example, differs between, say, the bland romanticism of the classic period and the more sexually aware articulations of heterosexual 'love' found in the horror movies of the seventies and eighties. Similar differences between periods can be found in other oppositions. Their referential scope has altered during the course of the genre's development, often, no doubt, for more general cultural and extra-cinematic reasons.

2 Each of the three types can take an open or closed form according to whether order is finally restored or whether we are left with the belief that the impulse to disorder will continue. In the event there are relatively few open knowledge narratives, though open invasion and metamorphosis forms are quite common in the seventies and eighties.

3 This hesitation between natural and supernatural explanations is, of course, fundamental to the literary genre Todorov calls 'the fantastic'. See Tzvetan Todorov, *The Fantastic* (Ithaca, New York, 1975), especially Chapter 2. It is notable that this explanatory tension is actually quite rare in the horror movie.

4 This distinction between the two horror-movie worlds is discussed at greater length in chapter 10.

# 6

## Events – Characters – Settings

There is a sense in which this chapter is about the 'pleasures' offered to us by the genre, though it is with some reluctance that I use the word 'pleasure'. This is not because of any doubts about the real pleasures afforded to genre audiences by horror movies, or even because I wish to claim those pleasures to be somehow unmerited or crass. My reluctance stems from the term's recent appropriation by psychoanalytically inclined film studies and its consequent restriction to those aspects of cinematic satisfaction most amenable to analysis in psychoanalytic terms. As I argued in chapter 1, this study is concerned with the kind of 'practical consciousness' of genre which, while not routinely articulated by audiences, is not thereby sunk into the murky depths of the unconscious. The pleasures that interest me, then, are rather more prosaic than those postulated by psychoanalysis. They revolve around narrative, character, style, tension, identification, verisimilitude, involvement: aspects of movie story-telling familiar to any movie-goer, if normally left implicit.

It is also important, then, that I do not seek to inquire from a culturally elitist perspective about the pleasures provided by horror movies. In the past that has all too often given rise to the argument that horror movies are so clearly peculiar, unpleasant and crude that their audiences must be at best unsophisticated adolescents, or at worst perverse and sadistic deviants. Less obviously, similar considerations lie behind the traditional inclination to subject horror movies, more even than any other genre, to psychoanalytic reduction. Since it is presumed to be self-evident that no normal person could actually enjoy this stuff as one might enjoy a proper drama or even a Western, horror movies must be tapping deep-seated desires, gratifying obscure and private needs. While I have no wish to deny the significance of repressed desires and needs, it does seem to me that the horror movie's pleasures are no more or less grounded in this substratum than are any other genre experiences. As we would with any body of film, therefore, we should initiate our inquiry into horror movie enjoyment in terms of its most basic elements, asking how it is that audiences generate and sustain their involvement in the genre's typical fictions.

Except in the case of almost entirely *ad hoc* pleasures (satisfying a desire to see photographic images of naked women, say, or violence or viscera), active involvement is a basic precondition for the enjoyment of all conventional forms of fiction. Unless we are involved in a story, unless we can relate to its characters and situations, the potential pleasures of a traditional narrative movie are severely restricted. There are still non-involved pleasures to be had, of course, whether in the respectable satisfactions of compartmentalized aesthetics ('such lovely photography...') or the more publicly dubious gratifications derived from sexual display. But for most audiences, for most of the time, a level of personal involvement is the *sine qua non* of movie enjoyment. What happens next has to matter; the fate of the protagonist must make a difference; the world in which the movie's story is told must be fundamentally plausible to a receptive audience.

Now, involvement is a complex social—psychological process, the more so in that it is constructed within historically variable cultural conventions. Furthermore, we normally do not respond to a fictional discourse in bits and pieces: we relate to the continuously developing whole, the fiction as it exists in our changing experience of it. Yet to actually analyse the character of our involvement in horror movies we must fragment that process, single out certain aspects for particular attention. In this chapter I shall be concerned with only three of the modes within which our involvement, and hence our pleasure, is constructed. First I shall focus upon *event* and its organization, a concern growing directly out of chapter 5's emphasis on narrative. The second section is organised around the idea of *character*, raising questions about character stereotypes and identification. Then, at the most general level, I shall examine some of the social and cultural terms within which the genre seeks to establish the verisimilitude of its typical *settings*. It goes without saying that these three do not exhaust the possibilities, even if they do cover much of the central ground.

### Event, Tension and Involvement

While most traditional narrative forms involve some degree of suspense in the structure and sequencing of the events that they narrate, both in detail (what will happen next?) and in the overall flow through disorder to order, the horror movie is particularly expected to generate tension. Popular genres are, typically, event-full in comparison with less popular forms and, even among the distinctively action-based genres, the horror movie is notably subject to the exigencies of event-centred narration. Whatever else we might expect, horror-movie conventions always lead us to anticipate pleasurable anxiety. Many have sought to define that pleasure in terms of what they consider to be two alternative strategies: the development of suspense, which depends on predictability in the sense of our expecting something to happen but not quite knowing when, and the use of shock, which achieves its aim by its very unpredictability. In the horror movie, of course, the two are often different aspects of the same process, for the shock — however it is achieved — figures as the expressive climax to suspense-generated tension. The conventionally accepted substance of the shock effect may change from time to time, as it has, for instance, in the passage from *secure* to *paranoid* horror, but its focal position in the formal dynamics of horror-movie narrative has remained more or less constant.

Within the order—disorder—order pattern, tension-generation works at both macroscopic and microscopic levels. Macroscopically, there is an overall rise throughout the whole narrative, ending in the movie's formal resolution. Microscopically, this pattern is composed of a series of shorter sequences of events, each following the suspense/shock tension-resolution pattern. As each microscopic section is built up and then climaxed we are, ideally, drawn further into the continuing cycle. Each phase pushes us a little more; each shock gives another turn to the screw. In what must be the most frequently invoked metaphor for the horror-movie experience, we are enthusiastic riders on a roller-coaster of growing tension and periodic shock. Of course, as the volume of genre-information available to us grows we learn what kinds of things to expect and we recognize the cues which tell us that something is about to happen, but — and this is the key to the shock-effect — we cannot predict the details of timing or the precise nature of the climactic event itself. When an audience has learned the appropriate genre conventions, it is the opposition between *general* predictability and *specific* imprecision that is the basis for the pleasures of suspense.

Consider the genre's biggest box-office success: *The Exorcist* (1974). A skilful and innovative combination of invasion and metamorphosis forms, it follows the orthodox pattern in precise detail. During the opening pre-rampage phase, the orderly and apparently happy life of mother and daughter is interrupted by tiny signs of impending invasion: noises on the stairs, thuds in the attic. As event follows event, the interruptions become more serious and the tension-climaxing shocks more overt: Regan urinating on the floor at the party; the icy temperature in her room; the 'help me' message that appears on her torso. And, of course, as the overall tension-level rises and as we become increasingly involved with the characters and their fates, the tension-building sequences become more frenzied and their associated shocks more extravagant. Once the rampage is in full swing, the transition from one level of tension to another is marked only by increasingly elaborate shock effects: obscene language, repulsive physical details, levitation and the like. By the time the film's final confrontation arrives, receptive audiences – and there were many of them – have been trapped in a rising cycle of tension, caught indeed on a giant roller-coaster which fulfils their expectations by hauling them to the top of the slope and hurtling them down again, while also contriving to do so without quite warning them about what they will encounter along the way.

Naturally, effective involvement is not simply a question of invoking the appropriate structure; if that were so, all horror movies would work as well, and on audiences as varied, as *The Exorcist*. Intensity of involvement depends on many factors, ranging from the construction and pacing of sequences through all the nuances of characterization, acting and dramaturgy. But event-oriented suspense is central to the genre whatever variation there is in other modes of involvement and in whatever period we care to examine. It is fundamental to the pleasures that horror-movie audiences derive from the experience, and, although the conventions governing its implementation may change (contemporary audiences, other than those making a deliberate historic leap, would find, say, the 1931 *Dracula* impossibly slow), the suspense requirement itself remains a basic constituent of the horror movie.

Inevitably that requirement has ramifications in other areas of the genre. Compared to many fictional forms, for example, the horror movie is restricted in the narrative space that it routinely allocates to characterization. To some degree, of course, that is true of all action-based genres, but the horror movie's special demands for tension-development are particularly restrictive. After all, if the genre requires an escalating pattern of event-driven suspense, little time remains for the kind of character-developing 'asides' found in other genres, since once a high level of tension is dissipated it cannot easily be re-established. Given such pressures, escalation is likely. Relative lack of characterization puts yet more emphasis on 'eventfulness' as a basis for involvement; this requires that even more resources are devoted to suspense and the tension that flows from it; and accordingly there is less potential for characterization. This tendency is common in all periods of horror-movie history, though it is true that the post-seventies horror movie has shown a growing inclination towards sheer eventfulness.

Both the horror movie's event-orientation and its central convention of regular suspense—shock cycles are important in understanding the place of violence in the genre. As do many popular genres, horror movies presuppose an essentially coercive universe: forms of coercion are the norm for narratively effective behaviour. Except in very few cases (most obviously in a handful of 'old-fashioned' ghost stories epitomized by *The Uninvited* (1944)), both the monster's threat and the combatant's response are fundamentally coercive. Consequently, violence is constitutive of rather than gratuitous to the genre. The dynamics of the confrontations that form the backbone of the horror movie's rampage phase are invariably based on the threat and application of violence. Even where expertise has a key narrative role, it is very rare for that expertise to succeed alone and very common for it to require the expert to employ violent solutions. Van Helsing has the knowledge to destroy Dracula; he also needs the wooden stake and the hammer.

If this convention is taken in conjunction with that which prescribes regular tension-generation followed by climactic shocks, then a characteristic pattern emerges. Though it would be possible to build tension and bring it to a climax without overt violence, it has become most common to do so in sequences punctuated by violent activity and reaching their climax accordingly. Of course, conventional critical perspectives on such matters extol the virtues of 'subtlety' and 'restraint' as exemplified in, say, the 'bus' sequence of *Cat People* (1943), where our heroine walks from lamp to lamp in the growing suspicion that she is being followed, and then, at the climactic moment, the loud noise of a bus braking, accompanied by its sudden appearance in frame, administers the final shock.[1] Most horror movies, however, are somewhat more forthright. Within the limits of prevailing censorship restrictions, they have invariably used graphic violence as a major element in both tension development and release, and as externally imposed restrictions have changed the genre has not been slow to follow. Modern horror movies have almost continuously extended both the detail and the variety of violent action, largely in pursuit of new ways of sustaining tension-based involvement. The kinds of activities routine in today's horror movies make many of their pre-sixties counterparts seem positively delicate, a development which has tempted some observers − often unfamiliar with the horror movie − to diagnose a brutalized and jaded audience in pursuit of ever more titillatory thrills. However, their very unfamiliarity betrays them, for even a superficial examination of horror-movie history suggests that the genre has always operated at one highly conventionalized edge of movie representations of violence, and therefore has always enraged those unacquainted with it. That is no more or less the case in the eighties than it was in the thirties or the fifties, and while there may well be important differences between old and new, they are not usefully summarized in slogans bemoaning today's 'excessive' violence.

Naturally there are other significant aspects of event-based involvement (including, for instance, conventionally established punctuation events commonly found at key narrative transitions), but none are of such general pleasurable significance as the suspense−shock cycle. The most basic expectations that audiences have of horror movies − expectations that have themselves been encouraged and developed during the course of the genre's history − presume that we will be afforded a cumulative experience of pleasurable tension and that this tension will be regularly interrupted by even more pleasurable shock effects. Other genres may create narrative suspense in a whole range of ways, but it is only the horror movie that wants to make us jump out of our skins as well. And that, if the seemingly inexhaustible genre audience is to be believed, is a rare pleasure indeed.

## Character and Involvement

Occasional observers of horror movies have a nasty habit of asking why it is that there is always some poor misguided soul who opens

the door to the cellar or to the attic or to the crypt when it's quite
clear that no sane person would even consider it. To the horror-
movie audience, of course, the answer is obvious. It's so we can sit
there shrieking 'don't open the door' secure in the knowledge that he
or she is going to do exactly that. Contradictory though it may seem,
this simultaneous desire for both danger and security is an element
which is constitutive to our involvement with many horror-movie
characters: an ambivalent sympathy for their predicament as in-
voluntary monster-fodder. After all, if no one actually opened the
door we might just as well go home.

Put more generally, and echoing this chapter's earlier claim that
horror movies are fundamentally event-centred, the genre's basic
strategy for involving us with its characters is dominated by the need
to sustain narrative impetus. To some extent, of course, that is true
of any popular film genre: we apprehend character as a secondary
consequence of the exigencies of narration, reading an individual's
behaviour in particular film situations, and confirming or reformulat-
ing our conception as more information emerges in the course of the
developing story. In horror movies, however, characterization is even
more story-dependent. In a thriller or a Western, say, sequences
conveying specifically characterizing information are quite common,
though strictly speaking unnecessary for narrative progress. Most
horror movies, by contrast, drastically limit such 'digressions',
primarily focusing audience attention through their tension-based
involvement with a restricted array of character types. It is rare to
find a horror movie that singles out individual protagonists for the
kind of sustained characterizing treatment routinely found in other
more 'serious' forms. In the non-pejorative sense of the term
stereotype, then, horror movies work by placing stereotypical
characters in cumulatively eventful situations. And while it is true
that all popular genres employ some form of this conventionalized
shorthand to define character, in the horror movie that process has
been pushed close to its limits.

What, then, are the genre's basic character stereotypes? In line
with its forced economy of characterization, the orthodox range is
simple enough. Without returning to the detailed distributions reported in chapter 2 (in tables 2.2 and 2.4), it is clear that the
genre's character resources may be conveniently classified into Experts,
Victims and Monsters. Of course there may be some cross-over
between these categories, and, as we have seen, there are variations

in different periods of the genre's history. But, for all that potential blurring of distinctions, this three-part division is useful for immediate organizational purposes.

EXPERTS

It seems appropriate to begin with experts because, formally at least, they are the genre's 'heroes'. The formal qualification needs to be emphasized, however, since the kind of involvement that they invite is not always that which is commonly presumed to be appropriate for the heroes of other genres. Although in strict story terms they may be their movies' protagonists, and although their capacity for autonomous action is an essential constituent of the genre's narrative progress through disorder to order, they are rarely afforded the same kind of attention routinely paid to heroic figures in other narrative forms. That is particularly the case where the movie's monster invites some degree of anthropomorphic sympathy, displacing audience involvement away from the official hero and onto the apparent 'villain'. There is some such displacement at work in, for instance, the classic versions of the Frankenstein story, in relation both to the monstrous creation and to the Baron himself, and it is notable that throughout the thirties expert monster-pursuers are among the least developed of major characters. One need only think of the lasting attraction of the 1933 *King Kong*'s eponymous monster, in comparison with the movie's generally uninteresting assembly of candidate heroes, to appreciate some of the ambiguities in our relations of involvement and identification with horror-movie characters.

Indeed, it is only really in the fifties that the expert is unreservedly given the attention that his (very few were female) formal narrative significance might suggest. To some extent, that decade's defenders against invasion are the descendents of Dracula's traditional opponent, Van Helsing; though fifties experts are generally permitted more in the way of 'human' character-traits than the stiff and bourgeois automaton portrayed by Edward Van Sloan in the thirties. The expert's character is particularly important, of course, in the vampire sub-genre, where the social and physical attractiveness of the monster is often central to our involvement. It is surely the case, for instance, that a considerable part of the success of the initial series of Hammer vampire movies depended on the delicate balance of our responses to both Dracula and Van Helsing as portrayed by Christopher Lee and Peter Cushing. Where Sloan's Van Helsing is, if finally effective, almost entirely lacking in charisma, Cushing's expert rivals Dracula himself. It is impossible to imagine Professor Van Helsing, in Sloan's account of him, clashing candlesticks together to form an impromptu cross or running the length of a banqueting table to tear open the drapes and let in the sunlight. Cushing's active physicality, displayed in these final moments of the 1958 *Dracula*, rescued the anti-vampire expert from the dry scholasticism and eccentricity of his traditional representation without in any way reducing the character's claims to expertise. His Van Helsing is both forcefully heroic and knowledgeable, an unusual combination in a genre which has generally separated the two traits in terms of age and attractiveness.

While not universal, this upgrading of the horror-movie expert became quite common during the fifties in both invasion and knowledge narratives. The scientific and military experts who spent so much of the decade prevailing over threats from space, from beneath the sea, or from other dimensions, were allowed to be heroes in ways almost unique to the period. Scientists, traditionally aged, dull and bespectacled (unless, that is, they were *mad* scientists) were even made personable objects for romantic sub-plotting, or, in the absence of such narrative digressions, took on almost superhuman qualities. Quatermass, as Brian Donlevy played him in *The Quatermass Experiment* (1955) and *Quatermass II* (1957) (in some contrast to Andrew Keir's more diffident 1967 characterization in *Quatermass and the Pit*) is an extreme example, but his sheer force of character and determined individualism were not untypical traits among his genre-contemporaries. In most fifties horror movies there can be no doubt about which characters invite our involvement, and, concomitantly, there is relatively little attempt to engage our sympathies with the period's monsters.

This unambiguous allegiance to the victorious expert barely survives the decade, however, and modern invasion and metamorphosis forms — whether dealing in psychosis, disease or demonology — have either relegated the expert to an ineffectual observer or eliminated the role altogether. Thus the psychiatrists who have featured in post-sixties psycho-movies are rarely able to harness their presumed knowledge to the task of defeating the threat. Like *Psycho*'s smug *ex post facto* explainer or *Halloween*'s peripatetic agonizer, horror-movie psychiatrists, and their knowledgable counterparts elsewhere in the modern genre, now generally operate at the periphery of events. In *Halloween* (1979) Donald Pleasence may bring a certain improbable conviction to his thankless role, but the character is never made available for any kind of direct emotional involvement. As so often in contemporary horror movies, it is the film's victims that constitute the main focus of our likely concerns and sympathies.

Experts, then, occupy a peculiar place in the repertoire of horror movie characters. Although any formal account of the stories told by many pre-seventies horror movies might suggest that the expert is a central focus for audience involvement, the actual telling of the stories generally puts the emphasis elsewhere. Narration gives the lie to formal structure. Only in the SF-influenced horror movies of the fifties does the pattern of invited involvement coincide with that of formal narrative position, and, significantly, it is only then that we lose the distinctive ambiguity so characteristic of the typical horror movies of other periods. In that respect, many of the fifties movies are as morally and emotionally black-and-white as their distinctive cinematography.

MONSTERS

The universal strategy for promoting audience involvement with the genre's monsters is to anthropomorphize them. Whether it is Frankenstein's creation as Karloff played it, Kong lovesick for Fay Wray, or Godzilla rescuing Japan from the perils of the Smog Monster, our sympathy is invited precisely to the degree that such patently inhuman creations exhibit human inclinations, emotions and loyalties. In contrast, it is difficult to feel involved with, say, the giant red jelly of *The Blob* (1959) or *Alien*'s (1979) ferocious carnivore; their motives remain opaque, as befits such thoroughly alien threats. Creatures of this kind are not characters. They are, rather, narrative functions given physical form — necessary if there is to be a story to be told, but requiring of us no more than a belief in the immediate reality of their threat. We can and do have complex responses to characters; narratively functional monsters are no more than that.

Broadly, then, horror-movie monsters sub-divide into 'aliens' and 'anthropomorphs', where the latter are routinely permitted sufficient depth of characterization to persuade audiences into some degree of emotional involvement with them. Historically, of course, anthropomorphs are the more common, as even a cursory examination of the distributions summarized in table 2.2 suggests. Indeed, many horror movies depend fundamentally upon the ambiguity of our responses to anthropomorphic monsters. Psychotics, mad scientists, vampires, mutations, ghosts, werewolves, are in significant part human. We are able to relate to them in ways other than simple fear or revulsion because they display recognizable human motives and concerns, however distorted by their status as monstrous threats. Like the central protagonists of classical gangster movies, a significant part of their fascination lies in their uneasy combination of human and inhuman traits.

Traditionally, of course, it is the vampire that has most frequently been taken to exemplify the anthropomorphic ambiguity of horror movie monstrousness, and, however overstated his acting might seem to modern eyes, Bela Lugosi's thirties rendering of Dracula has proved massively influential. Compared to his most famous silent predecessor (Max Schreck in Murnau's 1922 *Nosferatu*), Lugosi's vampire is elegant, attractive, sensual and, above all, shows few external signs of his alien nature. With only a handful of exceptions, it has been this kind of vampire that has subsequently dominated movie re-presentations, depending for much of its force on manipulating the ambivalence of our responses to a character composed of such contrasted bundles of traits. The vampire in this guise is evil and attractive, ruthless and charming, as well as voracious and sophisticated. He, or sometimes she, is both monstrous and human.[2]

Horror-movie anthropomorphism is also commonly found where monsters exhibit apparent or genuine metamorphosis. For example, the 'characterized psychotic' (Norman Bates in *Psycho* (1960), say, or Bob Rusk in *Frenzy* (1972)) is generally portrayed in such a way as to generate sympathy for the character, at least prior to − and sometimes after − our discovery that he or she is the monster. This places us in a curious position vis-à-vis the film's emotional and moral structure, having to change the focus of our involvement in mid-narrative. In the event we often find it difficult to do so, and the conjunction of monstrous and human in one character can then become a central element of our already ambiguously motivated pleasure in the narrative collision between threat and normality. When such ambiguity is pushed to its limits − as it arguably is in *Peeping Tom* (1960) − the experience can be very disturbing. That is rare, however, and most mainstream genre products remain on the comfortable side of our responses to the anthropomorphic monster, whether a psychotic, a werewolf or one of those demonic innocents that were so common during the seventies. Note, also, that most recent psycho-movies do not engage in this potentially disruptive form of characterization. The psychotic monsters of *Halloween* (1979) and *Friday the 13th* (1980) are almost entirely uncharacterised — in this respect they are closer to aliens than to anthropomorphs.

Among metamorphosing monsters, of course, the characterized psychotic has developed its own distinctive rhetoric. Often with such creations the moment of metamorphosis is unmarked by external signs, and the transition from human to alien is not simply unpredictable but, until the monster actually strikes, more or less undetectable. In contrast, traditional metamorphants — werewolves, for example — are caught up in a variously complex web of explicit ritual expectations. Werewolves traditionally metamorphose at the full moon, and most narratives contrive to make us aware of both that fact and the precise timing of the lunar calendar. Furthermore, the metamorphosis itself is a major set-piece in such movies (self-consciously so in recent examples like *An American Werewolf in London* and *The Howling* (both 1981)), preparing us for imminent violence and, perhaps more importantly, permitting us to safely compartmentalize the character, thus sustaining empathy with its human aspect whatever heinous crimes it may commit in lupine form. There is a sense, therefore, in which the wolf is seen as a separate character from the human who metamorphoses into it. Characterized psychotics, on the other hand, make such compartmentalization much more difficult. This character is indistinguishably human *and* monstrous, based not so much on an anthropomorphic rendering of a monstrous threat as on a diagnosis of monstrousness unpredictably submerged within human normality. This, of course, is a crucial feature of one branch of the modern psycho-movie, and I shall consider it in more detail in chapter 9. For the moment it will suffice to note that the characterized psychotic occupies one extreme of the continuum from anthropomorph to alien, while the likes of vampires, witches, werewolves, ghosts, mutations and mad scientist's creations range variously across it.

At the other, alien, end of the scale the selection of available characters (if they even deserve the name) is far less varied, and our potential for direct involvement with them is concomitantly restricted. Uncharacterized psychotics, threats from nature, abstract forces (such as radiation) and, most straightforward of all, the bug-eyed monsters of fifties invasion movies, do not exhibit character traits likely to attract us to them in any but the most superficial of narrative-enabling senses. Accordingly, character-based involvement in most films featuring such monsters is focused either on the appropriate experts (overwhelmingly so in fifties BEM movies) or, as has been the case in many modern horror movies where the status of the expert has radically declined, on the victims. The truly alien monster operates outside normal movie involvement. Even in those modern terrorizing narratives where the camera appears to accompany the monster (usually a male psychotic) as he stalks his female victims, it would be difficult to sustain an argument that the physical point of view imposed by the camera promotes our emotional involvement with the killer. As I shall suggest later, the application of this technique in, for instance, *Halloween* (1979) is more likely to work to extend our involvement with the psychotic's victims than with the uncharacterized monster itself.

In sum, then, the principal character-elements that determine the form of our involvement with horror-movie monsters depend, first of all, on whether the creature is an anthropomorph or an alien. In the latter case, resources of character involvement, such as they are, are always directed elsewhere — on experts and/or victims. If the monster is anthropomorphically conceived, then involvement can be variously complex. In simple cases, like the giant ape of *King Kong* (1933), the creature of *The Creature from the Black Lagoon* (1955) or even the monster from *Frankenstein* (1932), our involvement is broadly one of sympathy with the monster's predicament. In so far as such movies contrive to create pathos in their monster's narrative circumstances (usually by permitting it to express seemingly human desires and then ensuring that these desires are frustrated) they can unproblematically capture our sympathies on behalf of such unlikely subjects. But these are simple cases, and our relations of involvement with more complex anthropomorphs like vampires, characterized psychotics and werewolves, are much more elaborate and ambiguous than the diffuse feelings of sympathy we may have for poor bewildered Kong. There is no need to chart the full range here, and they will in any case feature as part of the sub-genre analyses of Part III. I shall note only that a significant part of the pleasures of psycho-movies like *Peeping Tom* (1960), *Psycho* (1960) and *Hands of the Ripper* (1971), or of vampire movies such as *Dracula* (1958) or *Martin* (1978), derive from the complexities of the emotional relationship in which we are placed with respect to these various movie monsters. Monstrous they may be; but they are never entirely alien.

## VICTIMS

Inevitably, victims or potential victims are the most numerous of horror-movie characters. For much of early genre history, however, they are also the least interesting, playing out their roles as monster-fodder and serving little more purpose than that. Though we may feel vaguely sorry for the doomed burghers who fall victim to Frankenstein's monster, or the half-suspecting young women into whom Dracula sinks his fangs, we are only really involved with them in the momentary tension of their capture or demise. Like the panic-stricken populace of *The War of the Worlds* (1953) and countless other fifties invasion movies, they are there to provide the human ground over which monster and expert, threat and defender, disordering and ordering impulses can battle it out. Second-class citizens of the genre, they are narratively indispensable because physically entirely disposable.

There are two kinds of exception to this sweeping generalization, their significance correlated with the relative status of the expert in modern and traditional horror movies. In the modern genre, where the expert has become largely peripheral, central characters are always also potential victims. In more traditional genre contexts where the expert remains a major figure, some victims emerge as distinctive supporting characters who stand in significant relation to the expert and with whom, therefore, we might be more than usually involved. Quite how much involvement can be sustained in this way is a function of other narrative and discursive elements, for supporting characters in all popular genres are notoriously subject to the vicissitudes of limited dialogue and minimal screen time. Thus, Harker, Lucy and Mina in most film versions of Stoker's original Dracula story could hardly be described as 'rounded' characters, and our capacity to become involved with their fates barely goes beyond that available to us in respect of any anonymous horror-movie victim. Many of the juvenile leads who featured in the romantic sub-plotting of the classic period are, in terms of involvement at least, barely distinguishable from the bulk of movie monster-fodder.

Consequently, there is little systematic that can be said about supporting characters as victims in traditional horror movies. As the genre changed, however, and as its typical experts ceased to reflect the old, wise, bourgeois gentleman model, so horror-movie stories conflated plot and subplot in such a way as to provide the expert with suitable romantic attachments. Accordingly, by the fifties it is quite common to find a male expert defending a female victim who is (or becomes) the object of his love. Whether that makes much difference to our involvement, however, is a moot point, for the genre's representation of passion and personal concern prior to the sixties is both schematic and expressively limited. It is only when the distinctive expert role loses its traditional significance that victims emerge as primary focuses for sustained identification. Up to then, they are no more than pawns in an event-dominated narrative game.

This change, of course, is part of a general pattern found in the modern genre which includes a drift towards more open narratives, the relative decline of the knowledge narrative, increasingly graphic representation of physical threats, as well as a less central role for the expert. All these changes make the genre's modern trend distinctively victim-oriented, whether the threat derives from disease, demons or the disturbed recesses of the psychotic mind. In this respect, abandoning the traditional polarity of expert and monster has had a kind of liberating effect on the genre, freeing modern horror movies from many of the character stereotypes of earlier periods. It's not that today's genre is without a reservoir of stereotypes on which to draw. The seventies and eighties have, rather, seen an extension of this range, and the victim, once the least characterized and most cardboard of horror-movie figures, is now frequently the genre's central focus of involvement.

That said, however, it is difficult to generalize about the kinds of character typifications available for modern horror-movie victims. In the emergence of 'everyperson' as the genre's non-monstrous centre of gravity we can certainly see differentiation of the horror movie's traditional character resources, an infusion of character types from elsewhere in popular culture. But the net effect of such developments is to absorb the horror movie's *dramatis personae* into a more general character pool, in which anybody can be made into a narratively convincing victim. Unsurprisingly, then, although particular sub-genres may exhibit certain stereotypical restrictions (many psychomovies, for example, feature college-age victims) almost no pattern covers the whole range of the modern genre. Even the common claim that eighties horror movies are generally distinguished by the relative youth of their principal protagonists will not bear too much ex-amination, since the significance of 'youth' in the context of, say, *The Evil Dead* or *Halloween II* is rather different from its significance in *Poltergeist* or *Cat People* (all 1982).

For such reasons, there seems no point in seeking a comprehensive typology of victims here. All that needs to be emphasized is the broad significance of the modern genre's concern with the victim as a major locus of involvement, a shift in the genre's character-structure which parallels that already described in relation to narrative. The decline of knowledge narratives, and the associated rise of more open-ended metamorphosis/invasion amalgams, entails a form of involvement based primarily on the victim role — with no effective experts and fewer anthropomorphic monsters it could hardly be otherwise. Taken by itself, this change has to be seen as, at the least, highly significant to the kinds of pleasures we can derive from the modern horror movie. Viewed in the context of the distinction between *secure* and *paranoid* horror, the changing nature of our involvement with experts, monsters and victims begins to fall into place as a further reflection of the genre's underlying pattern. In the remaining section of this chapter I shall consider features of the settings in which these characters are placed as yet another basis for involvement and, hence, pleasure. This, too, makes sense in the genre's larger developmental context.

## Setting and Involvement

It is a commonplace to invoke 'willing suspension of disbelief' in discussing the nature of our involvement in fictional worlds, all the more so where such worlds are remote from those of our everyday lives. And what could be more remote than Dracula's Transylvania or Kong's jungle? Yet, with its overtones of scepticism, the most common formulation of 'suspension of disbelief' — its source in Coleridge long forgotten — is surely misleading. We approach fictions already motivated to believe, prepared to be drawn into their worlds, wanting to be excited, moved, absorbed and captivated — 'willing', certainly, but willing to invoke a socially constructed commitment to believe what we see and hear rather than to suspend a natural inclination towards scepticism. We have long since learned the appropriate terms in which stories can be told, and a significant part of the pleasures to be had from their telling is in encountering and re-encountering those terms. We don't have to suspend anything to experience that pleasure; the capacity is already there, a product of our lifelong education in responding to fictions.

That is particularly clear in well-established genres, where the conventions of story-telling are necessarily given very specific interpretations. While genre-products are evidently intelligible to a general audience, they also rely upon more specialised conventions and practices. That is why genre audiences, although they are actually sophisticated 'readers' of genre stories, equipped with a practical consciousness of all the nuances of narration and setting, of style and character, are so often subject to condescension from non-specialized critics. They are able to enter the world of a genre film with an ease born of intimate familiarity, and can do so — initially at least — on the basis of a mere handful of cues. Fundamental to such 'cueing in' is the verisimilitude of the world presupposed in the film. Is this a familiar universe? Can we recognize its physical and social settings as convincing *within the genre expectations* that we routinely bring to bear? Does it 'work' in the ways in which we are accustomed to the products of *this genre* working? Such recognition facilitates our entry into the fiction, forming the ground in which more specific pleasures of involvement may be rooted. Characters and events are located within a setting. If that setting is implausible to its audience, then no amount of inventive story telling or subtle acting will make the fiction work.

Like other bases of our involvement, then, movie settings function in both general and particular referential contexts. The general context is that provided by the non-generic conventions which inform the creation of all plausible film worlds and determine the acceptable variety of narrative structures, as well as providing the materials from which appropriate characters, actions and events may be constructed: in effect, the cinematic conventions utilized in almost any fiction film. I shall not be much concerned with these general features here. The particular context is composed of the genre's own distinctive ways of creating and sustaining its worlds, and it is on such genre-specific functions that most of this discussion will focus. It is here, of course, that genres often develop their most specialized conventions and, to a genre outsider, appear to make their most outrageous demands upon our credulity. Accordingly, it is the shared settings or 'worlds' of horror movies that most dramatically distinguish them from other fictional experiences.

The obvious starting point for any account of the generic world of the horror movie lies in its physical character; and, for all the importance of the supernatural in many areas of the genre, representation of its physical world has been surprisingly naturalistic. Or perhaps this not so surprising, given the popular cinema's general commitment to standards of verisimilitude based in photographic emulation of the real world of visual experience. Though visual style may have undercut the extremes of naturalism at certain periods in horror-movie history (most notably in the thirties, and rather less consistently in the late fifties and early sixties), a physical order broadly that of our everyday experience remains a dominant assumption. Few horror movies invite our involvement in terms other than as proxy participants in an apparently 'real' physical, social and psychological setting.[3]

Within that general format, though, there is much room for manœuvre, both in substance and representational style. Typical products of the thirties, for instance, were often given a period setting in what looked like a kind of stylized nineteenth century, whether in *Frankenstein*'s middle-European village, *Dracula*'s Transylvanian mountains or *The Werewolf of London*'s fog-shrouded London. The fact that *The Werewolf of London* is not alone in actually being set in the twentieth century has little effect on the sense of *elsewhen*, of distance, lent to many of these movies by their settings. They exist, as it were, in a nineteenth century of the mind. Castles, old manor-houses, country inns and elaborate laboratories repeat themselves from film to film, forming a highly distinctive setting and, no doubt, serving to divorce the fictions from their audience's immediate context of experience. Over time these period settings came to be associated with specific audience expectations, and, as well as giving pleasure by virtue of their very distinctiveness, they developed a characteristic rhetoric of involvement different to that found in the vast majority of horror movies. It is therefore important to note that, contrary to popular stereotypes (accurately pastiched in *Young Frankenstein* (1975)), this much remarked feature of the genre's formative years did not survive for long. By the forties, horror-movie settings were predominantly contemporary and mundane, a pattern that continued even when Hammer and their various imitators set about renewing the Gothic tradition in the late fifties.

Unsurprisingly, then, it is the eruption of abnormality into a mundane setting that has formed the genre's most common means of narratively exploiting its physical environment. For all its expression-istic flourishes of composition and camerawork, for instance, one of the more strikingly effective moments in *The Haunting* (1964) derives its undoubted power from the matter-of-fact way in which we are shown a solid wooden door bulging inwards as a consequence of the supernatural force behind it. Similar effects are achieved in our first sight of the tiny alien reptile of *Twenty Million Miles to Earth* (1957) as it stands on an ordinary table-top roaring defiance; of the school climbing frame suddenly laden with crows in *The Birds* (1963); of the lurching zombie who appears from nowhere in the opening scenes of *Night of the Living Dead* (1970); of the extraordinary voice emerging from the possessed girl of *The Exorcist* (1974); of the shark's fin speeding through the waters of the hitherto-safe lagoon in *Jaws* (1975); of the demonic black car inexplicably terrorizing the peaceful town of *The Car* (1977); and the gnarled tree that smashes through a suburban bedroom window to snatch the child in *Poltergeist* (1982).

What such diverse examples share is a recognition that to fracture a naturalistically represented physical order is, simultaneously, to affirm both the precariousness and the significance of that order. And, as we have already seen, that is a tension fundamental to our most basic involvement in many horror movies. Thus, although phy-sical and natural credibility is obviously a requirement of any movie setting, it has a particular significance for the horror movie. Since the genre depends upon the introduction of the *in*credible, and since its distinctive event-focus typically means that horror movies devote relatively little time to the task of detailing setting, the most imme-diately effective strategy is to set stories within a prosaic and familiar everyday. It is, therefore, the period Gothic extravaganzas, so notable in the beginning years of the genre, which have subsequently proved to be the deviant form.

This contrast — between the stylized world of the Gothic tradition and the more naturalistically represented world that dominates the rest of the genre — captures the most general dimension of variation of the horror movie's physical settings. That does not mean that there are not other differences to be found. Different narrative types and sub-types clearly have an affinity for particular settings, and specific settings (laboratories, old houses, small towns, woodlands, etc.) have been variously significant at different stages of the genre's development. Overall, there is also a broad correlation between physical setting and secure or paranoid horror. For instance, the worlds characteristic of paranoid horror are almost never given period settings; they are most commonly located in contemporary suburbs, in enclaves at the edge of civilization, or within the homes of their protagonists. There is good reason for such a pattern, given the typical narratives of paranoid horror, but to properly appreciate that it is first necessary to extend consideration to the genre's distinctive social settings.

Horror movies are relatively simple in the kinds of social worlds that they presume — even by comparison with other popular genres. Unlike the Western, for example, they rarely digress into the minutiae of community activities except as an incidental background to more narratively central events: the villagers' festivities interrupted by the father carrying the dead girl in *Frankenstein* (1932) are, after all, hardly on a par with the extended and celebratory 'Sunday morning sequence' in *My Darling Clementine*. In part that reflects the fact that the fundamental structuring devices of the horror movie's social worlds always involve division. So, for example, traditional knowledge and invasion narratives generally presuppose a social division between experts (both good and bad), who are at the centre of events and capable of autonomous action, and potential victims, who exist at the periphery and are thus dependent upon expert intervention. At different times this centre—periphery structure has been given various social inflections. In the classic Gothic horror movie, for instance, experts commonly belong to the bourgeoisie or even to the aristocracy, their superiority to ordinary folk underlined at every opportunity. Even mad scientists — most notably Frankenstein himself — could thus unproblematically be construed as both villains and heroes, their social superiority placing them beyond the scope of everyday moral judgements.

In the knowledge and invasion narratives of the fifties such crude distinctions of class (generally embodied in European period settings) were replaced by equally crude distinctions between a meritocratic elite — military, scientific and occasionally governmental — and an undifferentiated and largely anonymous mass of victims. In seeking to save the world, or at least the American Way of Life, experts acted in the interests of all. In actually succeeding, as most of them did, they also justified their own meritocratic status. Those familiar with the public concerns of the fifties, or with the influential social thought of that time, will detect a crude but recognizable version of the Mass

Society argument here. The image of a mass who are in need of protection and guidance from an appropriately qualified elite was central to conservative applications of Mass Society ideas, and in the West's then-prevailing climate of anti-communism and xenophobia it is not surprising that such themes should find their way into the horror movie.

In effect, then, the traditional (*secure*) horror movie employs a simple centre—periphery model of significant social relations, its detailed content varying from period to period. This is not to suggest that other sources of social division are insignificant. Gender, for example, is an important structuring device which, in the traditional genre, is reinforced by the more general centre—periphery division. In pre-seventies horror movies it is very rare to find women occupying the narrative and social focus other than as victims, and where this is not the case — as in movies focusing upon female vampires from *Dracula's Daughter* (1936) to *The Vampire Lovers* (1970) — the crucial locus of expertise and ultimate success invariably remains male. In this, of course, the horror movie is much like every other popular genre, presuming a relation of dependence between male and female which typically affords the male opportunities for autonomous action and, in a microcosm of the more general social model, relegates women to the periphery of heterosexual love and/or family relations. Significantly, part of the distinctive threat posed by the female vampire stems from precisely this aspect of the horror-movie world: in rejecting the 'normal' terms of male—female relations, she constitutes a threat to one of the genre world's basic ordering systems — a threat dramatized in periods of relaxed censorship by the overt lesbianism of many such characters. Thus, as I shall argue in more detail in chapter 8, the female vampire — like her male counterpart — embodies an essentially sexual threat to the presumed stability of socio-sexual relations, a threat made the more comprehensive in her case because it derives from the routinely unrepresented domain of female sexuality.

It is easy to see why a centre—periphery model should be so basic to the social world of secure horror. The requirements of narrative closure, of successful intervention by experts, of survival of the main features of order, lead to a social setting in which proper distinctions are made between relevant character types and in which the dimensions of defensible order are clearly laid out. A model based on appropriately interpreted centre—periphery relations (appropriate, that is, to the changing character, often externally determined, of audience expectations) serves that purpose admirably, generating an easily accessible image of social relations and a related ordering division between characters. We know where we are in such a world. That is not true, relatively speaking, in the world of paranoid horror.

Basically, the social world of paranoid horror has lost the sense of order embodied in the traditional centre—periphery model. Indeed, from a traditional viewpoint the social worlds of many modern horror movies are all periphery and no centre, a development reflected in the fact that in the contemporary genre all characters, major or minor, are potential victims. The social order of modern horror is typically the social order of the victim's world. At its most general this is not a distinctive order at all, but ranges over a variety of possibilities. It is here that 'everyperson' has emerged as the genre's major protagonist, his or her social homogeneity limited only to age (mostly youthful), nationality (mostly American) and presentability (mostly attractive). In other respects, today's horror-movie prota-gonists can come from any and all social locations, even if they do remain predominantly male and white. It is true, of course, that female protagonists are more significant in the modern genre, and that they are permitted more autonomy and resourcefulness than were the 'heroines' of earlier films. The sole survivor of *Halloween*'s rampaging psychotic, for example, or of *Alien*'s salivating monstrosity (both 1979), forcefully played by Jamie Lee Curtis and Sigourney Weaver respectively, are afforded a degree of effective participation in the action all but unheard of prior to the seventies. Nevertheless, they and their sisters remain significant exceptions to the continuing pattern of male domination of the genre's central situations. Women have always featured as horror-movie victims, and it is therefore to be expected that they should *seem* more prominent in a period of victim centrality. Whether that implies a new gender-structure for the genre is another matter entirely. The occasional inversions found in female revenge movies like *Death Weekend* (1976) or *The Slumber Party Massacre* (1983) are so rare as to seem more like novelties than indicators of a trend.

The principal exceptions to the general lack of distinctiveness of the modern genre's social world revolve around the family. As I have already observed in chapter 4, horror movies in the seventies and eighties have often used the family as both source of and target for their typical threats, a practice that raises the possibility of a distinctively family-based conception of horror-movie disorder. In fact it is difficult to make any reliable generalizations about the horror movie family other than to emphasize its evident importance as a basic ordering structure in the genre's social setting. The trend towards family-oriented horror is part of a larger pattern discernible in recent horror movies and reflecting what might be thought of as the increasing *proximity* (physical, psychic and social) of the fictional threat. The growing emphasis on internal threats, on metamorphosis, on disease and on the likelihood of destructive forces emerging from and/or attacking the family unit, together constitute a central focus of paranoid horror. I have observed elsewhere that this indisputable emphasis on the family does not unproblematically lead to the conclusion that repressed insecurities about the institution are being returned to us in the guise of popular culture. While individual readings may be constructed in support of such a thesis (especially of films like *The Texas Chainsaw Massacre* (1976), where a kind of family unit itself becomes the threat) the overall pattern is sufficient only to suggest that the horror movie family — which includes surrogate groupings such as the isolated survivors in *Zombies* (1980) — is mostly invoked as a precarious locus of order in an increasingly threatening and disordered universe.

The shared significance, then, of families into which monsters are born (*The Omen* (1976) or *It's Alive* (1975)), families invaded by monstrousness (*The Exorcist* (1974) or *The Shining* (1980)), and families besieged by monsters (*The Amityville Horror* (1980) or *Poltergeist* (1982)) lies in their thoroughgoing paranoia. As do so many modern horror movies, these films postulate a world in which the disordering impulse is immanent rather than contingent, and in which the final bastions of our identity — our physical being, our mental stability, our immediate social environment — are crumbling in the face of overpowering threats. Thus, just as it is easy to see the rhetorical potential of the centre-periphery model for traditional narrative forms and secure horror, so it is clear how the family comes to be a key element in the social settings of paranoid horror. It is the most obvious and easily represented *social* analogue to the threatened mind or body of the modern genre. Consequently, it is important not to overemphasize the family's significance in recent horror movies. The more far-reaching development is that which I have sought to summarize in describing the modern genre as paranoid, an informing paradigm which finds expression in many aspects of post-seventies horror. In this context, so-called 'family horror', like 'body horror',[4] can be seen in perspective as one strand in the modern genre's reformulation of the horror-movie universe, a distinctively social embodiment of a pattern also realized in the context of physical and mental disorder.

Only one general observation about the genre's social settings remains to be made. Throughout its history, whether paranoid or secure, knowledge narrative or metamorphosis narrative, stylized or naturalistic, the horror movie's typical social worlds have involved constraint. Indeed, at its most general level the genre universe itself is coercive; effective actions — whether on the part of monsters, experts or victims — invariably require their perpetrators to use force. Of course, the horror movie is not alone in that emphasis. As I have already argued, most popular 'action' genres require resort to coercive means in order to resolve their central narrative problems. In the horror movie, however, there is little opportunity even to contemplate alternatives. In a Western or a thriller there is often room for reflection upon the coercive necessities; even, occasionally, some attempt to pose other possibilities. In the horror movie — its universe and our involvement founded on both the fascination and the fear of violence — there is finally a Hobbesian state of nature: 'continual fear and danger of violent death; and the life of man, solitary, poor, nasty, brutish, and short'. As a general setting that, too, is some part of the genre's appeal to us.

Notes

1 Lewton himself dubbed such moments 'busses', so named because of this sequence. See Joel E. Siegel, *Val Lewton: the Reality of Terror* (London, 1972), pp. 31–2.
2 This generalization may be slightly misleading in that the late sixties saw some increase in a more bestial conception of the male vampire, though without really altering the conventional physical attributes. See chapter 8 for a fuller discussion.
3 'Real', here, refers to constructed verisimilitude and not to any claim that there is or ought to be some fixed relation between the world of a fiction and a privileged world of natural or social 'reality'. Without quotation marks the term 'real' has become so laden as to be almost unusable in discussing fictions—perhaps even quotation marks are not enough! For just some of the issues in relation to the cinema, see Christopher Williams (ed), *Realism and the Cinema* (London, 1980).

4 The family has been a central focus for many recent discussions of
modern horror, influenced particularly by Robin Wood's work. See his
contributions to Andrew Britton, Richard Lippe, Tony Williams and
Robin Wood, *American Nightmare: Essays on the Horror Film* ( Toronto,
1979). See also Tony Williams, 'Horror in the Family' *Focus on Film*, 36,
(1980), pp. 14–20; Tony Williams, 'American Cinema in the '70s: Family
Horror', *Movie*, 27/28 (1981) pp. 117–26; and, for a discussim from a
slightly different point of view, Vivian Sobchack, 'Bringing It All Back
Home: Family Economy and Generic Exchange', in Gregory A. Waller
(ed), *American Horrors: Essays on the Modern American Horror Film*,
(Urbana and Chicago, 1987) pp. 175–94. For some interesting observations on the modern horror movie's concern with the body see Pete Boss,
'Vile Bodies and Bad Medicine', pp. 14–24 and Philip Brophy, 'Horrality
– the Textuality of Contemporary Horror Films', pp. 2–13 both in
*Screen*, 27, 1 (January/February 1986).

# Part III
*Science, Supernature, Psyche*

# 7
# *Mad Science*

The belief that science is dangerous is as central to the horror movie as is a belief in the malevolent inclinations of ghosts, ghouls, vampires and zombies. In just over a quarter of the films included in this study (264), science is posited as a primary source of disorder, and in 169 of them that impulse is given flesh in the person of a 'mad scientist'. Though such 'madness' encompasses both the familiar obsessives, who devotedly and misguidedly seek knowledge purely for its own sake, and those traditional villains who want no more than to rule the world, all mad scientists share one characteristic. They are volitional. Disorder in these movies is a direct consequence of individual scientists' actions. In the other 95 science-based films, it is not so much the direct actions of scientists that occasion the threat as it is unanticipated consequences of scientific investigation and discovery. Either way, science gets the blame. However, the degree to which individual scientists are assumed to be responsible is significant both for the kinds of threat involved and for the genre's typical responses to the ensuing disorder.

Before pursuing such details, however, I must first describe some of the more general features of science-based horror movies. I have already suggested that science is of primary importance to the horror movie only during the genre's first 30 years. Though statistically it is true that just over half the total of science-based horror movies date from after 1960, this has to be seen in the context of a massive expansion in all kinds of horror movies during the sixties, seventies and eighties. If we examine numbers of science-based horror movies as a proportion of the whole genre, then both the pre-sixties peaks and the subsequent decline become apparent.

133

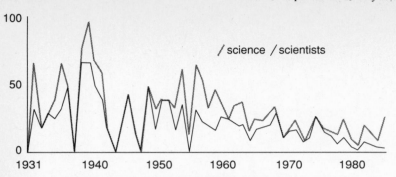

**Figure 7.1   Percentage of threats in horror movies
caused by science/scientists**

Figure 7.1 also suggests that, other than in the second half of the
fifties, the pattern of scientist-caused threats broadly follows the
more general distribution of science-based movies. The gap that
opens up in the fifties, and, incidentally, in the late seventies and
eighties (although the scale of figure 7.1 is such as to make that less
clear) is a reflection of the different evaluations of scientist's responsibility found in the movies of those periods. With growing
public concern about atomic energy during the fifties, the idea of
science *unwittingly* causing disaster becomes more common, a pattern
that is repeated in the late seventies and eighties, where scientific
'side-effects' give rise to pollution and ecological imbalance. A similar
shift is apparent in the relative proportions of different kinds of
monsters in different periods. When mad scientists are in the ascendant,
and individuals are thus responsible for the threat through their own
actions, monsters are mainly medical creations more or less directly
descended from the Frankenstein prototype. During periods of indirect scientific responsibility, however, accidental mutations become
much more common, as a consequence first of radiation and, later,
of pollution.

   This distinction between direct and indirect responsibility is a basic
parameter of the conceptual context from which science-based horror
movies may plausibly generate disorder: their 'threat-structure'. By
the same count, there is a corresponding 'defence-structure': a set of
conventional resources that are drawn upon by the genre's fictions in
constructing their defences against the disordering impulse. In the
case of science-based horror movies, dominated as they are by the
knowledge narrative, the major resources for defence lie with coercive

authorities such as the police or the military, with scientists and scientific knowledge and, as in all horror movies, with 'ordinary' people. The underlying opposition here is that between defence based upon an appeal to authoritative 'others' (police, military, scientists) and that based upon individual self-reliance. It is, no doubt, a consequence of the genre's tacit authoritarianism that the years in which 'ordinary' people become the major focus for defence are also the years in which threatening monsters are most likely to be victorious.

More of that later. For the present I want to examine the whole range of science-based horror movies with a view to distinguishing periods which differ systematically in their characteristic conceptions of threat and defence. By looking at percentage distributions of mad scientists, medical creations and mutations, it is possible to establish broad indicators of direct and indirect responsibility. Similarly, the distribution of defenders among police and military, scientists and ordinary people gives some indication of the balance of self- versus other-reliance. Detailed examination of these figures on a year-by-year basis suggests four main periods: 1931–1950; 1951–1964; 1965–1976; 1977–1984. The films of each period are homogeneous in their assumptions about threat and defence, but those assumptions differ quite dramatically from one period to the next.

Differences among the various periods can be summarized conveniently in tabular form. To keep things simple I have combined the individual indicators, and rather than expressing the distributions in their original percentage terms – which would be as misleading in its numerical detail as it would be difficult to read – I have condensed them down to three levels: LO, MID and HI.[1] Bearing in mind that this is intended only as a general framework to help order subsequent discussion, that seems an acceptable simplification.

Table 7.1 Threat and defence in science-based horror movies

|  | Threat | | Defence | | |
|  | Direct | Indirect | Authorities | Scientists | Ordinary people |
|---|---|---|---|---|---|
| 1931–1950 | HI | LO | MID | LO | LO |
| 1951–1964 | LO | HI | HI | HI | LO |
| 1965–1979 | HI | MID | MID | MID | HI |
| 1977–1984 | LO | HI | LO | MID | HI |

Shifts in distribution of responsibility for the threat are clear enough. From 1931 to 1950 and 1965 to 1976 there is a distinct emphasis on threats produced directly by individual scientists. I shall look at this in more detail later, but it is worth noting now that these are the periods in which the Frankenstein tradition is most prominent. The years of high indirect responsibility are, predictably, 1951 to 1964 when the significance of atomic energy is particularly apparent, and 1977 to 1984 when pollution plays a similar role. The picture is not as clear in relation to defence, for it is complicated by the fact that military defenders were almost unknown before the fifties. For this reason the MID that appears in the 'authorities' cell for 1931 to 1950 is probably an underestimate, and, as detailed examination confirms, this period is quite heavily inclined towards non-military authorities as the most significant basis for defence. If that is the case, then the overall pattern becomes a little clearer. After 1965 there is a growing commitment to ordinary people as the primary locus for defence: this is true of 72 per cent and 80 per cent of films in the two periods respectively. Before 1965 the figure is correspondingly low (below 30 per cent) and there is much more emphasis on the defensive role of authorities.

At their most general, then, the periods conceptualisze threat and defence in the ways expressed in table 7.2.

**Table 7.2   Summary of threat and defence in science-based horror movies**

| | Defence | |
| | Authorities | Self-reliance |
|---|---|---|
| *Threat* | | |
| *Direct* | 1931–1950 | 1965–1976 |
| *Indirect* | 1951–1964 | 1977–1984 |

Against this background I shall document the principal features of each period in turn, although because of the post-1965 decline in science-based horror movies I shall concentrate on the first two periods.

### The Secret of Life: 1931–1950

If you drew up a family tree of science-based horror movies in these two decades you would find a solid trunk in which scientists cause

disorder as a consequence of their commitment to science, one substantial branch in which they use science for their personal evil ends,
one tiny branch in which disaster is accidental and a few odd twigs.
A little less fancifully, you might observe that the bulk of this period's
mad-scientist movies fall squarely within the *Frankenstein* tradition.
They postulate commitment to science as a central source of disorder,
and their key protagonists are devoted to the pursuit of knowledge at
the expense of humane values. This science is dominantly medical,
concerned particularly with creating life or with transforming the
already-living. Where it gives rise to humanoid monsters, such creatures are generally afforded a degree of anthropomorphically grounded sympathy, and their creators are permitted the luxury of partly
defensible scientific motives. These men (they all are) are not simply
mad, bad and dangerous. They have higher aspirations, and although
most narratives do contrive to demonstrate the corruption consequent upon obsessive pursuit of knowledge, they also allow that
relations between scientific and human interests may be genuinely
problematic.

Even someone as finally unredeemable as Dr von Niemann in *The
Vampire Bat* (1933) is permitted an impassioned speech about the
glory of science. 'Mad?', he says, 'Is one who has solved the secret of
life to be considered mad? Life, created in the laboratory. No mere
crystalline growth, but tissue, living, growing tissue that moves,
pulsates, and demands food. ... What are a few lives when weighed
in the balance against the achievements of biological science? Think
of it. I have lifted the veil. I have created life. Wrested the secret of
life from life.' Of course, the fact that von Niemann finally comes to
a sticky end (shot by his vengeful assistant) narratively demonstrates
his obsession to be truly insane. Yet the line dividing movie madness
from genius is often less clear: science, however threatening, also has
its potential for good. It is notable, therefore, that although existing
authorities are the major narrative resource for dealing with those
who stray from the path of scientific propriety, many of the period's
monsters and creators are finally destroyed not by those authorities
but by each other, as if in implicit recognition of their joint sins.

· As an example of the most famous dynasty of mad scientists – and
instead of *Frankenstein* itself, which I have already considered in
some detail – let us look at its 1939 second sequel: *Son of Frankenstein*.
Sometimes criticised as rather more overwrought than its two predecessors (it is, after all, the source for most of the better jokes in
*Young Frankenstein* (1975)), *Son of Frankenstein* clearly exhibits

many features basic to the tradition. Set in that odd expressionist *elsewhen* found in so many early horror movies, *Son of Frankenstein* begins with Wolf von Frankenstein, his wife Elsa and their small son Peter travelling from the modern world to a village which, for all practical purposes, belongs in a Universal Studios' vision of the European nineteenth century. Early in the story's development it is clear that the new Baron has inherited more than just an aquiline nose from his infamous father, and the movie's generically essential assertion of scientific values comes in a letter that father has left for him: 'If you, like me, burn with the irresistible desire to penetrate the unknown, carry on. Even though the path is cruel and tortuous, carry on. Like every seeker after truth you will be hated, blasphemed and condemned.' Frankenstein, inspired by these words from the past, and later shown his father's tomb on which someone has chalked 'maker of monsters', takes up a symbolically burning torch and, using it as a pen, alters the crude epitaph to read 'maker of men'.

The terms have been set, and our involvement now is both with the growing pace of events (what happens next, and when?) and with the shifting balance of humane versus scientific values. On the one side are ranged the characters of Elsa, who grows increasingly distraught, the child, who is carried off by the monster at the film's climax, and Inspector Krogh, the film's principal representative of the forces of order. Arrayed against them we are given Ygor, the elder Frankenstein's former grave-robber now motivated by revenge, and the Creature, the familiar physical caricature of the 'men' Frankenstein aspires to create. And at the crux is Frankenstein himself, focus of science's destructive and creative impulses, the prototypical obsessed scientist.

Yet, as is so often the case in the thirties Frankenstein tradition, these character oppositions are ambiguously rendered. In terms of narrative resolution, of course, 'good' triumphs, with order restored, the family reunited and the village, drenched in rain at the story's opening, now happily sunlit. In the film's detailed realization, however, things are not that simple. Elsa, like all such female characters, is portrayed as weak and dependent, hardly a focus for serious identification. The villagers are not distinguished by their civility or strength of character — they are willing to form a riotous mob at a moment's notice — and, of the representatives of authority, only Krogh (played to the hilt by Lionel Atwill) is permitted any dignity or, indeed, credibility. Our involvement is with Frankenstein and the Creature rather than with the official forces of good. When Karloff's Creature studies his unprepossessing reflection in the mirror, drawing Frankenstein next to him the better to make the comparison, we are touched far more than we are by Elsa's fear or Peter's irritating precociousness. Even the vengeful Ygor attracts more sympathy than the self-righteous burghers who once tried to hang him.

I do not want to make too much of *Son of Frankenstein*'s ambiguous view of the perils of mad science. As in most mad-scientist movies, there is no doubt here about the fundamental disordering potential of scientific knowledge. Yet, throughout the 'trunk' films of the 1931–1950 family tree there is some sense that selfless devotion to science is not entirely negative. Thus, for example, all the mad-scientist movies of 1932, the foundation year, including *Dr Jekyll and Mr Hyde, Dr X, Frankenstein* and *Murders in the Rue Morgue*, show some positive evaluation of scientific inquiry, however qualified by reservations and uncertainties. Fear of science is not straightforward here, for it is tempered by ideas about the need for progress and the inevitable price of that need. Predictably, this is less true of those mad-scientist movies in which the scientist's central motivation is not commitment to science itself, although even then – as with, say, *The Hands of Orlac* (1935) – medical science can be construed as socially responsible. Overall, though, the uncomplicated evil of Lugosi's Dr Vollin in *The Raven* (1935) typifies such movies. 'Try to be sane, Vollin' is the plaintive request of one character about to undergo torture. As well ask a river to flow backward, so simplistically and irreducibly mad is the doctor.

These two types of mad science – as an overwhelming commitment and as a means to other evil ends – dominate the thirties and forties, although by the time the thinnest variations appear in 1946 (*Dr Renault's Secret, Face of Marble, Frankenstein Meets the Wolfman, House of Frankenstein*, and *Jungle Captive*), commitment to science lacks the apparent cogency and passion of the early Frankenstein series. Many of the familiar accoutrements are still there, including appropriately elaborate experimental apparatus, stereotypical juvenile leads, intermittent comic relief and ritual obeisance to the need to discover the secret of life. But like most forties horror movies, these films simply rework the basic conceptual materials of the decade before.

What, then, are those materials? The vast majority of early mad science films revolve around the familiar life/death polarity, and they take four main forms. Centrally, of course, there are the movies in which anthropomorphic monsters are created from scratch, of which the best known are the three initial Frankensteins: *Frankenstein* (1932), *The Bride of Frankenstein* (1935) and *Son of Frankenstein* (1939). Secondly, there are movies that deal with the restoration of life to the dead, whether by virtue of a mechanical heart, as in *The Walking Dead* (1936) and *The Man They Could Not Hang* (1939), by injecting a serum, as in *Before I Hang* (1941), or even by preserving a brain without a body as in *The Lady and the Monster* (1946). The third group, perhaps a little less extravagantly, proposes the creation of more basic living elements: tissue in *The Vampire Bat* (1933), or the flesh substitute of *Dr X* (1932); while the fourth group − with some nods in the direction of the theory of evolution − seeks to create ape−humans of one kind or another. These films run the gamut from *Murders in the Rue Morgue* in 1932 through to the likes of *Dr Renault's Secret* and *Jungle Captive* in 1946.

Compared to this concern with creating life, alternative conceptions of mad science in this period are minor. There are other applications of medicine of course, not least the kinds of transformations wrought in the two adaptations of *Dr Jekyll and Mr Hyde* (1932 and 1941). And there are other bases for transformation, including something called 'thought-content' transfer in the first British-made contribution to mad science, *The Man Who Changed His Mind* (1936), as well as those in the better-known *The Invisible Man* (1934) and *The Electric Man* (1941). These last two are more significant, however, because they are among the few early horror movies to incline towards an indirect conception of scientific threat: the invisible man is driven mad by the unanticipated irreversibility of the process, while Chaney's electric man is started on the road to monsterdom by a rail accident. In both cases, though, concern with the indirect effects of science is marginal. There is only one film of this period which really anticipates that feature of fifties horror movies, and that is Universal's Karloff/Lugosi vehicle of 1936, *The Invisible Ray*. Overtly concerned with questions of moral responsibility in science, this early venture into what will subsequently be seen as SF/horror gives us a scientist rendered insane and finally destroyed by his discovery of the highly radioactive substance, 'Radium X'. It would be nearly 20 years before this theme − the indirect dangers of nuclear science − would finally come into its own.

Overall, then, this period's characteristic image of mad science revolves around inhuman ambitions which, by their very nature, give rise to inhuman threats. In seeking to interfere with the fundamental processes of life, science is trespassing in areas forbidden to it — a belief occasionally given crude religious justification, though more often simply taken for granted. Dazzled and corrupted by the prospect of progress, scientists ignore the proper limitations, the everyday values, and loose their misconceived beasts upon an unsuspecting world. In this situation only established authorities are in any position to combat the threat, and even they find it difficult. All too often it requires a change of heart on the part of the scientist, or even a rebellion on the part of the monster, to restore a sense of order to the world. In this view, then, scientists are very powerful, their capacity to manipulate nature undoubted and all-embracing. As one character observes in *The Electric Man* (1941), 'this theory of yours isn't science — it's black magic.' Nevertheless, whether by coercion, expertise, change of heart, or all three, order is invariably restored and the pre-science world once more made secure. The secret of life is safe — for the moment, at least.

## The Price of Progress: 1951–1964

During the fifties the vision of science presumed by science-based horror movies changes quite dramatically. While films of the thirties and forties regularly gave us scientists causing disorder because of their overwhelming commitment to science itself or because they could bend science to satisfy their personal desires, in the fifties those traditions are joined by a third. A new branch grows on the family tree, and a new conceptualization of science-as-threat emerges. The heart of this change lies in the gradual loosening of the hitherto close relation between individual scientists' activities and the ills generated by scientific progress. Science is still frightening, certainly, but increasingly it is its accidental and unanticipated consequences which threaten the world. The most prominent cause of such disorder is to be found in atomic energy, and later I shall describe some of the terms in which this newly discovered threat is articulated. Before turning to that, however, it is first necessary to trace the fate of the archetypical mad scientist, Frankenstein, and those of his genre descendents still seeking the secret of life.

There is some continuity between the mad medicos of the forties and those of the early fifties, not least because a number of films which were actually produced in the USA during the war did not surface in Britain until a decade later — among them, *The Mad Monster* and *The Case of the Missing Brides* (both made in 1942 and released in Britain in 1952), *Lock Your Doors*, *Return of the Ape Man* and *Captive Wild Woman* (made in 1943 and distributed in 1951) and the 1945 *House of Dracula* (a partner in parody to *House of Frankenstein*), which didn't turn up in Britain until as late as 1957. These distributional quirks apart, however, the fifties genre does introduce a few of its own 'life creating' scientists, though most of them lack the characteristic ambiguities of their thirties predecessors. *Frankenstein 1970* (1958), *Teenage Frankenstein* (1958) and *Frankenstein's Daughter* (1959) are, by any standards, crude caricatures. The principal exception to this simplification is Hammer's *The Curse of Frankenstein* (1957), a film which can be taken to represent one limit of fifties developments in mad-science movies. Subject to much controversy on its first release, this early Hammer success is a relentlessly downbeat variation on the familiar theme; with its small cast and almost spartan settings, it relates to earlier Frankensteins rather as an austere chamber piece might relate to a grandiose romantic symphony. There is no affirmative return to familial bliss here, no optimistic restoration of order. The Baron goes to his execution terrified but unrepentant, a man sufficiently obsessed with his desire to create life to have murdered for it. The movie's final image is not the conventional one of happiness restored, but a silhouette of the guillotine on which Frankenstein is about to die.

Yet, in this reading of the character (played by Peter Cushing, as he would be in many subsequent Hammer productions), Frankenstein is not simply evil. Arrogant and superior, perhaps, but his subjection of moral standards to the requirements of science is achieved in the course of the story's telling and not presumed at its beginning. Only slowly do we realize that the Baron is prepared to go to any lengths; that — as Paul, his increasingly unwilling assistant, tells him — 'you can't see the horror of what you're doing.' Unlike traditional movie versions of the Frankenstein story in which stereotypical concepts of good and evil are held in uneasy balance, *The Curse of Frankenstein* shows us the Baron progressively corrupted. This aura of growing evil is reinforced both by the brutishness of Christopher Lee's monster in comparison with the pathos routinely invoked in the Karloff account of the character and by the film's evident fascination with viscera – in its time shocking, as several contemporary reviewers suggested.

Unsurprisingly, then, compared to its predecessors *The Curse of Frankenstein*'s vision of science lacks celebratory mystique. The laboratory scenes, once dominated by equipment used to stage spectacular and even playful displays of pyrotechnics, are now distinguished by the sickly reds and greens of retorts filled with unnamed chemicals. There is much blood in this Eastman Colour laboratory – in a memorable touch, Frankenstein absently wipes his bloody hand on his elegant jacket – and the Baron's obsession becomes increasingly sordid as organs are purloined from any available source. The familiar generic aspiration to create life is no longer expressed in noble speeches made by men whose eyes are fixed, metaphorically and literally, on some distant point. Indeed, the only lengthy dissertation on science in *The Curse of Frankenstein* comes from the aged Professor Bernstein just prior to his murder by the brain-seeking Baron. For Bernstein it is the world that is to blame:

> Is the world ready for the revelations that scientists make? There's a great difference between knowing that a thing is so and knowing how to use that knowledge for the good of mankind. The trouble with us scientists is that we quickly tire of our discoveries. We hand them over to people who are not ready for them while we go off again into the darkness of ignorance searching for other discoveries which will be mishandled in just the same way when the time comes.

Though it can hardly apply to the Baron's ruthless single mindedness in *The Curse of Frankenstein*, this speech does express a view of science that becomes increasingly common in the horror movies of the fifties and early sixties. Behind it lurks the generalized fear that, powered by science and technology, the engine of change is out of control, that 'progress' may not be the unqualified force for good that we presume it to be and that individual scientists – however well-disposed – are neither responsible for, nor in control of, the outcome of their researches. Such a fear is clearly central to the many films that focus on the adverse and usually monstrous side-effects of atomic energy, but it also permeates some of the period's more traditionally framed horror movies. Take *The Fly* (1958), for instance, one of the most commercially successful mad-science movies of the fifties, and the first to be produced by a major studio (Fox) in both colour and CinemaScope. *The Fly* presupposes the familiar stereotype of the obsessed scientist whose precipitate haste to complete his research brings disaster. In the event, he is the victim. Testing his matter-transfer apparatus on himself, he unwittingly enters the machine in company with a fly, emerging with the fly's head and one claw-like hand, and his own head and arm imposed on the insect. With no hope of reversing the process, he destroys his notes and his equipment, persuades his wife to co-operate in crushing his body in an industrial press and leaves his brother to restore familial order with his wife and child.

A clear enough variation on the Frankenstein model, then. Yet where the scientist, André, differs from so many of his predecessors is in the almost absolute sympathy that the film accords him. He could hardly be described as 'mad' even to the limited extent of, say, Wolf in *Son of Frankenstein*, and his disastrous haste is never motivated by a desire for self-aggrandizement. It is, rather, based on his wish to help humanity by exploiting the positive potential of his discovery. In many ways, and unlike traditional mad scientists, he is not at fault; like all of us he is a victim of the modern age, turned into a creature of pathos as much as one of horror. After he demonstrates the matter-transfer effect to his wife, they discuss its promise and its dangers:

| | |
|---|---|
| Helene: | It's frightening. It's like playing God. |
| André: | God gives us intelligence to uncover the wonders of nature. Without that gift nothing is possible. |
| Helene: | Oh André, I get so scared sometimes. The suddenness of our age: electronics, rockets, earth satellites, supersonic flight. And now this. It's not so much who invents them. It's the fact that they exist. |
| André: | But you're not frightened of TV, or radio, or X-rays, or electricity, or that the earth is round. |
| Helene: | No, but everything's going so fast, I'm just not ready to take it all in. It's all so quick. |
| André: | Just do like Philippe [their young son] does; accept them as part of our normal life. They're facts, wonderful facts. |

*The Curse of Frankenstein* and *The Fly*, then, represent either extreme of fifties 'mad science', though it is the latter which more closely reflects the period's general image of science and scientists.[2] Thus, while the price of progress is very high in the films of these years, individual scientists are often relatively blameless. As I have already observed, this is the era in which the expert is most in demand and most successful in dealing with a wide variety of movie threats, not simply those created by science itself. Many of these experts are also scientists, their specialist knowledge recognized as both dangerous and essential, their expertise irreplaceable. This concurrent positive and negative evaluation of science is not new, of course, but it is given additional force in the fifties, both in the distinctive interpretations of familiar genre conventions in a film like *The Fly*, and, more clearly, in the evolution of those SF-inclined horror movies whose thirties ancestor was *The Invisible Ray*.

Some of these films, like *The Fly*, feature scientists whose pursuit of scientific goals is admirably motivated but misplaced in its effects. Deemer, for example, the biochemist in *Tarantula* (1956), is researching nutrients in the hope of solving the world's food problems, work which kills him and his staff as well as releasing an overgrown spider into the local community. Typically, only a combination of expertise and the military finally eliminates the threat, destroying the hapless arachnid by bombing it with napalm. Similar accidents generate a creature that takes nourishment from atomic energy in *Fiend Without a Face* (1959), an injured war survivor whose treatment with a re-growth compound derived from reptiles turns him into an alligator mutation in *The Alligator People* (1959) and a scientist whose exposure to an experimental gas makes him a death-delivering monster in *Hand of Death* (1963). These, and many films like them, are distinctive in that their scientific researchers are not obsessed, nor are they evil: they are simply unlucky. In trying to improve the lot of humanity they have the misfortune to destroy themselves or others. Science here neither corrupts nor commits blasphemy, but it is, by its very nature, a risky enterprise, and for that reason it can be dangerous. That, of course, is the price of progress.

In such narratives, science is still in the control of individual scientists, even if its results are unpredictable. However, in the most distinctive contributions to the genre in these years, science's adverse effects are generalized — above all in the presumed threat of radiation and nuclear explosion. From *The Beast from 20,000 Fathoms* in 1953 through *Them!* (1954), *X the Unknown* (1956), *Godzilla* (1957), *Behemoth the Sea Monster* (1959) and scores of others all the way to *The Horror of Party Beach* in 1964 runs the theme of monsters awakened, created or attracted by atomic energy. *Them!*, a considerable box-office success of the mid-fifties, is typical. Opening with only intimations of the threat to come — a carefully constructed sequence in which a child is found wandering dazed in the desert — the film goes on to postulate giant ants which have mutated as a consequence of 'lingering radiation' from the first A-bomb tests. Experts are summoned (an entomologist and his daughter) and, in co-operation with the appropriate authorities, they finally corner and destroy the surviving ants in the Los Angeles drainage system. Shot in naturalistic style, *Them!* lacks the self-consciousness about science evident in many older mad science movies. Here science is simply taken for granted, as indirectly responsible for disorder, but also vital to any attempt to combat it. Like several of its contemporaries, the movie implies that other mutations can be expected as an inevitable consequence of continuing research into atomic energy, a prediction splendidly rendered in an apocalyptic biblical quotation: 'And there shall be destruction and darkness come over creation. And the beasts shall rule over the earth'.

As, indeed, they seek to do for much of the decade, perhaps most extravagantly in the Japanese productions that give us huge prehistoric creatures freed by atomic explosions: *Godzilla* (1957), *Rodan* (1958) and *Gigantis the Fire Monster* (1960). Quite overt in laying the blame at the door of nuclear energy, these Toho Compary products were dubbed and re-edited for the American and European markets. They usually climax with their respective monsters laying waste to Tokyo, but finally vanquished by the full might of science and the military. Nor are they alone. The pattern remains the same whether we are dealing with the mutated molluscs of *The Monster that Challenged the World* (1957) or the radioactive liquid of *The H-Man* (1960), the radiation-consuming thing of *X the Unknown* (1956) or the monsters generated from radioactive waste in *The Horror of Party Beach* (1964), the irradiated mutant of *The Cyclops* (1957) or the giant locusts of *Beginning of the End* (1960). Some form of radioactivity disrupts the normal order of the natural world; a monstrous excrescence goes on the rampage; science and coercive authority successfully avert total disaster. Within this format, though individual scientists do occasionally despair of the future (Dr Serizawa in *Godzilla* commits suicide, having saved the world and thus witnessed the destructive potential of his discovery), science's moral complexities are rarely given the kind of explicit consideration common in the Frankenstein tradition. Scientific discovery has simply become part of the order of things.

In the fifties, then, the inhuman ambitions of individual scientists are far less to the fore than they were in the previous two decades. Though there are still cases of science used for evil ends, as well as one or two traditional mad scientists, the sub-genre's major emphasis is on unintentional and often accidental threats. This, combined with the evident importance of scientists in resisting the disordering impulse, paints the familiar moral ambiguity of the Frankenstein tradition onto a much larger canvas. No longer the special quasi-magical activity of thirties mad science tucked away in old houses and Gothic castles, science now is more prosaic and more all-embracing. Penetrating into every corner of our lives, the science developed in fifties horror movies is a constitutive part of our everyday world, its admired and feared exponents harbingers of both progress and disaster, its most common threat — radiation — unseen, but a potential invader of any area of our activities. Perhaps, then, the most symptomatic image of fifties science-based horror movies is not Godzilla laying waste to Tokyo or the giant ants struggling for their lives in a city sewer. It is the eponymous hero of *The Incredible Shrinking Man* (1957) desperately seeking just to survive in a universe which no longer offers him a secure and central place.

## Carry on Screaming: 1965–1976

For the connoisseur of mad science these years do not offer an embarrassment of riches. Traditional obsessive scientists are thin on the ground, and the most striking innovation of the fifties — un-anticipated nuclear threats — almost disappears. Only a handful of films in the mid-sixties follows that theme, including two additions to the Toho cycle of Japanese nuclear monsters: *Godzilla versus the Thing* (1965) and *Frankenstein Conquers the World* (1967). After that, several years go by before the genre shows some inclination to renew the old mutation tradition (though not now derived from radioactivity) in the form of giant rabbits in *Night of the Lepus* (1973), intelligent carnivorous cockroaches in *Bug* (1975) and a whole bestiary of overgrown creatures in *The Food of the Gods* (1976). More interesting than this revival, however, is the emergence of a truly apocalyptic vision of human mutation and disease, a conception which only fully comes into its own later in the seventies and eighties. The earliest examples of this trend in a science-related context are *It's Alive!* (1975) and *Shivers* (1976), although in the case of the former the causal connection with science is rather attenuated. At least the aphrodisiac parasites of *Shivers* are a direct product of scientific research; the mutant infant of *It's Alive!* is only hypothetically a consequence of pharmaceutical shortcuts, and ideas about the perils of science play almost no part in the film. As it will be in later eco-apocalypse movies, science in *It's Alive!* is no more than a background facilitator of disaster.

More of that later. For the present it is enough to observe that by the late sixties, science as a major source of horror-movie threat is in serious decline. Although other areas of the genre both expand and innovate in this period, science-based horror movies do not. One symptom of this is their tendency to resort to implausible combinations with other horror-movie traditions and even with other genres. The revealingly titled *Jesse James Meets Frankenstein's Daughter*, made in the USA in 1965 but not given British distribution for nine years, suggests something of the splendid lunacy of the trend. It is a development in which pastiche, parody and even slapstick comedy are not uncommon, usually based on the presumption that constant overstatement of the genre conventions is an effective substitute for comic invention. This strategy is shared by films as diverse as *Carry on Screaming* (1966), *Horror Hospital* (1973), *The Thing with Two Heads* (1974), *The Rocky Horror Picture Show*, *Young Frankenstein* and *Flesh for Frankenstein* (all 1975), with varying degrees of box-office success. Even in movies not overtly presented as comic, there is a general tendency to resort both to camp humour and to black comedy; regrettably, not all of it is as ingenious as the running gag in *Scream and Scream Again* (1970) in which a character continually awakes in a hospital bed to find himself minus yet another limb! These and other more frantic attempts to soup up the traditional formulae reflect the fact that, for audiences and film-makers alike, the unleavened mad-science story is no longer sufficient in itself, and it is significant that some of the period's more striking films − *The Creeping Flesh* (1973), for instance − attempt to weld together aspects of the hitherto separate horror-movie domains of science and supernature.

With the science-based genre in such evident disarray it is hardly surprising that Frankensteinian scientists, corrupted or destroyed by their devotion to science, are rare, and even they are given little opportunity to articulate the genre's standard rationalizations for their actions. Take, for example, two of the Hammer Frankenstein films of the period, both of them directed by Terence Fisher and featuring Peter Cushing in his customary role. They give us a much changed Baron. In *Frankenstein Must Be Destroyed* (1969) he is embittered and ruthless; any sympathy that we may feel is directed at the film's pitiable monster. In *Frankenstein and the Monster from Hell* (1974) he rules cruelly and implacably over a lunatic asylum, and his scientific researches seem no more than an extension of that closed and authoritarian world. Thus, even allowing for Fisher's and Cushing's general toughening up of the role, these later Frankensteins are a far cry from the progressively corrupted figure of their first joint endeavour, *The Curse of Frankenstein* (1957). With scientific aspirations no longer a credible reference point, there is a growing tendency for the Baron's motivations to fall back into a residual 'evil' category, thus further precluding the moral ambiguity so important in earlier genre visions of the dangers of science.

Nor is Hammer alone in deserting the familiar terrain. The idea that science is likely to lead astray its more enthusiastic exponents is given only perfunctory treatment in those few movies which actually allow for that possibility. *The Curse of the Fly* (1965) boasts none of its predecessor's evident concern with the risks of progress, resorting instead to an increasingly frenetic mixture of horror movie, detective story and melodrama. This is symptomatic of a more general attempt to reinforce the failing sub-genre from almost any source, a trend further accelerated by late-sixties relaxation of censorship restrictions and subsequent changes in horror-movie conventions governing sexual representation. Most such developments, at least in relation to science-based movies, resemble *Lady Frankenstein* (1972) in their crude attempts to incorporate as much explicit sexual activity as possible, however implausible that may be; though some — notably *Doctor Jekyll and Sister Hyde* (1971) — succeed in combining new and old without rendering both entirely unconvincing

In this context it is hardly surprising that the majority (over 60 per cent) of science-related horror movies distributed between 1965 and 1976 invoke science as no more than a quasi-magical means for pursuing non-scientific ends. Whether one seeks to rule the world by reanimating refrigerated Nazi soldiers as in *The Frozen Dead* (1967), or merely to capture the heroine's heart by mutating into a jellyfish and killing off the romantic opposition as in *Sting of Death* (1968), science serves only as an unexplicated instrument of evil. Though many favourite mad-science enterprises do remain credible — creating

life, preserving youth and beauty, developing animal/human mutations – the concept of science to which they relate has lost whatever
distinctiveness it once had. Science is no longer intrinsically frightening,
and scientists, whichever side they are on, are much diminished.
Indeed, the idea of the expert scientist as a bastion against all manner
of threats has virtually disappeared by the seventies. Instead, the
most likely source of successful resistance is the lay person, inexpert
by definition, and there is even some suggestion that scientific expertise
might be a positive disadvantage. It is this widespread decline in the
efficacy of science which is, finally, the most distinctive feature of the
period's science-based movies. By the late seventies and eighties it
has become so common that even the most explicitly science-oriented
of horror movies actually pay little attention to science.

### Altered States: 1977–1984

Inevitably, then, by 1977 the Frankenstein tradition is in full retreat.
There are mad scientists, certainly, but few of them behave as they
do out of devout commitment to science, and even those movies in
which that is a rhetorical possibility minimize its significance in
favour of other narrative and discursive concerns. Thus, *The Island
of Dr Moreau* (1977) rapidly loses sight of Burt Lancaster's initially
altruistic scientist in favour of graphically presented mutations; the
science of *Altered States* (1981) finally seems rather less significant
than the elaborate hallucinations that it occasions; and *The Blood of
Dr Jekyll* (1984) bears only a formal resemblance to the familiar
Jekyll and Hyde theme – as one might expect from so individual a
director as Walerian Borowczyk. Given that these three films are
about as close as any in this period to giving us mad scientists who
are corrupted by their commitment to science, it will be apparent
that the evolution of that particular horror-movie form is now
effectively at an end. Even a conceit as inspired as a mad scientist
called Dr Freudstein, in *The House by the Cemetery* (1983), is
contained in a film which has far more to do with Lucio Fulci's
visceral zombie movies than with the familiar world of mad science.

   Such energy as there is in science-based movies of the eighties is as
much a spin-off from other areas of the genre as an indigenous
product. Leaving aside oddities like *Silent Rage* (1982) (which seeks
to combine mad science with the martial arts through the person of
former Karate champion Chuck Norris), the principal inputs to the

much reduced eighties sub-genre involve zombies, ESP, epidemic spread of disease, ecological disaster and sometimes all of them at once. Most of these films are narratively open-ended and many of them feature drastic human metamorphoses. Most, too, stretch the connection with science to its limits. In *Blue Sunshine* (1977), for example, the epidemic of psychosis is laid at the door of a type of LSD used by its victims 10 years previously, but the relation of that to the science of its manufacture is irrelevant to the film. Even the somewhat closer connection postulated in *The Crazies* (1978) — the precipitator of disaster is a biological weapon accidentally released into a town's water supply — is framed more in terms of the threat posed by military and state than by science. What was once a consequence of scientific over-ambition or individual misuse of knowledge is now part of the activities of the very authorities who used to be central to our defence.

This presumed conspiracy between the institutions of science, state, military and industry is a thread running through many modern horror movies and not simply those which make overt reference to science. Nor is the relationship always simple. In *Piranha* (1978) the rampaging fish have been created (by science) as weapons for use in Vietnam. Accidentally released into a local waterway, their existence the subject of a military cover-up, they can only be destroyed by polluting the water with chemical waste from a convenient factory — if, that is, they *are* totally destroyed, for like most such films, *Piranha* keeps its options open. In other circumstances, however, pollution has the opposite effect. The spreading mutations of *Prophecy* (1979) are a consequence of mercury poisoning from a local lumber mill; the humanoid nasties of *Monster* (1981) are the accidental product of DNA experimentation to increase the yield of local salmon; and the giant reptile of *Alligator* (1982) mutates as a result of eating the animal remains from a big corporation's hormone experiments.

It should be obvious from even these brief descriptions that science functions strictly instrumentally in most of these movies. If thirties mad-scientist films were, at some level, about science and its dangers, those of the eighties are clearly about something else. Falling firmly within the *paranoid* category, they postulate a world under threat of imminent destruction, and one in which the authorities are either helpless in the face of epidemic mutation, or corruptly involved in its genesis. Science here is one among a range of ways in which power can be exerted over a desperately resisting population; scientists one tool among many. Science has become the servant of other interests, and the 'price of progress' — the key issue for fifties mad science — no longer has any meaning or relevance.

## The Evolution of Horror-Movie Science

Earlier in this chapter I used the metaphor of a family tree, its trunk composed of films in which science corrupts ambitious scientists, its first branch representing science appropriated by those who use it for non-scientific ends, and its second branch formed of films in which science is a dangerous source of unexpected and unintended terrors. These three constitute distinct traditions within science-based horror movies, and although there is inevitably some interpenetration among them — most obviously in relation to the kinds of science typical of the different periods — it does make sense to consider the general evolution of the sub-genre in these terms. To this end, figure 7.2 offers a broad summary of the 'branches'.

The two arrows at the head of figure 7.2 indicate the most general differentiating factor underlying the three traditions. At one extreme lie those threats which are deliberately created ('motivated'), and at the other those which are neither intended nor anticipated ('accidental'). Ranged between are a variety of mixed types, the most historically significant of which involve an overwhelming commitment to science which leads to disorder precisely because such commitment excludes all other considerations. Of course, the boundaries between types are not always as clear as the diagram might suggest. For simplicity's sake, however, I have assumed sharp distinctions, so that the shaded columns of figure 7.2 can be taken to represent the rough distribution of films within each tradition.

In each column the strongest shading represents a high density of films per year; lighter shading reflects significant numbers of films, though now rather more scattered; and no shading at all means very few indeed. So, for example, between 1930 and the early fifties there are only two or three films that fall clearly within the 'unexpected' category. Note also that density as represented here is density *within* the sub-genre. As I have already suggested, after 1965 science-based movies are decreasingly significant in the overall genre, both in numerical terms and in terms of their contributions to new genre-developments. Thus, the fact that the 'instrumental' tradition is heavily shaded throughout the sixties, seventies and eighties has to be understood in the context of that more general decline. It certainly does not imply that this tradition is massively significant in the horror movie of those years.

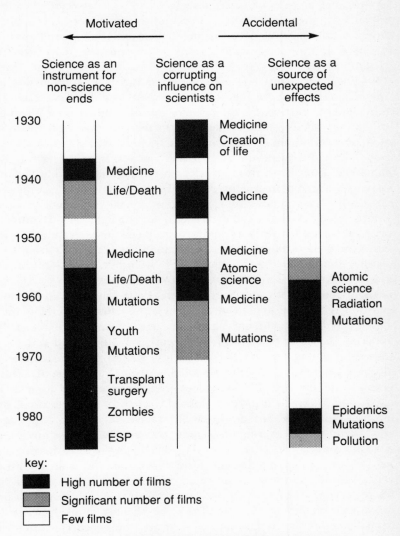

**Figure 7.2    Evolution of science-based horror movies**

The remaining information summarized in the labels down the side of each column is illustrative, suggesting only some of the scientific practices and associated threats that are prominent at different stages of the genre's development. While it would be possible to draw up a very detailed account of, say, the sequence in which specific scientific disciplines appear in the genre, I have not sought to do so. As well as the practical difficulties of presenting such information, a proliferation of detail at this stage would serve to obscure the more general pattern.

It is clear both from figure 7.2 and from the detailed discussion of this chapter that, over the sub-genre's first two decades, it is the individual scientist who is the primary disordering impulse. Whether he (as they all were) uses science to further his own non-scientific ends, or ignores human values in obsessive pursuit of scientific knowledge, the subsequent threat to order derives from an essentially individual deficiency. His is, in effect, a moral failing, and as such it can easily be repaired. However difficult it may be to eliminate threatening scientific creations, their source − the individual scientist − must either be destroyed or made to see the light. In the simplest cases the mad scientist is straightforwardly evil, and, given appropriately equipped authorities, he can be annihilated equally straightforwardly. But in the more complicated 'science corrupts' tradition, simple destruction is inappropriate: moral weakness must be resolved by moral reform, with, ideally, the scientist destroying his own creation and thus redeeming himself in the sight of his family and the world.

It is this 'science corrupts' tradition, of course, that conceptually underlies the other two branches of figure 7.2. Remove its potential for moral ambiguity and the possibility of individual redemption, and you are left with the simple villains of the 'instrumental' tradition. Retain the moral complexities, but shorn of their individual focus, and the result is a threat posed by scientific progress itself. By the mid-thirties the former was well-established, its very simplicity and adaptability ensuring its continuous survival throughout the genre's history. The latter, however, took longer, only achieving its fullest development in the late fifties. In the earlier individualistic versions of the science/humanity dilemma, resolution always involved the reassertion of human over scientific values. Later, with the threat more accidental than motivated and the scientist as likely to be a defender of society as a source of disorder, the benefits of progress are taken to counterbalance the attendant risks. What were almost mystical ambitions in the corrupted obsessives of the thirties have become everyday matters of fact by the fifties, and although nuclear science is clearly something to be feared in these movies, they propose neither its abandonment nor its control. Science is now simply too effective to be suppressed.

Up to the mid-sixties, then, science is frightening because it is a powerful and destructive tool in the wrong hands, because its goals and values are inimical to those of established order, and because in facilitating 'progress' it endangers our lives and our futures. For much of the time these fears are articulated in a medical context and in relation either to the creation of life or the resurrection of the dead. The dominance of such practices is only challenged by the growing visibility of nuclear energy in the fifties and the concomitant nightmare of both unanticipated and intended mutations. In the event, this is the developmental high point of the sub-genre, the only period in which all three traditions are in full swing. After 1965 the instrumental tradition makes most of the running, recycling many of the familiar mad scientist narratives but with minor variations derived from whatever form of scientific activity was currently attracting public attention: transplant surgery and extrasensory perception are two examples from the seventies. Most such films invoke science in a fairly desultory way, such that − compared to the thirties, forties, and fifties − there is no sense of scientific knowledge itself posing a threat. Indeed, even in the late resurgence of the 'accidental' tradition it is clear that science is no longer a power to be respected or feared, for its once-resourceful exponents are now unable to resist the epidemics, mutations and ecological disasters that characterize the period.

What kind of sense might be made of this? Or, more specifically, in what kind of cultural context might such a pattern seem coherent to its audience? At the very least it presupposes a changing public evaluation of science and scientists, one which runs the gamut from fear to disillusion and disinterest. In the thirties and forties the horror movie conceptualizes science as dangerous at every level. It creates monsters, aids evil and corrupts intelligent men and women. The fact that much of this science is medical in emphasis does not disguise the generality of the presuppositions necessary to make these stories work. It is not medicine which is on trial here, but scientific knowledge, whether represented by ideas which run counter to accepted beliefs or by people who are too clever for their own good. The common culture presumed by these films is anti-intellectual, conservative, and rigid. It looks to authority to deal with all difficulties, and demands that deviants conform or perish.

Yet there is a chink in this armour. The high-flown ambitions that once were only articulated by wild-eyed mad scientists slowly become part of a more prosaic social world. Science is domesticated, at least to the degree that its everyday technological benefits are presumed to be apparent. Progress becomes a public watchword. In the fifties, although nuclear energy emerges as one of the major fears of the century, science is also widely accepted as the pre-eminent form of modern knowledge. Scientists join the very authorities whose principal function it once was to hold them in check. There is a certain irony in this, of course, and a definite discrepancy between the enormity of the nuclear threat and the credibility afforded to fifties science. Was our culture really trying to teach us 'to stop worrying and love the Bomb'? After all, the irradiated monsters that are so common in those years invariably succumb to authoritative intervention, leaving our world secure in its commitment to the further benefits and risks of scientific progress. In this ideology of technocratic certainty, one form of conservative culture has been exchanged for another.

Once a visionary threat, then, science by the mid-sixties has been assimilated into the institutional structure of capitalist society. In our general culture, as in the horror movie, it is no longer a topic of controversy. As something potentially frightening, science recedes into the background, a taken-for-granted feature of everyday living, and the science-based horror-movie dwindles into insignificance. Only late in the seventies does science recur as a significant horror movie topic, and then only in negative terms. Many areas of culture have evinced a degree of paranoia in the seventies and eighties – an apparent mistrust of other people, of institutions and of established authorities. The horror movie, definitionally paranoid in an everyday sense, is also paranoid in the more distinctive ways that I have described earlier in this volume. In this context, horror-movie science becomes, at its worst, part of the repressive apparatus of the big corporations, of the military and of the state, or, at its best, a fast-crumbling defence against apocalyptic social and physical collapse.

It's hardly surprising. In a world in which ordinary people can be unpredictably transformed into cannibalistic zombies, a belief in science seems particularly inappropriate. Throughout the modern genre, expertise – the meat and drink of science-based horror movies

– has been devalued. As civilization collapses all around them in *Zombies* (1980), a TV interviewer talks to a stereotypically bearded and black eye-patched scientist in a now barely functional studio. The scientist, despairing and exhausted in the face of an intractable situation, asserts the faith of experts everywhere. 'We've got to remain rational, logical, logical, logical...' He sinks into hypnotic repetition of 'logical' and the interviewer's voice rises above his: 'Scientists always think in those kinda terms. It doesn't work that way. That's not how people really are.' But the scientist doesn't even hear him: '...logical,' he continues, 'we have no choice. It has to be that way. It's that or the end.' In the event, of course, the end is exactly what it proves to be, both for the civilized world and for horror movie science.

Notes

1  The MID category in any period indicates a figure which is close to that for the whole 264 films; the other two categories reflect significant variation above or below that level.
2  Interestingly, David Cronenberg's powerful 1986 remake of *The Fly* minimizes the 'price of progress' subtext in favour of an approach which dwells on the metamorphosis and brings out the internal potential of the story. In these respects the, two films reflect many of the crucial differences between secure and paranoid horror.

# 8

## Lurkers at the Threshold

If, to borrow a title from Lovecraft, there is always a lurker at the threshold, in the horror movie it most frequently lurks on the border dividing the prosaic everyday from threatening supernature. A third of the movies in this research (339) posit supernature as a primary source of disorder — significantly more than any other single domain posited. Furthermore, supernature is a constant feature of the genre's threat-structure. Science, as we have seen, is decreasingly important after the mid-sixties. The psyche, as we shall see in chapter 9, first emerges as a major factor during that same period. But it is only for a very few years in the fifties that supernature shows any real sign of decline, and that proves to be short-lived. For much of the genre's history, supernature provides the threat in between 25 per cent and 50 per cent of each year's films. Figure 8.1 summarizes that pattern.

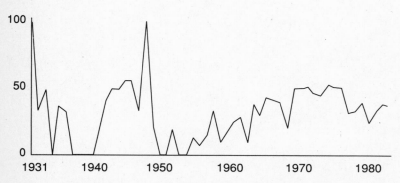

**Figure 8.1   Percentage of threats in horror movies from supernature**

Ignoring the distorting effect of the two 100 per cent peaks (in 1931 and 1948), the graph shows how evenly supernatural horror movies are distributed across the 50 years relative to the other sub-genres depicted in figures 7.1 and 9.1. Though there is a steady rise from the late fifties to the mid-seventies, there are no changes as evidently dramatic as those found in relation to science or the psyche; supernature is clearly both the genre's most pervasive and its most stable fount of disorder.

Of course, not all supernature-based films invoke the same concept of supernature. Ninety of these movies feature vampires (easily the genre's most frequent supernatural threat), and it will be clear to even a casual viewer that the kind of supernature presupposed in most vampire movies is very different to that found in, say, demonic possession stories like *The Exorcist* (1974). To explore the development of supernatural horror movies, then, it is necessary to pinpoint the different kinds of supernature that routinely inform the genre. In pursuit of that task I shall propose some categories. Note, however, that these categories — like those that structured the discussion of science in chapter 7 — are not simply snatched from the air; they have been developed and modified in the course of analysing the movies themselves.

As with science, a basic factor is the degree to which supernatural threats are a direct consequence of human actions — *dependent* threats, in the term used earlier in this book — or whether they are *autonomous* sources of disorder emerging unbidden from supernature. The most common sub-genre realization of dependent threats involves magical manipulation of some kind by magicians, witches, satanists and similarly disposed aspirants to supernatural powers. This 'manipulative' supernature, as I shall call it, is under human control — though often precariously — and is therefore directly related to human motives and human failings. Such a supernature is in principle intelligible to people, once initial scepticism is overcome, and therefore might be turned to other purposes. The analogy with mad science is obvious enough, though few supernature-based films ever develop it as far as a fully fledged knowledge narrative with all its attendant moral ambiguity. In the main, manipulative supernature serves its exponents much as science has served evil characters throughout the genre's history: as a powerful means for achieving unacceptable ends.

Non-manipulative supernature, on the other hand, generates different narrative possibilities. Here we are at the mercy of ghosts, vampires, ghouls, werewolves, demons — representatives *par excellence* of humanly inexplicable threats from another order of reality. In this context a further distinction is helpful, if only to alert us to an important feature of the evolution of supernature-based horror movies. Though all attacks from unmanipulated supernature are definitionally invasions, there are significant variations in the emphasis actually given to the threat's invasive character. In some movies our bodies, minds and immediate environment may be overwhelmed by invading supernature, the fabric of our everyday world ripped apart by a malevolent and intrusive power. The demonic invasions common in post-seventies horror movies typify this pattern. In other cases — traditional vampire movies for example — there is less sense of violent personal invasion. Here supernature is represented as a domain coexistent with our own, and while its products may prey on us, they do not routinely threaten the fundamentals of our humanity. Clearly this difference is a matter of degree, but one which is sufficiently marked at the extremes to merit distinguishing between 'coexistent' and 'invasive' supernature. Accordingly, I shall speak of three types of horror movie supernature, manipulative, coexistent and invasive, and I shall use these terms to structure the discussion that follows.[1]

By exploring a number of indicators of each type, it is possible 'statistically' to identify boundaries at which one or another comes to prominence. This suggests a division of supernatural horror movies into three main periods, each distinctive by virtue of a relative emphasis on one type of supernature. The emerging pattern can be seen in table 8.1, where the most significant forms of defence are also summarized. As in chapter 7 and for the same reasons, I have used a division between LO, MID and HI.

**Table 8.1  Threat and defence in supernature-based horror movies**

|  | Supernatural threat | | | Defence | |
|---|---|---|---|---|---|
|  | Coexistent | Manipu-lative | Invasive | Authorities | Ordinary people |
| 1931–1954 | HI | LO | LO | MID | MID |
| 1955–1974 | MID | HI | LO | MID | MID |
| 1975–1984 | LO | MID | HI | LO | HI |

First, a comment about defence. In sheer percentage terms, 'people' are the main defenders throughout the supernatural sub-genre. The table entries for defence, then, actually reflect the *relative* balance between 'authorities' (primarily experts and police) and ordinary people, and the table's most distinctive feature is the dramatic decline of authoritative defence in the seventies and eighties in favour of a kind of 'self-reliance'. The same pattern was encountered in science-based movies, and it is one found throughout the modern genre.

As far as supernature is concerned, the tabulation is quite clear, even if the contrasts between periods are a little over-stated. Both coexistent and manipulative types are to be found in all periods, and their cell labels thus represent relative rather than absolute dominance. Of the three forms, it is the invasive which changes most dramatically, the post-sixties rise of invasive supernature signalling a decline in both the other types. Nevertheless, it is reasonable to suggest that 1931 to 1954 are primarily the years of coexistent supernature, 1955 to 1974 those of manipulative supernature, and 1975 to 1984 those of invasive supernature. How that works out in detail can be seen by looking at each period in turn.

## Children of the Night: 1931–1954

Let us begin with the most famous of all children of the night: Count Dracula. Subsequent commentators have always had difficulties in accounting for the remarkable box-office success of *Dracula*, Universal Studios' first 'sound' horror movie and its biggest money-maker of 1931. They observe, rightly, that even by the standards of the day the film is slow and stagy, that many of its dramatically central events actually take place off-screen and that, at times, its narrative is well nigh incoherent. Obvious rhetorical opportunities fall by the wayside. The 'Lucy' subplot, for example, merits only a single shot of her nocturnal forays and two secondhand accounts, via Mina and a newspaper report. Even her ultimate fate remains obscure. More centrally, the ritual confrontations between Van Helsing and Dracula often seem to be restricted by the conventions of polite staging (the film's primary source is Hamilton Deane's play), and they certainly lack the sheer physical energy found in some later movie versions of the story. Dracula even suffers the final ignominy of an off-screen staking to the accompaniment of an implausible groan, and compared to *Frankenstein* (1932), Universal's other major thirties original, *Dracula* seems both static and uneventful.

It is revealing, however, to consider some of the film's more obviously innovative and positive characteristics, both because of their likely appeal to period audiences and — more important here — because of their significance for subsequent representations of vampirism and supernature in the horror movie. *Dracula* is, after all, the first product of the classic genre and the undoubted base-line for subsequent vampire movies. During the 1931—1954 period a quarter of supernature-based films feature vampires, and most of them owe a clear debt to this film, the first of their kind.

The obvious place to begin is with the movie's visual style. Like many of its immediate successors, *Dracula* is heavily influenced by the 'German Style' in lighting, design and cinematography, shot as it was by the *émigré* German cameraman Karl Freund. These highly stylized visuals are most noticeable in the wilder Gothic settings — among the high windows and arches of Castle Dracula or in the shadowy crypt of Carfax Abbey — but stark contrasts of light and shade recur, if inconsistently, throughout the movie. And it is surely this visual style that, even today, can give the film's first reel such a powerful impact, from Renfield's midnight ride to the castle on a bat guided coach to his final soporific collapse as Dracula's three 'brides' approach him. It is conventional to view the film's 'expressionist' techniques functionally — as means of heightening the movie's sense of mystery and doom. But, plausible though that is, it is important to make the more prosaic point that the very novelty of this style may well have proved a significant attraction in 1931. In a movie context dominated by flat lighting and naturalistic sets, even a film oscillating as wildly as *Dracula* between Gothic excess and routine dullness could seem strikingly new.

However, the 'German Style' is hardly unique to this film; it is common to most early-thirties horror movies. To get at the distinctive contribution of *Dracula*, it is necessary to examine the movie's construction of character and narrative, and in particular to attend to its conception of Count Dracula himself and Bela Lugosi's singular reading of the role. Retrospective criticism has treated Lugosi much as it has treated the film as a whole — puzzled that such obvious overstatement could have made so considerable an impact. But the more interesting question is to ask what it was that Lugosi's Dracula actually introduced to the movie-going public? Although vampires were not entirely new to the cinema in 1931, it was Lugosi's version that was to prove most influential.

That can be appreciated immediately in the comparison between Lon Chaney's admittedly fake vampire in *London After Midnight* (1927) and Lugosi's 'real' one four years later — both films, incidentally, directed by Tod Browning. The Chaney figure is patently evil and physically repulsive, a recognizable descendant of Max Schreck's extraordinary vampire in *Nosferatu* (1921). Lugosi, however, is essentially human in all outward signs, comporting himself as a stereotypically stylized foreign aristocrat. Constantly clothed in full evening dress, only the strange rhythms and accents of his verbal delivery ('I am...Draacula') and the studied lighting of his 'hypnotic' close-ups serve as permanent reminders that he is both malevolent and alien. Simultaneously monstrous and human, he represents a force of evil supernature concealed behind a sophisticated and conventionally attractive human exterior, a force that coexists with and preys upon our secular world.

If that were all, of course, it would not be much: a familiar enough vision of the supernatural. But such a characterization also permits, perhaps even encourages, something which was to become a central feature of the rhetoric of the vampire movie. Almost unique among classic horror-movie threats, that posed by vampirism presumes a particularly intimate relation between vampire and victim. Sucking blood from the throat — though it can, and would later, be presented as both bloody and violent — puts the two parties in an unusually extended and close relationship. Unlike the normal run of death-dealing monsters, classic vampires are therefore permitted a degree of apparent delicacy in their activities, and the physical form in which it became conventional to represent the moment of blood-taking has many of the external signs of the loving and erotic embrace. There is no need, therefore, to construct elaborate analogies between blood and semen, as do some psychoanalytic accounts, to establish the irreducibly sexual character of the vampire/victim relationship. Once given a presentably human figure as the vampire, demonstrating parallels with sexual activity does not require esoteric symbolic interpretations; it arises quite routinely from straightforward similarities in situation, posture and action.

Consider such moments in *Dracula*. There are half a dozen of them, one each with Renfield, the flower girl and Lucy, and three with Mina. As the narrative passes from one to the next we are made increasingly aware of the dimension of intimacy and sexuality. With Renfield it is almost entirely absent. Dracula dismisses the hungry 'brides' with an imperious gesture, and, as the camera tracks in on the unconscious Renfield, the Count bends over him in a medium-long shot, the scene fading well before physical contact is made. With the flower girl, however, there is a positive embrace. We see her over Dracula's shoulder as he approaches through the London fog and she comes forward to offer him a buttonhole. Looking into his face she freezes; there is a reverse shot of his key-lit eyes, another reverse to a close-up of her face as she stands hypnotized, and then a medium two-shot from slightly behind her as he bends forward and she leans submissively backwards into his arms. He could easily be kissing her.

More pointed still, three of the remaining incidents take place with their female victims in bed, throats bare, arms lying languidly on the bedclothes, unable and unwilling to resist. In each case the scene fades before blood flows, much as, in that most widespread of censorial conventions, love scenes were routinely faded before they became too explicit. Consequently, each remains suggestively ambiguous. Also, inasmuch as first Lucy and then Mina are shown to be fascinated by the Count, literally and metaphorically hypnotized by him, their submission carries clear overtones of sexual consumma-tion, an impression confirmed by Mina's subsequent unprecedented mood of satisfaction and well-being. This sexual dimension is further underlined in the film's remaining act of vampirism. Mina emerges into the night-time garden, sees Dracula waiting, and walks purpose-fully toward him. In long shot, he opens his arms and his cloak, and as she embraces him he closes the cloak around her − a picture of the willing victim in search of sensual pleasure. Evidently the film's most famous advertising slogan − 'The Strangest Love Story of All' − was not entirely inappropriate.

None of this humanizing of the vampire means that we are con-strained to become positively involved with him in the way in which we are with, say, Frankenstein. Although there are brief appeals to our sympathy in *Dracula* − most notably in Lugosi's melodramati-cally tragic declaration that 'to die, to be really dead, that must be glorious' − this Dracula certainly would not merit Silver's and Ursini's label, 'sympathetic vampire'.[2] Of course, there are some sympathetic vampires in this period, but they are greatly outnumbered by their more unremittingly evil and powerful brethren. Only *Condemned to Live* (1935) and *Dracula's Daughter* (1936) give us apparently unwilling vampires, a circumstance which in the former leads to suicide and in the latter to a psychiatrist and a final self-sacrifice. But most vampires of these early years follow some version of the original pattern, whether performed by Lugosi himself, as in *The Return of the Vampire* (1946), by John Carradine in *House of Frankenstein* (1946) or by Lon Chaney Jr, as the improbably named Count Alucard in *Son of Dracula* (1947).

For the most part, then, the classic vampire is thoroughly evil, but by virtue of his powers – physical, mental and, by implication, sexual – he is able to captivate and control others, especially women. The source of this power, the supernature that he embodies, is non-manipulative: it is a fixed feature of the movie's universe, requiring neither apparatus nor human interference for its continued operation. Like the supernature of most thirties horror movies, it represents a coexistent or parallel domain from which powerful forces emanate. But because it is made manifest in a presentable human form, it is all the more effective a threat, using against us our own suppressed desires for sensuality, for excitement and for immortality. Dracula's victims are always, in some sense, willing victims, and, unlike those horror movie monsters who simply bring death and destruction, Dracula threatens us through our own weaknesses. It is hardly surprising, therefore, that apart from the authority and expertise required for the application of wolfbane, crucifix and wooden stake, the quality most needed to oppose the vampire is sheer power of will. When Van Helsing resists Dracula's hypnotic powers – the only person in *Dracula* to do so – it occasions reluctant admiration from the vampire. 'Your will is strong, Van Helsing', he says, and it is clearly only this self-control, neatly expressed in Edward Van Sloan's rigidly repressed performance, that enables the anti-vampire expert to fulfil his or her narrative function. Only by self-control can Dracula be prevented from exploiting human desires and passions. Most characters, and especially women, are unable to muster such discipline.

Although vampire movies dominate the supernatural sub-genre in the thirties and forties, they do not exhaust it. These are also the years in which such genre notables as the zombie, the mummy and the werewolf first put in an appearance. None of them, of course, initiate quite the major tradition begun by *Dracula*, but all offer a distinctive contribution to subsequent developments in horror-movie supernature. Most werewolf movies – in this period including *The Werewolf of London* (1935), *The Wolf Man* (1942) and *Cry of the*

*Werewolf* (1945), as well as an assortment of mixed cases like *House of Frankenstein, Frankenstein Meets the Wolfman*, and *Return of the Vampire* (all 1946) – share the vampire movie's conception of coexistent supernature, but in the context of a metamorphosis narrative which generally seeks sympathy for the doomed monster. This monster-as-victim formulation was to become the definitive convention of the werewolf sub-genre, partly, no doubt, because of the difficulty of establishing and retaining audience involvement in werewolf movies. Unlike vampires, werewolves simply kill their victims – though they may infect them – so if our involvement is to extend beyond the basic 'what happens next?' it can only focus on either expert defence or on the lycanthrope itself. It was the latter that prevailed, giving rise to a vision of the werewolf as a sympathetic and even a tragic figure, an unfortunate victim of supernature.

The other main supernatural traditions that originate in the thirties presume a somewhat more manipulative conception of supernature, though not as clearly as in later periods. Take the 'Mummy' series of films, for example. As the pattern repeats itself, from the original *The Mummy* in 1932 through *The Mummy's Hand* (1941), *The Mummy's Tomb* (1942), *The Mummy's Curse* (1946) and *The Mummy's Ghost* (1947), there is remarkably little change: the mummy, accidentally or deliberately revived by magic, seeks to be reunited with its lost love who is conveniently reincarnated in the person of the female lead. Clearly there is some potential here for sympathetic characterization, and there are obvious narrative opportunities to draw out affinities between supernature, love and the erotic. In practice, however, that potential is not often realized, and, apart from the occasional *frisson* – the mummy's chilling revival in the 1932 film is a good example – these movies do not contribute greatly to sub-genre development.

To some degree this is also true of zombies, whose incarnations in thirties and forties horror movies share very little with their cannibalistic descendents of the seventies and eighties. The focus of these early films lies more with the magician who creates the zombies, and with his or her motives, than with the hapless victims themselves. In the likes of *Revolt of the Zombies* (1936) and *King of the Zombies* (1941) the improbable goal is to create a zombie army for purposes of world conquest, and although *White Zombie* (1932) and *I Walked with a Zombie* (1943) are more interesting because they invoke supernature in a sexually charged context, early zombie films remain a somewhat stunted branch on the genre's evolutionary tree.

The real focus of the sub-genre of this period lies with the vampire, although the underlying pattern can be more clearly seen in entirely another kind of film: *Cat People* (1943). Here, Irena's metamorphosis into a panther is occasioned by sexual arousal, as direct a link between sexuality and supernature as can be found, and the movie is replete with oblique references to the threatening realm of female sexuality and the erotic. Of course, the equation connecting supernature to repressed desire is rarely as straightforward as it is in *Cat People*; most vampire movies do not pose an unproblematic correspondence between sexuality and supernature. But they do constantly allude to some such relation, both in the physical representation of vampirism and in specific features of narrative and characterization. So, although it would be going too far to say that coexistent supernature directly reflects our sexual fears, it is clear that sexuality plays a crucial part in the basic workings of the sub-genre. It is also clear that supernature acts on and through the will, the vampire's powers being explicitly or implicitly hypnotic. Accordingly, only when faced with a stronger will can the vampire be defeated, and the period's all-important experts, while certainly requiring specialist knowledge, also need to develop a unique internal discipline. Thus it is that among horror-movie experts, those who combat classical vampires must be authorities indeed: rigorous, infallible and immune to the temptations that afflict the rest of us. Against such powerful threats only absolute rectitude will suffice.

## Covens, Cults and Conspiracies: 1955–1974

During the thirties and forties manipulative supernature was most commonly invoked in its simple form: magic as an individual weapon, a tool in the hands of evil people. It was rare to find horror movies conceptualizing supernature as a focus for collective beliefs, and, although some such assumption is implicit in the zombie movie's image of voodoo, even there most films revolved around the magician rather than the voodoo congregation. Almost the only exception to this dominantly individualistic focus was the RKO/Lewton production *The Seventh Victim* (1944), which dealt with a group of urban American 'diabolists'. Like most of the Lewton productions, *The Seventh Victim* is hardly typical of the period. Not many horror movies are framed by lines from John Donne — 'I runne to death, and death meets me as fast/And all my pleasures are like yesterday' —

and *The Seventh Victim* exhibits little or nothing of the paraphernalia of Satanism that would become familiar to later horror movie audiences. If it is an ancestor of modern black magic movies, then it is a very distant one.

It is not really until the sixties that things start to change, and any attempt to characterize supernatural horror movies between 1955 and 1974 has to begin by recognizing the growing importance of manipulative supernature as a focus for collective belief. From the simple curse structure of *Cult of the Cobra* in 1955 to the rather more sophisticated pursuit by Satanists in *Race With the Devil* 20 years later, the single largest group of manipulatively supernatural horror movies presume the existence and efficacy of alternative systems of belief and worship, their supernature crucially distinctive in its capacity to attract unquestioning adherents. To believe that supernatural power can be harnessed by those appropriately equipped simply supposes that there is an alternative and manipulable order of reality. Actually to worship a supernatural power is to translate that belief into collective commitment and action, a process that threatens to permeate our immediate social world and implies that apparently ordinary people might turn out to be unexpectedly malevolent. While individual magicians can harm us, destroy us, even send us to un-imaginable dooms, they do not usually seek to compete with our everyday beliefs. Cabals and cults do precisely that.

It is this, of course, that lends witchcraft films an additional edge in exploiting the magic sub-genre's narratively central transition from scepticism to conviction. At its simplest, in traditional individualist versions of the form like *Night of the Demon* (1958) or *Night of the Eagle* (1962), tension flows from our growing recognition that if the film's central investigator is to stand any chance of success, he or she must first recognize that there *is* a genuine magical threat. We find ourselves positively willing these aspiring experts to believe the evidence. In more collectivist variations, however, while progress from scepticism to belief can be important, our involvement and our consequent feelings of tension are often more complicated.

Take for example *Rosemary's Baby* (1969). The film constrains us to identify almost exclusively with its central character, Rosemary, if for no other reason than that hers is the principal point of view in the movie's every scene. We learn what she learns; we come to believe what she believes. As she is progressively convinced that a group of Satanists is seeking to sacrifice her as-yet-unborn child, so we too are convinced. Though we do suspect something about the child's paternity that she does not, by and large there is no gap between her perceptions and ours — in contrast to, say, *Night of the Demon*, where we are certain that Karswell is using black magic long before Dr Holden believes it. Thus we experience little or no tension of the familiar 'will she find out in time?' form. Tension flows instead from the very impossibility of Rosemary convincing anyone else that the threat is not simply a product of her disturbed mind; that there really is a conspiracy. In one of the movie's most striking sequences she tries to persuade a new doctor of her story, first on the telephone and then in person. We, by now thoroughly involved with her, are conscious both of the urgent need to persuade him, and of the counter-productive paranoid image that she is presenting. Our feelings of tension and doubt build steadily throughout the episode, so, when the doctor seems to believe her but then summons her own doctor, himself a conspirator, it is for us a predictable double blow. The conspiracy now encloses both Rosemary and the audience that has so wholly identified with her.

It is this conspiratorial element that can make witchcraft movies so distinctively threatening. In a conspiratorial world we may be surrounded by Satanists without ever knowing — at least, not until it is too late. Of course, the narrative prominence of conspiracy can vary. In *Rosemary's Baby* it is quite significant, as it is, in their different ways, in *The Brotherhood of Satan* (1972), *The Wicker Man* (1974) and *Race with the Devil* (1975). All these films depend on our growing awareness of quite how pervasive is the conspiracy and our recognition that all too few of the movie's apparently normal people are actually what they seem. It is significant that these cases all come from quite late in the period, partly a consequence of *Rosemary's Baby*'s influence, and partly a reflection of the genre-wide trend towards paranoid horror. Prior to the seventies, witchcraft movies presumed a basically secure world. While all the examples quoted above end with their threats undefeated, most earlier such films — for instance, *The City of the Dead* (1960), *Witchcraft* (1964), *The Kiss of the Vampire* (1964), *The Witches* (1966) and *The Devil Rides Out* (1968) — finally restore order by eliminating their covens, cults and conspiracies.

Again, it is a matter of emphasis rather than absolute divisions. Manipulative supernature in the sixties and early seventies encompasses a range from conspiratorial Satanism to magical curses, from pagan sects to avenging reincarnations. Certainly the period is dominated by a growing concern with Satanic cults and conspiracy, but there remain substantial numbers of movies based on a more individual conception of magical threats. *Night of the Demon* (1958), *Night of the Eagle* (1962), *The Haunted Palace* (1966), *The Reptile* (1966) and *Revenge of the Vampire* (1968)[3] are all evidence of such a thriving tradition. In this universe, individual magicians seek revenge and domination through their occult knowledge, curses pass down the centuries to be visited on unwitting descendents, and sceptical aspiring 'experts' finally find the knowledge and belief that will allow the powers of good to triumph.

As I have already observed, there are some formal similarities between such stories and the typical knowledge narratives of mad science. The key difference, however, lies in the central role played by belief. If mad-science movies are primarily about knowledge and its attendant dangers, those concerned with manipulative supernature are more about the need for, and the risks of, belief and faith. To combat a magical threat we must substitute belief for scepticism, and to combat a conspiracy of believers we must provide an alternative set of beliefs. Taken to the limit, such a view offers one of the most Manichaean of horror-movie visions, its world circumscribed by forces of light and dark, good and evil. In this period few films totally foreground the terms of this contrast, though it is quite clearly implicated in the battle for Simon and Tanith in *The Devil Rides Out* (1968) and in the attempt by the cult leader, Angel, to seduce the priest in *Blood on Satan's Claw* (1971). It is also a feature, though in transmuted form, in two of the period's most original attempts to extend the genre's terms of reference: *Witchfinder General* (1968) and *The Wicker Man* (1974). Neither film commits itself to the existence of supernature as such, but both play successfully on the social consequences of such beliefs and on the complexity of our received views of good and evil.

Needless to say, such reflective horror movies are uncommon. For the most part, manipulative supernature — like others of the genre's basic informing conceptions — occasions a straightforward threat and defence pattern in which arcane knowledge plays a central part. In such a world expertise is crucial both in creating and in resisting the threat, though it is notable that from the late sixties onward there is a considerable decline in the effectiveness of defenders, expert or otherwise. At the same time there is an extension of the collectivist potential of many witchcraft movies which, after *Rosemary's Baby*, feeds neatly into the paranoid tendencies of the modern genre. But it is probably *Witchfinder General* which best expresses the incipient despair of the late sixties and seventies. At the end of Reeves's powerful film the young lovers, innocents both, have been destroyed by their society's willingness to accept superstition and persecution. Richard is reduced to frenzied physical destruction of Hopkins, the witchfinder, and Sara has been tortured to the point of insanity. The film closes on her long drawn-out scream of despair, a terminal response to a world which has lost all sense of security.

Although manipulative supernature is central to the supernatural sub-genre of this period, there still remain a number of films firmly based on the coexistent tradition. At their heart, as in the thirties and forties, lies the vampire movie, though now evolving in several directions. One development, perhaps best epitomized in the massively successful Hammer *Dracula* of 1958, takes up the traditional conception. Christopher Lee's Count is, on the surface, an icily polite aristocrat, physically attractive and clearly fascinating to the film's female characters. Even without the advantage of social contact with Lucy and Mina, essential to the operation of the 1931 film, he has a remarkable effect. Lucy lies on her bed awaiting his arrival with an expression of eager anticipation, while the apparently securely domestic Mina returns from his attentions looking radiant and behaving coquettishly. For all Van Helsing's protestations that a vampire's victims experience simultaneous attraction and repulsion 'similar to addiction to drugs', it is the women's evident desire for Lee's powerfully sensual Count that is most striking.

Van Helsing himself, here played by Peter Cushing, has all the traditional qualities of the anti-vampire expert: knowledge, resourcefulness and will-power. In the movie's skilfully orchestrated climax he is even able to fake unconsciousness in the very jaws of the vampire so as to overcome Dracula's superior strength, and his general account of the character projects a sense of self-contained devotion to duty. Quite obviously, then, this *Dracula* belongs firmly in the established universe of the vampire movie, its world given renewed vigour in the film's forceful colours and insidiously disturbing camera movements.

For all its traditional framework, however, there are some signs of thematic change in the 1958 *Dracula*. When Harker is confronted by the female vampire early in the film, Dracula deals with her in a frenzy of violence, in some contrast to the imperious gesture which serves the same purpose in the 1931 version. Eyes blazing, blood round his mouth, he hurls her aside with an animal shriek, the vampire's bestial nature here given expression for almost the first time. There is no need for this Dracula to establish animal connections by metamorphosing into a bat or making mawkish remarks about 'the children of the night': it is quite clear that in his unrepressed physicality he *is* a beast as well as an apparently sophisticated human being. In the years that follow, it is this shifting balance between beast and human, unbridled ferocity and refined tastes, which forms one basis for diversifying the vampire movie. When Christopher Lee next plays the Count for Hammer in the 1966 *Dracula − Prince of Darkness* his character has been reduced almost to a cipher. Although still an impressive physical figure, he is given not a single line of dialogue, a restriction which all but eliminates the ambiguously human aspect of the role. With minor variations, this restricted characterization was to continue through almost all Hammer's period vampire films with Lee, including *Dracula Has Risen From The Grave* (1968), *Taste the Blood of Dracula* (1970) and *The Scars of Dracula* (1970), as well as in the improbably updated *Dracula A. D. 1972* (1972). The vampire as decadent sophisticate survives only in an implausibly mutated form in *The Satanic Rites of Dracula* (1974), in which Lee's vampire turns up as a modern property developer, and in a cluster of innovative vampire movies set in contemporary America: among others, *Count Yorga, Vampire, House of Dark Shadows* (both 1971) and *Blacula* (1973).

By this time, of course, a more permissive attitude to censorship had encouraged much greater sexual explicitness in all horror movies, a trend unsurprisingly and enthusiastically embraced in the vampire movie. As well as an obvious increase in female nudity, this gave rise to the so-called 'sex-vampire'.[4] The French film-maker Jean Rollin is usually invoked as a key innovator here − with, for example, *Sex and the Vampire* (1971) and *The Nude Vampire* (1973) − but his work can hardly be said to have featured prominently in the commercial mainstream in Britain. In any case, the basic conception of the sex-vampire was already apparent several years earlier in *Dracula − Prince of Darkness*. In that film, besides the dehumanizing of Dracula himself, we are given a female vampire who exhibits rather more than the customary hint of sexual voraciousness. Helen, forcefully played by Barbara Shelley, is transformed by Dracula from a repressed, disapproving and dull woman into a thoroughly voluptuous figure. Her attempts to vampirize her brother-in-law and her sister are laden with sexual overtones. 'Come sister,' she says, and when Diana nervously asks for her husband, the reply is apposite and suggestive: 'You don't need Charles.' The point is driven home, literally and metaphorically, in the extraordinary imagery of her final demise. Held down by several monks and staked by the movie's anti-vampire expert, Father Sandor, she writhes as if her body were possessed by an irresistable sensual force. Given the limits imposed by mid-sixties censorship, she is surely a prototype for the aggressively sexual female vampires who would all but replace their male ancestors in the following decade.

The oft-cited source for the most prominent female sex-vampires of the early seventies is Sheridan Le Fanu's novella *Carmilla*. Given a moderately faithful adaptation in Hammer's first real venture into the area with *The Vampire Lovers* in 1970, it later provided the studio with general inspiration for two more films involving lesbian and bisexual female vampires — the three films together sometimes referred to as the Karnstein trilogy. They feature sex very prominently: even *The Vampire Lovers*, which follows the main outline of Le Fanu's story, is far more explicit about its lesbian element than was its source, and positively strident compared to Vadim's somewhat restrained 'art movie' version, *Blood and Roses* (1962). Both Ingrid Pitt in *The Vampire Lovers* and Yutte Stensgaard in *Lust for a Vampire* (1971) bring a considerable charge of sensuality to the vampire role, enticing young women into becoming their victims by first seducing them sexually — a process presented to us in vivid detail as Mircalla caresses one naked body after another. The Stensgaard vampire is also heterosexually active, not simply to procure blood but for its own sensual pleasure, a perfect embodiment of the movie's concept of voracious female sexuality. Even the imagery is overflowing with overt sexual references. In one of the most striking scenes in the third of the Karnstein group, *Twins of Evil* (1971), the current Count Karnstein resurrects Mircalla. An exquisitely beautiful figure, she vampirizes and seduces him, and her suggestive stroking of a large candle as she does so would have been an almost inconceivable conjunction of images just a few years earlier.

With these films, then, the vampire movie's loose coupling of the sexual and the supernatural is foregrounded to an unprecedented degree, as it is also in a number of other seventies vampire movies, including those, like *Countess Dracula* and *Daughters of Darkness* (both 1971), which were based upon the Elizabeth Bathory legend. What effect does this have on the sub-genre's overall conception of sexuality and supernature? In the traditional genre world of the male vampire the supernatural threat is channelled through presumed human weakness, notably unrepressed female sensuality. Women, the films seem to suggest, lack the will necessary to resist the vampire's temptations. They can be all too easily transformed by desire, no longer safely domesticated by the restraining structures of family and marriage. Destruction of the vampire, and hence of unbridled sexuality, restores social as well as natural order. Of course, the films vary in the degree to which they foreground this theme. Not many are as explicit as Peter Sasdy's *Taste the Blood of Dracula* (1970), in which two daughters of the Victorian bourgeoisie are transformed by the vampire's attentions and used by him to kill their respective fathers. But most of them clearly present a world of repressive familial order constantly threatened by the rampant sexuality of its female members.

Much of that remains intact in the more sexually explicit vampire movies of the seventies, though with a heightened sense of the disruptive potential of specifically female sexuality. In the traditional conception, women could be tempted from the path of righteousness by appealing to their repressed desires, an appeal that remained heterosexual inasmuch as the figure of temptation was represented within established conventions of male attractiveness. The addition of lesbianism, at least in the way it is portrayed in these films, yields yet another layer of threatening female sexuality. Here women are not simply lured away by their inability to resist sensuality; they are seduced by yet another version of that very sensuality. Thus is the heterosexual domain effectively excluded – though not unambiguously. Most of these films also include a great deal of female nudity, in which young women are offered as a pleasurable spectacle for the appreciation of the viewer – in horror movies in Britain, as like as not, a male viewer. This, together with the potential for voyeuristic pleasure to be derived from watching the women's love-making (itself highly conventionalized), suggests a form in which narrative implications are constantly undercut by the manner in which the tale is told, the threat of female sexuality defused both by narrative closure – most of these vampires are finally eliminated – and by subjecting the women involved to male erotic contemplation.

This concern with sexuality is the most prominent feature of the period's conception of coexistent supernature, though it is largely limited to the vampire movie. Elsewhere there is no clear pattern. Naturally, the major traditions are represented: in werewolf movies, for example, such as *The Curse of the Werewolf* (1961), *I Married a Werewolf* (1964) and *The Boy Who Cried Werewolf* (1964). And some of the period's ghost stories – most notably *The Innocents* (1962) and *The Haunting* (1964) – do reflect an affinity between supernature and sexuality simialr to that found in the vampire movie. But whatever the individual significance of such oddities, the most elaborate and revealing developments in coexistent supernature are to be found among the period's vampires, and for a few years in the early seventies they outnumber even the well-established representatives of manipulative supernature. Interestingly, it is also in these years that invasive supernature first emerges, though since its principal development is in the later seventies and eighties I shall defer consideration until the next section of this chapter. If some films therefore appear 'out of order' it will underline the fact that, with a growing emphasis on all three types of supernature, the early seventies was a period of expansion and innovation for all supernatural horror movies.

## Day of the Demon: 1975–1984

It is widely agreed that *The Exorcist* (1974) marks a crucial transition in the modern horror movie. The film was enormously successful – sources disagree about precise figures but, other than *Jaws*, which barely merits the genre designation, it remains the largest earner of all horror movies – and it paved the way for several big-budget films designed to attract a much wider audience. Without *The Exorcist*'s success it seems unlikely that *The Omen* (1976) and *The Amityville Horror* (1980) would have found their way into production on the scale that they did, let alone have generated two sequels each. *The Exorcist* was also highly controversial, yet, for all the fuss that it provoked, it made the genre briefly respectable, as its two Oscars and eight nominations might suggest. Condemned from the pulpit by no less a moral authority than the Archbishop of York, it ran to packed houses in that cleric's city and across the world. For the horror movie, the day of the demon had arrived.

Possession had not been a common horror-movie theme prior to

*The Exorcist*, though it had figured occasionally in witchcraft stories: in *The Possession of Joel Delaney*, for instance, two years earlier. But possession in *The Exorcist* was different: violent, graphically physical and provocative. Though by no means the source of the idea, it popularised the notion of youthful innocence masking horrific evil, killed off its experts as if their sacrifice were a necessary precondition for the restoration of order, showed us a happy domestic lifestyle progressively destroyed and generally assaulted the sensibilities of its audience as directly as it could. *The Exorcist*'s demon was without any doubt the most extravagant embodiment of invasive supernature that had yet appeared in the genre.

A plethora of imitations followed, including *Abby, Devil Within Her, Magdalena − Possessed by the Devil* (all 1975) and *Cathy's Curse, House of Exorcism, Naked Exorcism*, and *The Sexorcist* (all 1977). These films, some of them slavish copies of the original, were dominantly individual in their emphases. The focus of invasion, and hence the whole thrust of their narratives, lay with the possessed person and her (they were mostly female) mental and physical collapse. But as the decade progressed this characteristic individualism gave way to a more generalized and apocalyptic invasion. Though there were still cases of individual possession − in *The Amityville Horror* (1980) and *Amityville II: the Possession* (1982), for instance, or even *The Shining* (1980) − they were increasingly embedded in a more widespread context of supernatural disruption. Although the Amityville films do work partly by postulating a possessed individual, much of their power derives from an invasive threat to the stability of the family unfortunate enough to take up residence in the malevolent house. Compared to *The Exorcist* it is our *social* lives that are invaded here, and rather less the fabric of our bodies and minds.

The social focus for such invasion can cover a scale from the individual right up to the whole of social order. Nor are individuals exposed only to simple possession: *The Entity* (1982) and *Incubus* (1983) posit bodily invasion by supernatural rape, while *The Evil Dead* (1982) subjects its victims to all sorts of physical abuse as well as to the conventional demonic possession. At a more socially elaborated level, families serve as the focus for invasion in the Amityville films in *The Shining* (1980) and in *Poltergeist* (1982); communities are invaded, by a satanic car in *The Car* (1977) and a crew of vengeful ghostly sailors in *The Fog* (1980); and, most general of all, the world itself is put at risk by the presence of the Antichrist in *Holocaust 2000* (1978) and the three 'Omen' films: *The Omen* (1976), *Damien: Omen II* (1978) and *The Final Conflict* (1981).

What these and other films of the period share is a conception of unrestrained supernatural forces attacking us with a directness and vigour hitherto unimagined, and doing so from the *inside* of our minds, bodies and fundamental social institutions. On top of that, and typically for paranoid horror, these narratives are often left open, the threat, at best, temporarily held at bay. Whether directed at small groups or 'civilization as we know it', the invasive supernature of the late seventies and eighties takes on a positively apocalyptic tone. Experts, if there are any, are helpless (except in occasional optimistic and closed variations like *Poltergeist*), and ordinary people are left to fend for themselves in a world in which the everyday things that we consider most secure are no longer to be trusted. Houses, cars, trees, television sets, all the routine apparatus of suburban life, can be unpredictably imbued with supernatural malevolence, a trend which attains its apotheosis in Wes Craven's remarkable success, *A Nightmare on Elm Street* (1985). Although it falls just outside the time limits of this research, Craven's film has to be mentioned here for its sustained and systematic destruction of the apparent fixity and solidity of small-town life, and for its visual embodiment of supernature in precisely evoked dream imagery. For all its nods and nudges to the American youth audience, *A Nightmare on Elm Street* is as effective and serious a piece of paranoid supernatural horror as one is likely to encounter.

Much of this dramatic expansion is at the expense of the well established domains of coexistent and manipulative supernature, especially in the eighties. Thus, although both vampire and werewolf traditions still exist, they develop, if at all, in eccentric ways. Even that most striking creation of the seventies, the sex-vampire, although still apparently thriving in the predatory young women of *Vampyres* (1976), barely survives the year. True to the well-established pattern of rise and decline, the late seventies vampire movie rapidly collapses into forms of pornography, as *The Horrible Sexy Vampire* (1976) and *Dracula Sucks* (1980) might suggest; into pastiche in *Love at First Bite* (1979); and even into self-conscious 'artiness' in the David Bowie vehicle *The Hunger* (1983). These were not inventive years for the vampire movie or for coexistent supernature more generally; perhaps only *Martin* (1978) is genuinely innovative, playing on and with the classic conventions. For that originality alone, it merits more attention here.

Martin, apparently a disturbed teenager but possibly also an 84-year-old vampire, constantly protests to his ageing cousin that he does not 'believe in the magic', chewing garlic and fingering a cross to prove it. His is instead a bloody and literal vampirism set in a decaying and depressed suburban world, a subject for cheap laughs on a radio phone-in show on which he is dubbed 'The Count' and treated as just another nut. Armed with a package of hypodermics he scrupulously puts his victims to sleep before stripping and caressing the women and razoring open a vein from which to drink. As ever in the vampire movie, sexuality is to the fore, and Martin's need for blood is intimately related to his shyness about what he calls 'the sexy stuff'. 'Someday maybe I'll get to do it awake,' he tells the phone-in host, 'without the blood part.'

In the movie's riveting opening sequence these basic terms of reference are established. Joining the Pittsburgh train, Martin selects his victim, prepares his syringe and, with it held like a pirate's knife between his teeth, picks the lock to her compartment. There are no magically opening doors here. As he is about to enter, there is a brief subjective shot of a nightgowned woman welcoming him with open arms, like so many Minas and Lucys before her, but, in the event, what actually follows is a frenzied and unremittingly physical struggle until the forcibly injected drug takes effect. With both parties naked, Martin now enacts a strangely tender simulation of love-making, kissing and stroking the woman's inert body, until, at last, in direct analogy to orgasm, he spills her blood across his own chest just before drinking it. The act of vampirism is no longer a metaphor for sex; it *is* sex. Thus, when Martin finally does do it 'without the blood part', he is doomed. His desire for blood partly undermined, he becomes careless and, reduced to attacking a homeless drunk, he is almost caught, escaping only because the pursuing police are distracted by more familiar crimes. Meanwhile, the bored and depressed housewife with whom he has been having sex cuts her wrists, and Martin's cousin, the film's superstitious aspiring expert, believes Martin to be responsible and so stakes him. This denouement is a nicely ironic comment on the tangle of beliefs and confusions that surround both supernature and sexuality — inside and outside the vampire movie.

*Martin*, for all its virtues, is hardly representative, and the best-known movie expressions of coexistent supernature in the eighties have been more concerned with metamorphosis than vampirism. *An*

*American Werewolf in London, The Howling* (both 1981), *Cat People* (1982) and *The Company of Wolves* (1984) all make impressive use of the tradition in their different ways, but not on a scale which competes with the evident genre supremacy ˋof invasive supernature. Even the generally more adaptable manipulative subgenre seems to mark time during these years. Though the mid-seventies still offer familiar stories of witchcraft and Satanism − *The Devil's Rain* (1976) and *Satan's Slave* (1977) for example − they are in clear decline as the decade comes to an end. There is no real pattern to be found here, and the period's most striking expressions of manipulative supernature are isolated works by highly original directors or variously improbable amalgams of several traditions − and sometimes both.

*Carrie* (1977), for instance, was hugely successful with its over-wrought tale of repression, pubescence and psychokinesis. In the same year, *Suspiria* offered even more fancy camera work than did Brian de Palma in *Carrie*, while paying far less attention to the demands of coherent narrative. *Suspiria* is a witchcraft story, to be sure, but one which works − if it works at all − as a sustained assault on our apprehension of colours, sounds, shapes and movement. The presence of witchcraft seems no more than an excuse for its director, Dario Argento, to indulge a passion (and an undoubted talent) for wild visual and aural effects. More orthodox than *Suspiria*, *Halloween III: Season of the Witch* (1983) yokes together elements of mad science, psycho-movies and Celtic witchcraft to create a self-conscious genre amalgam (*Halloween* on TV, echoes of *Alien* as androids lose heads and limbs, a final image borrowed from *Invasion of the Body Snatchers*) which is left narratively open as much out of genre self-consciousness as because the film's proposed apocalypse demands it. Yet another distinctive work, Larry Cohen's *Q − the Winged Serpent* (1983), tells a darkly humorous story of Mexican magic and moral retribution, with a pterodactyl-like god conjured up by human sacrifice and hunting for food among the skyscraper dwellers of New York.

The very diversity of these four films suggests how incoherent the manipulative tradition has become by the eighties. It is invasive supernature that dominates these later years, its paranoia, its emphasis on internality, its routine resort to open narrative reflecting similar patterns seen elsewhere in the modern genre. In many ways this invasive tradition is a simplification of the horror movie's con-

cept of supernature, most clearly so in comparison with the sometimes
quite complex network of relations between sexuality and supernature
characteristic of the more elaborate coexistent-and manipulative-
based films. Invasive supernature tends to shortcircuit that in favour
of direct, shocking and graphically physical attack – a paranoid
vision of a world imbued with inexplicable supernatural malevolence.

## The Evolution of Horror-Movie Supernature

As with science, it is possible to map the overall development of
horror movie supernature in diagrammatic form. Once more there
are three main branches to the evolutionary tree, here given by the
three basic concepts of supernature introduced at the beginning of
this chapter. The diagrammatic conventions of figure 8.2 are as
before. In each column the strongest shading represents a high relative
density of films per year, the lighter shading reflects significant
numbers of films, and no shading at all means very few. Naturally
the boundaries are not as sharp as the diagram seems to suggest: its
function is to provide a general summary, not a precise and detailed
delineation. I have also indicated the kinds of threats given most
emphasis at different stages of the genre's development, but it will be
apparent to any reader of the earlier sections of this chapter that
these labels are far from exhaustive. They are intended only to
represent the principal features of what is a complicated pattern.

Note that coexistent supernature occupies a focal position in the
diagram, necessarily so given its central historical importance. Other
than in the fifties, when supernatural horror movies of any sort were
very rare, movies based on coexistent supernature are distributed in
significant numbers throughout horror-movie history. Unsurprisingly,
then, coexistent supernature is the genre's root conception of the
supernatural. Its assumption of a separate and autonomous order of
reality is the conceptual base-line from which the other two variations
are constructed. Emphasize the possibility that with the aid of
appropriate knowledge, supernatural powers might be controlled,
and the concept of supernature begins to shift away from the coexistent
and toward the manipulative. Emphasize the capacity of supernatural
threats to erupt violently into our ordered everyday world to rend its
basic fabric, and you begin to develop an account of invasive
supernature. Both possibilities are implicit in the initial coexistent
conception.

But this is to anticipate. Staying for the moment with the coexistent category, it is clear that vampire movies are the dominant form, and that they rise and decline in three distinct cycles. The first, mainly derived from the terms of reference of the 1931 *Dracula*, is the sphere of the sophisticated and apparently human vampire. The second cycle, still dominated by male vampires, develops an alternative conception emphasizing the vampire's bestiality, while the third is

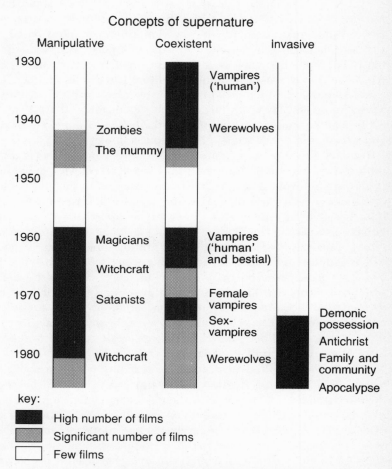

Figure 8.2 **Evolution of supernature-based horror movies**

distinctive by virtue of its preponderance of female sex-vampires. Throughout these variations the vampire movie exhibits a constant concern with sexuality, posing a kind of elective affinity between what it represents as ill-understood, unpredictable and powerful forces which emerge from both supernature and sexual desire. In the vampire movie, at least, there is no doubt that human sexuality is centrally related to the mysterious threat of supernature.

But is this also to be found elsewhere? Within the coexistent category it is certainly true that most movies are at some level concerned with sexuality. This is the case, for instance, in the principal cycle of films that alternate with the vampire movie, films based on metamorphosis in general and werewolves in particular. Sometimes the relationship that they pose is direct, in that it is sexual desire which occasions the metamorphosis. More often it is indirect, the sexual dimension only implied by the manner in which the creatures' depredations are typically represented. Predictably that is more explicit in the genre's later years — in the lupine love-making of Bill and Marsha in *The Howling* (1981), for example.

There is also a powerful thread of sexuality running through the other two supernatural traditions. Many witchcraft movies, individual or collective, invoke a sexual dimension, often as an integral feature of magical or satanic ritual, as if the orgiastic release of repressed sexuality allowed supernature itself to be apprehended, the two powers inextricably intertwined. In such a context it hardly needs esoteric analysis to recognize that the routine oppositions of good versus evil and individual versus conspiracy are frequently joined by a third, opposing the purity of love to the excesses of unrestrained sex. Similar concerns are also found in movies grounded in invasive supernature, where demonic possession commonly leads to violent and aggressive sexual behaviour and, in a significant minority of films, where unconfined sexual activity appears to call forth punishment from the realm of supernature.

Although few of these invocations of sexuality pose a straightforward link with the supernatural, the vast majority — in whichever of the three traditions — assume that there is *some* relationship and that malevolent supernature and unbridled sexuality both fall on the side of evil. They are threats to proper social and moral order and they must be repressed, whatever causal relation is assumed to connect them. In different periods, of course, the sexual element takes different forms, some of which have already been detailed earlier in this chapter. At a very general level, however, it is worth emphasizing the degree to which aggressive female sexuality has become a prominent element in the supernatural threat-structure of the seventies and eighties. Supernatural horror movies have always been inclined to represent women as less able to resist the conjoint threat from sex and supernature. But in the last 15 years, that gender imbalance has been reinforced in all sorts of ways, and especially in the significant narrative role given to sex-vampires, possessed or supernaturally endowed adolescent girls and sexually aggressive witches.

How can we make cultural sense out of such developments? To begin to do so we must imagine a culture in which female sexuality has become a public issue in substantially new ways, and in which such sexuality has also been routinely interpreted as socially and individually threatening. Historical factors like the uneven distribution of change in women's social status, the emergence of vocal women's movements in many western societies and the declining credibility of traditional marital values and their associated gender roles have undoubtedly contributed to confusion and fluidity in contemporary conceptions of female *and* male sexuality. Such social stresses, such mismatches between beliefs, actions and institutionalized expectations, inevitably pervade our cultures where − depending on the forms available − they are given highly mediated and conventional expression. There is nothing automatic about the process, but in supernatural horror movies it is to be found in the modern extension of the genre's traditional concern with the threat of female sexuality, as well as in the emergence of paranoid horror more generally. It is, therefore, only in this context of cultural change and conflict that we can make sense of recent sub-genre evolution; in chapter 9 we will encounter significantly similar features in the growth of horror movie psychosis.

Clearly, then, sexuality is a central organising feature of the sub-genre. It does not tell the whole story, which it is considerably complicated by shifting emphases on different types of supernature at different stages of genre evolution. This is particularly clear in relation to paranoid horror and seen at its most dramatic in the sudden expansion of the invasive tradition in the mid-seventies. Even a cursory examination of figure 8.2 underlines the degree to which invasive supernature is distinctively a product of the modern genre, although the sheer ferocity of many invasive movies is not confined to them. Indeed, as the supernatural sub-genre differentiates along the lines of the three concepts of supernature, a process that becomes increasingly complex after 1960, all its products become more explicitly horrific, more graphic in their representation of physical horror, more sexually forthright, and more likely to leave their central threat finally undefeated. In effect, the sub-genre's evolution involves both vertical and horizontal differentiation. The further down figure 8.2, the more diverse is the supernatural horror movie in terms of its spread across the three traditions but the more homogeneous it becomes in terms of the shared presuppositions of paranoid horror.

By the late seventies and eighties, then, whatever the concept of supernature, there is an increasing sense of a secular world besieged by threats from beyond. The invasive tradition expresses that very economically, but it is also the most prominent feature of the modern sub-genre taken as a whole. Back in the thirties the lurker at the threshold, for all its power, always had the door slammed in its face. Expertise, faith and self-discipline combined to provide a foundation against which vampire and ghost, zombie and ghoul, were helpless. Fifty years later and the house itself is imbued with supernatural malevolence. In the typical narratives of paranoid horror, the defences protecting this world from the other have long since disappeared. Van Helsing is in his grave, the old remedies do not work and the lurker has crossed the threshold for good.

## Notes

1 Note that this is a practical distinction closely related to divisions within the materials, not a logically constructed typology.
2 See the discussion in James Ursini and Alain Silver, *The Vampire Film* (New York and London, 1975), pp. 89–95.
3 *Revenge of the Vampire*, Mario Bava's remarkable 1960 movie, is perhaps better known to *aficionados* as *Black Sunday*. It was notoriously refused a British certificate until 1968.
4 For a very useful discussion of the emergence of the sex-vampire, see David Pirie, *The Vampire Cinema* (London, 1977), ch. 5.

# 9

## *The Sleep of Reason*

Along with supernature and science, there is one other major source of horror-movie disorder: the human psyche. In 270 of the films considered in this book, the principal threat is that posed by madness, most commonly homicidal psychosis. Unlike 'mad' scientists, however, horror-movie madmen are not visionary obsessives, glorying in scientific reason as they single-mindedly pursue their researches. They are, rather, victims of overpowering impulses that well up from within; monsters brought forth by the sleep of reason, not by its attractions. Horror-movie psychotics murder, terrorize, maim and rape because of some inner compulsion, because the psyche harbours the dangerous excesses of human passion.

There is thus an interesting symmetry between the distinctive madness of mad science and that of the murderous psychotic. The former is focused outside the individual, on knowledge, and it is the scientist's all-encompassing desire for scientific truth that overcomes restraint. In mad science, therefore, the mind is unbalanced by obsessive attention to what is otherwise a perfectly legitimate ambition. In horror-movie psychosis the threat is far more internal, the mind itself potentially unsound. In its very nature, these films suppose, the psyche nurtures the seeds of its own destruction, and the *contingent* corruption occasioned by a desire for knowledge is replaced by a seemingly *immanent* threat from the unconscious. Mad science is the price exacted for human knowledge, ambition and progress; horror-movie psychosis is deep-rooted human malevolence made manifest.

It is significant, then, that the decline of mad science is almost exactly matched by the rise of the horror-movie psychotic, the genre replacing one form of 'madness' with another during the course of the sixties. It is significant because mad science, however dangerous, always remains within human control, its concern with reason laying it open to reasoned refutation. As I argued in chapter 7, classical mad science is the epitome of *secure* horror. Horror movie psychosis, however, is already edging towards the *paranoid* in its fundamental conception of an unpredictable threat from within, and the shift from mad scientist to mad slasher is a move from reason to unreason, from the relative security of human thought and volition to the absolute insecurity of inhuman impulse. Horror-movie psychosis trades on our fear of what is hidden within ourselves. In its world, any of us might suddenly be transformed into unpredictable and inexplicable killers.

This essentially paranoid conception grows ever more widespread after 1960, with only a handful of psycho-movies reaching our screens prior to that year and *Psycho* itself. The general pattern is apparent in figure 9.1 (note that to show this pattern clearly figure 9.1 represents numbers per year of horror movies featuring insanity and not pro-proportions of the total number of horror movies).

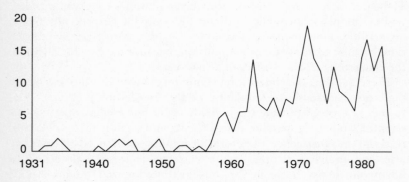

Figure 9.1    **Number of horror movies featuring insanity**

The dramatic increase that begins in the late fifties and is sustained in the decades that follow is not simply a function of the genre's general expansion. The overall proportion of psycho-movies also increases, climbing as high as 50 per cent in the early eighties. In this context, then, it is tempting simply to ignore the thirties, forties and fifties, which comprise, after all, only a couple of dozen films. I shall not quite succumb to that temptation, if only because some of the root conceptions of horror movie madness are tentatively laid out in the early years, though I shall inevitably focus most attention on the post-sixties genre.

At a general level I want to suggest a broad distinction between two types of horror movie insanity. Note that these types are not derived from any coherent psychoanalytic or psychological theory; they simply reflect the two principal horror movie strategies for representing insanity. In the first, to which I shall apply the label 'madness', insanity is framed within an essentially melodramatic context, its victims evidently and often grandiloquently off their heads. In the second type, for which I shall reserve the label 'psychosis', insanity is conceptualized rather more naturalistically. So while those suffering from 'madness' are invariably seen to be living in a different world from the rest of us, a world of heightened perceptions, those suffering from 'psychosis' are placed firmly within the same conceptual domain as the sane. Insanity, here, is an emergent feature of the prosaic everyday.

Naturally the boundaries between these categories are somewhat blurred, less blatant forms of madness shading into the more extravagant cases of psychosis. But these two types do represent a *real* distinction in the history of the psycho-movie — as with the categorial systems of the last two chapters, they are not nominal constructs — and they provide almost the only discriminatory framework that applies right across the sub-genre. In comparison with science and supernature, therefore, the conceptual world of the psycho-movie is relatively undifferentiated. For this reason the task of 'statistically' describing basic patterns of threat and defence is quite straightforward, with defence distinctive only in its predictably growing emphasis on 'ordinary people' in the seventies and eighties. Examination of the detailed distributions suggests the following general tabulation.

Table 9.1  Threat and defence in psycho-movies

| | Threat | | Defence | |
|---|---|---|---|---|
| | Madness | Psychosis | Authorities | Ordinary people |
| 1931–1959 | HI | LO | HI | LO |
| 1960–1974 | MID | MID | HI | MID |
| 1975–1984 | LO | HI | MID | HI |

As before, I have employed general indicators rather than numerical data. Prior to 1960, of course, there are few films in which the principal threat is insanity — only a couple of dozen — and so the two HI entries recorded in this period relate to only a small base of films. Thereafter the rate of growth is very striking. That is not to say that the earlier period is entirely without interest, but it does mean that the 1960 boundary is clearly marked both in terms of sheer numbers and because of rapid crystallization of the two central traditions. After 1975, madness goes into some decline and psychosis becomes the dominant horror-movie vision of insanity — a development closely associated with the distinctively modern emphasis on paranoid horror. But before exploring the detail of those changes, we must give some consideration to the prehistory of horror-movie insanity.

## Intimations of Insanity: 1931–1959

In the thirties, forties and fifties there are few films that even vaguely conceive of threatening insanity, and they pay little attention to either the mechanics or the sources of insane behaviour. True, the mid-forties saw a brief vogue for overtly Freudian conceptions of the psyche, a concern also found elsewhere in the popular culture of the period, but Freud and psychoanalysis are invoked as no more than superficial sources of credibility in films like *Bewitched* (1945) and *The Spiral Staircase* (1946), and such films are in any case not numerous. More representative are the madmen of, say, *The Mystery of the Wax Museum* (1933), *The Climax* or *Phantom of the Opera* (both 1944), men who have been emotionally and, in two cases, physically disfigured, but whose consequent 'madness' is merely an excuse for the narratives that the films present. Certainly insanity is not really the *subject* of these films: their protagonists' actions might lead us to designate them 'mad', but we have no clear sense of their madness as leading to their actions. Indeed, Claude Rains's character in *Phantom of the Opera* is so refined as to be more eccentric than insane, and the film barely merits the designation 'horror movie'. Similarly with the likes of *The Invisible Ghost* (1941) and *House of Mystery* (1943), which straddle the boundary between horror movie and detective thriller, their status as horror movies as much derived from Bela Lugosi's presence as from other generic credentials.

In most of these films madness is simply a bucket from which to pour strange and dangerous actions, and in the thirties it is only in *The Black Cat* (1934), *The Raven* and *The Hands of Orlac* (both 1935) that we can glimpse anything more. In the Lugosi/Karloff vehicle *The Black Cat* (directed by Edgar Ulmer), though both main characters could be described as insane, it is really the extraordinary fabric of the film's settings that serves to suggest a kind of endemic madness, a world at odds with itself. In *The Raven*, again with Lugosi and Karloff as a pair of notional madmen, Lugosi's Vollin — for all his obsession with Poe and torture — remains an orthodox period-product, a classic 'mad genius'. Karloff's Bateman, though, suggests a more interesting extension of the standard disfigurement and insanity equation, as he is driven even further into violence by Vollin making one side of his face hideous and showing him the result in a room full of mirrors. But neither film evokes insanity with quite the directness of *The Hands of Orlac*, where Dr Gogol's obsession with Yvonne Orlac achieves an intensity that makes rather more sense in the context of the film's original title — *Mad Love*.

An air of delirium surrounds Peter Lorre's performance as Gogol, at its most remarkable in his first appearance watching Yvonne playing a torture tableau in Paris's Theatre des Horreurs. Bracketed by two images of Lorre's shaven-headed features, the scene invokes a complex of interlinked references to violence, obsession, voyeurism, eroticism and torture which together form the terms in which we subsequently understand Gogol's insanity. The first shot tracks in on his half-shadowed face as the torture begins, his one clearly visible eye focused with startling intensity on the woman stretched out on the torturer's frame. The second shot, at the performance's end, shows us that same eye slowly closing in a kind of orgasmic satisfaction as her screams of pain reverberate around the theatre. It is a genuinely disturbing moment, the like of which would not be found again in horror movie madness until films like *Psycho* and *Peeping Tom* a quarter of a century later.

There is, then, no really distinctive pattern to be found in these first two decades, though that does not mean that there was no consistency whatsoever in the genre's developing conception of insanity. With the benefit of hindsight, it is possible to see how films like *The Mystery of the Wax Museum* and *Phantom of the Opera* stand at the beginning of a tradition in which insanity can only be conceptualized as a blatantly obvious form of 'raving' madness, a tradition continued in the early fifties in *House of Wax* (1953) and

*The Mad Magician* (1954). Similarly, there are some respects in which *The Hands of Orlac* evokes a form of insanity that is covert and only intermittently manifests itself, providing an early example of what would later emerge as movie psychosis. After 1960 both these incipient conceptions were to develop into established traditions in movie representations of insanity.

## Something Nasty in the Woodshed: 1960–1974

Though *Psycho* (1960), seen in terms of its subsequent impact, may well be the outstandingly influential film of this period, the most striking overall feature of the sixties, if not the seventies, is the consolidation of 'madness' as the prime horror movie expression of insanity. Most insane protagonists of these years are mad in the grand manner. They move in a world of high melodrama, whether that of the wax museum maniacs of *Chamber of Horrors* (1966) and *Nightmare in Wax* (1970), the lunatic relatives confined to the attics and cellars of *The Black Torment* (1964), *The Shuttered Room* (1967) and *The Beast in the Cellar* (1971), the disturbed old ladies of *What Ever Happened to Baby Jane?* (1962) and *Hush...Hush Sweet Charlotte* (1965), or the morbid obsessives of *The Fall of the House of Usher* (1960) and *The Premature Burial* (1962).

The last two are particularly interesting in that, along with other of Corman's somewhat free adaptations from Poe, they push the melodramatic tradition close to its limits. *The Fall of the House of Usher*, *The Pit and the Pendulum* (1962), *The Premature Burial* and even the more supernaturally inclined *The Tomb of Ligeia* and *The Masque of the Red Death* (both 1964) share a distinctly heightened sense of the mental instability of their central characters, capturing it in a florid visual style which underlines the peculiar grandeur of their folly. Most compelling in this respect are *The Fall of the House of Usher* and *The Pit and the Pendulum*, giving us a world in which overstatement is the norm, colours are artificial, rich and intense, compositions fill the 'scope frame with elaborate formality and our typical vantage point is an uneasily prowling camera. On top of that, the star of both films is the syrupy voiced Vincent Price, whose penchant for stagy over-playing contributes enormously to the movies' singular mood of self-conscious unreality.

In such a world madness is a morbid disposition inherited at birth or created as a consequence of fearful physical or mental tortures. It encompasses the physically disfigured, the despairingly romantic, the phobically obsessive, and those poor souls who — in Stella Gibbon's memorable phrase from *Cold Comfort Farm* — encountered 'something nasty in the woodshed'. Such movies are often period pieces, their settings generally physically isolated and socially aristocratic: decaying country houses well-suited to the requirements of mad axe-wielding relatives. Where there has been nastiness in the woodshed, it is invariably familial. Take Billy, for example, in Francis Coppola's first film, *The Haunted and the Hunted* (1964), who kills his sister and creates an underwater memorial to her, touchingly engraved with the words 'Forgive me Kathleen.' He eliminates several relatives before he is discovered. Or Carol, in William Castle's characteristically wild Joan Crawford vehicle *Strait-Jacket* (1964), who, having seen her mother murder her father and his lover, subsequently takes to the axe herself. Both these films have nominally contemporary settings, though a castle in Ireland and an isolated farm still provide plenty of old fashioned potential for what the *Monthly Film Bulletin* review of *Strait-Jacket* rather nicely described as 'that old Grand Guignol'[1].

This, then, is the mainstream of horror-movie madness in the sixties: high melodrama and modern variations upon Grand Guignol. Insanity was invoked in other horror movie contexts, of course, but usually as more of a narrative convenience than a central feature. So there are notionally insane figures in horror movies of the period whose madness is little more than a label for evil intentions — the sadistic central villains of *Horrors of the Black Museum* (1959) and *Circus of Horrors* (1960) are early examples. Or, perhaps more interesting and certainly more numerous, there are a number of convoluted thrillers that revolve around an attempt to make someone believe that he or she is going mad. Taking their inspiration from Clouzot's *Les Diaboliques* (1954), though adding rather more in the way of shocks and explicit violence, they encompass a range from *Taste of Fear* in 1961, through *Maniac* and *Paranoiac* (both 1963), *Nightmare* and *Strait-Jacket* (both 1964), and on to late variations like *Fear in the Night* (1972). While they evidently share the mainstream belief that madness can be caused by appropriate woodshed experiences — their plots generally depend on it — these offshoots of *Les Diaboliques* are more concerned with the manipulative effects of the *threat* of insanity than with the state of insanity itself.

The single genuinely new development of the sixties is most cogently expressed in the first films of the psychosis tradition, above all in

*Psycho* and *Peeping Tom*. These two mark the beginning of the modern psycho-movie, and their release within months of each other (*Peeping Tom* first, in the spring of 1960, and *Psycho* later in the summer) is one of the more fascinating coincidences of horror-movie history. Of course, it could be argued that this was no coincidence, that by the late fifties most capitalist cultures were already accelerating away from post-war repression and towards a market and commodity driven concern with sexuality and personal gratification. The vision of insanity embedded in *Psycho* and *Peeping Tom* is, on this account, no more than the dark side of that development, the new 'price of progress' in a genre world where mad science had ceased to play that role. It is a case that can be made about the whole pattern of horror-movie history in the sixties and seventies, a shift in focus of which these two films were merely the extraordinary precursors.

So extraordinary were they, in fact, that they provoked even more critical abuse than had been levelled at Hammer's big successes with *Dracula* and *The Curse of Frankenstein* two years earlier. In a now infamous observation, one British critic (Derek Hill in *Tribune*) claimed that 'the only really satisfactory way to dispose of *Peeping Tom* would be to shovel it up and flush it swiftly down the nearest sewer'.[2] Responses to *Psycho* were a little more restrained, but still dubious about the film's probable effect on impressionable minds and about its makers' allegedly perverse intentions. None of this seems to have greatly harmed either film at the box-office, and *Psycho* (backed by a carefully designed publicity campaign) was a huge success. Still, however inappropriate and overstated were the press responses, there is little doubt that *Psycho* and *Peeping Tom* were seen as both innovative and disturbing by 1960 audiences, partly because of the then unusual detail with which they represented violence, and partly because they so clearly departed from the genre's traditionally *secure* view of insanity.

Neither feature can be viewed in isolation from the other. Thus, while it is true that violence in both films is quite explicit, the shower murder in *Psycho* is as notable for what it does not show as for what it does, and the violence of *Peeping Tom* is more a violence of situation than of visceral detail. Focusing on a killer whose weapon is the sharpened leg of a tripod, and who films his women victims as they are impaled and as they see a distorted reflection of their own terror in a mirror mounted above his camera, *Peeping Tom* is clearly violent. But to chart the terms in which *Psycho* and *Peeping Tom* are innovative and disturbing, it is necessary to go beyond superficial claims about violence, asking instead how each film, taken as a whole, might have been perceived by its genre-educated audience. Or, another way of posing the same question is, what are the principal ways in which *Psycho* and *Peeping Tom* changed the horror movie's conception of insanity?

The first and most obvious contrast with tradition is to be found in the relative naturalism of both films — relative, that is, to the prevailing melodramatic idiom. In *Psycho*, of course, a carefully contrived naturalism is signalled from the beginning. The camera pans across a cityscape, and the titles 'Phoenix, Arizona', 'Friday, December the eleventh', and 'Two forty-three p.m.' successively slide into shot. The imagery is, as it remains, monochrome and matter-of-fact, while the camera selects one window out of the hundreds visible and slips under its partly closed blind on what proves to be the first of several voyeuristic penetrations. The prevailing tone is a kind of documentary, candid camera if not exactly *cinema verité*. *Peeping Tom*, too, for all Powell's characteristic dependence on stylized colour, is naturalistic compared to the excesses of, say, *The Fall of the House of Usher*: this film opens with Mark's viewfinder perspective on a prostitute victim as he stalks her, and continues in a similar vein of film-within-film reportage. In neither case, of course, does this naturalism function as an absolute reference point; these are not products of conventional social realism. They are, rather, naturalistic in the ways in which they establish a framework of 'normality' from which our two psychotics emerge — part of the process of conceptualizing insanity as a constant potential in the everyday order of things.

Thus, although we know that Mark is a killer from the very beginning of *Peeping Tom*, we never conceive his insanity in the way that we do, say, that of the Vincent Price character in *The Pit and the Pendulum*. We apprehend Mark as a quite ordinary, rather shy, lonely figure whose fearsome capacity to kill is contained within his generally calm normality. He does not belong in the world of Grand Guignol, his insanity worn on an anguished face or expressed in a grandiose gesture. Similarly, Norman in *Psycho* (whose insanity and guilt, remember, are never established until almost the end of the film) appears strange when we first encounter him, but only slowly enters our perceptions as potentially homicidal. In retrospect we see all the signs, but while 'innocently' experiencing the film (almost impossible now, so well known has *Psycho* become), we feel only an emerging sense of imprecise disturbance. Things are somehow wrong, but quite how wrong always remains to be seen.

That 'wrongness' is very distinctive, of course, and both films presume strikingly similar terms for comprehending it. Our understanding of Mark and Norman is framed by a number of narrative and stylistic references to sexuality, voyeurism, repression and the expression of sexual desire in violence. Norman watches through his peephole as Marion undresses, thus releasing the desires which precipitate 'mother's' repressive attack on the showering Marion, a kind of rape with an appropriately phallic knife.[3] Mark, used by his psychologist father as a guinea-pig in experiments on fear, pursues his female victims with an even more patently phallic weapon, subsequently deriving sexual satisfaction from watching his films of the murders. In one sense, of course, both characters are traditional victims of nastiness in the woodshed: Mark in consequence of his father's experiments, Norman because he killed his dominating mother and her lover and then mentally resurrected her. But in terms of the cluster of ideas that the films invoke to contextualize their behaviour, they are anything but traditional. *Peeping Tom* and *Psycho* do not offer a coherent theory of psychosis – there is no reason why they should – but they do redirect the genre towards different ideas about insanity. Their overt concern with repressed sexuality, voyeurism, gratification through violent attack and women as victims is central to the burgeoning psycho-movie tradition of the next 25 years, though not always with quite the same reflexive potential as these two films. *Peeping Tom*, especially, has the capacity to make audiences uncomfortably aware that they too are voyeuristic participants in a violent spectacle.

This still does not quite answer the question with which I began: what made these two films disturbing? It does go some way towards an answer, however, because it emphasizes the degree to which both *Psycho* and *Peeping Tom* departed from the familiar terms in which movie insanity had hitherto been safely contained. Mark and Norman represent a potential eruption of disorder into an everyday, prosaic world, no longer happily distanced by archaic settings or Grand Guignol overstatement. But they also go further. Both films devote time and narrative resources to binding us closely to the perspectives and circumstances of their central psychotics. In *Psycho*, famously, our identification with Marion – for a third of the film its apparent star and key character – is savagely disrupted by her murder, and, given our belief at that stage that Norman is the pathetic victim of a dominating and now murderous mother, the focus of our involvement shifts to him. This, of course, is uncomfortable, becoming the more so as we find Norman's behaviour less and less acceptable. And in *Peeping Tom*, although we always know that Mark is insane, he is played as someone with whom we would normally expect to empathize, whose romance with Helen might, in another context, form the basis for a touching love story. Again we experience discomfort, caught between character traits that attract our sympathy and overt behaviour which undermines it. And even though both narratives are 'properly' resolved, their threats officially eliminated, the uneasiness remains. Mother's grinning skull superimposed on Norman's face at the end of *Psycho* reminds us that the unexpected always lurks within, that psychosis is endemic. It is this *paranoia* that *Peeping Tom* and *Psycho* bequeath to the next generation of psycho-movies.

Throughout the sixties and seventies, then, there is a steady stream of movies whose central psychotics are born of the same family as *Psycho* and *Peeping Tom*. Several are specifically derived from the two founding films. Thus, *The Psychopath* (1966), *Twisted Nerve* (1969), *The Fiend* and *The House that Screamed* (both 1972) all give us young male psychotics who are in some sense products of dominating mothers. In *The House that Screamed* the murderous son even sets about constructing a woman assembled from the bodies of his victims, his mother naturally providing the model for female perfection. Interestingly, given subsequent developments, not all are predisposed to female victims: Mark in *The Psychopath* and Martin in *Twisted Nerve* kill for reasons other than sexual sublimation or misogyny. Even so, sex is a prominent feature in most such psycho-movies: *The Fiend*'s religiously motivated psychotic slaughters prostitutes in the belief that this is the only way that they can be saved, while Peter in *Straight on till Morning* (1972) murders only women, subsequently listening to tapes of the killings.

None of these variously effective sub-*Psycho* exercises added much that was new to the genre's conventions for representing psychosis; for the most part they simply rehashed the basic assumptions familiar from *Peeping Tom* and *Psycho*. But there are a few isolated psycho-movies of the period that did contribute something distinctive to the pattern of subsequent genre evolution. The earliest of this oddly assorted group is *Repulsion* (1965), which traces a young woman's collapse into homicidal psychosis in almost documentary detail while implying some imprecise connection between sexuality, repression and insanity. Carol is not really a female Norman Bates, however, since we experience her insanity not as something threatening within normality but more as a symptom of its breakdown. Nevertheless, she paves the way for a distinct tradition of murderous female psychotics, finding less downbeat expression in *Play Misty for Me* (1971), whose inexplicably assertive knife-woman nearly manages the impossible task of slaughtering Clint Eastwood, and *Blood Sisters* (1973), in which Brian De Palma rings the Hitchcockian changes by inverting the male psychotic female victim relationship of *Psycho*.[4]

A female psychotic also features in *Hands of the Ripper* (1971), but what makes that film especially interesting is not so much her presence as that of the Victorian doctor who seeks to cure her. Like many a movie psychiatrist (he is a late Victorian follower of Freud), Dr Pritchard fails to understand the character and magnitude of the psychotic threat. So convinced is he of his own expertise that he precipitates several deaths including, in the end, both his and his patient's. *Hands of the Ripper* plays cleverly on the ambiguity of candidate explanations, posing a range of possibilities between possession and hysteria, supernature and psyche, and not conclusively committing its narrative to any of them. Faced with this over-determination, expertise proves incapable of offering either satisfactory explanations or effective therapy, and Pritchard's rallying cry — 'I can cure her' — has a hollow ring. Finally, faced with the devious complexity of the human psyche, he has to concede defeat.

In *Hands of the Ripper* we, at least, know the source of Anna's murderous inclinations, even if we remain uncertain about the precise mechanism connecting past to present. In *Targets* (1967) we have no idea why Bobby Thompson suddenly shoots his wife and parents and takes to sniping at passing cars on the freeway and at customers in a drive-in cinema. He does it in the same matter-of-fact way that he conducts his everyday life, and, apart from his collection of guns, there is nothing to distinguish him from any other young man with a safe job and a comfortable home. Normality and psychosis blur together, and what is explained, however sketchily, in *Peeping Tom* and *Psycho* is now given no explanation whatsoever. In the movie world heralded by *Targets*, and further developed over the next 15 years, psychosis becomes an inexplicable but constant constituent of everyday life.

Another variation on that pattern is apparent in *Frenzy* (1972), Alfred Hitchcock's blackly comic portrait of a terrifying psychotic set in a kind of pastiche England. Barry Foster's Bob Rusk is charming, friendly, helpful, considerate and murderously insane. His strangling of his women victims is sexually motivated in that he kills them as 'punishment' for their enforced submission to his sexual wants. This point is made with fearsome intensity in the film's central killing, a rape accompanied by the repeated invocation 'lovely', then followed immediately by his post-orgasm hatred: 'You bitch,' he screams, 'women, they're all the same. . . .well, I'll show you.' Though the power of this sequence is unusual — it is extremely disturbing — its attention to the detail of both rape and killing was to become increasingly common through the seventies, as was its image of psychosis as an expression of unexplained misogyny.

The obvious extension of that, of course, is the 'terrorizing narrative', in which an often unexplained male psychotic terrorizes, perhaps rapes and certainly murders an array of young women. An early example is *Fright* (1971), which poses the now classic situation of the solitary female baby-sitter attacked by, in this case, the insane former husband of the household. There is some attempt to characterize the psychotic, but the real focus of the film is in the strong potential of the terrorizing process for creating tension, the logic of which inevitably undercuts any consideration of the causes of psychosis. Thus, as the terrorizing narrative develops in the late seventies, it all but dispenses with explanations of insanity, turning instead towards a narrative type which ruthlessly excludes characterizing digressions or any non-functional concern with setting.

By the end of the seventies these innovatory fragments had fused into a highly commercial form. In various combinations this involved some or all of the following: graphic portrayal of violence; insanity conceived as a routine expectation in everyday life; declining efficacy of experts, whether coercive or psychiatric; little or no explanation for psychotic behaviour; violent misogyny as a central element in psychosis; and a narrative structure dominated by the tension requirements of the terrorizing narrative. These conventions are central to the psycho-movie in its third phase and were, in the end, to make the horror-movie psychotic the most successful boogey man in the modern genre.

## The Boogey Man: 1975–1984

Unsurprisingly the melodramatic tradition in movie representation of madness all but disappears from the genre after 1975. Only a handful of films paint their lunatic central characters with the broad brush strokes once so common, and most of them would hardly qualify as unproblematic descendents of *House of Wax* or *The Fall of the House of Usher*. Thus, while it may well be that Leatherface in *The Texas Chainsaw Massacre* (1976) is as wild a madman as any in the genre's history — and few previously were able to go on the rampage decked out in a leather mask and armed with a chainsaw — Tobe Hooper's insistently extravagant shocker as much reflects the rural nightmares of *Straw Dogs* and *Deliverance* as it does horror-movie Grand Guignol. Of course, there is an element of the latter's characteristic overstatement in *The Texas Chainsaw Massacre*'s frenzied family group, just as there is in *Homebodies*' (1977) array of crazed pensioners, *Death Trap*'s (1978) crocodile feeding madman, or in the cannibalistic hill people of *The Hills Have Eyes* (1978). But, other than as open pastiche — *The Phantom of the Paradise* (1975), perhaps — true horror-movie 'madness' declines into insignificance in the modern genre.

Psychosis, though, is everywhere, and if *Psycho* was the key reference point for its sixties development, the equivalent influence in the eighties is John Carpenter's hugely successful *Halloween* (1979). The differences between the two films are, in many respects, the differences between the decades. From the very beginning of *Halloween* we know who is responsible for the killings. What is important is the terrorizing process itself, and our concern for his victims as Michael pursues and kills a succession of high-school students. Thus, *Psycho*'s characteristic dependence on misdirection to sustain and manipulate our involvement is alien to *Halloween*. Tension here is not a question of 'What's going on?', but more 'Who will he get next and by what method?'. Accordingly, unlike Norman Bates, *Halloween*'s Michael is entirely uncharacterized. In the film's prologue he slaughters his elder sister for no reason that we ever discover, and, as he continues on his homicidal way, we learn nothing that casts light on his motives. At the very end of the film Laurie, the only survivor among the movie's young females, distractedly observes: 'It *was* the boogey man.' 'Yes,' replies the film's psychiatrist, 'as a matter of fact it was.'

Not that *Halloween* was the first out-and-out youth-focused terrorizing narrative in the modern genre. That honour probably belongs to the Canadian movie *Black Christmas* (1975), which has its psychotic killer menacing the occupants of a sorority house at a Canadian college. Concealed in the attic, he makes crazed telephone calls to the young women downstairs (a contrivance which recurs in a variation on *Fright*'s trapped baby-sitter in *When a Stranger Calls* (1980)), periodically emerging to stab yet another victim. The film is a stylish and sometimes ironic exercise in promoting tension – one killing is nicely intercut with a children's choir singing christmas carols – effectively employing wide-angle lenses and a prowling subjective camera to invoke the killer's murderous forays. By dint of careful misinformation – we assume that all is resolved – the film ends on our realization that the psychotic is still up there in the attic, the only survivor helplessly tranquillized below.

Some features of the terrorizing pattern also occur in *The Town that Dreaded Sundown* (1977), in which a ferociously violent masked killer attacks young couples who park in out-of-the-way places to make love, as well as more peripherally in Alfred Sole's remarkable *Communion* (1977) and in *The Eyes of Laura Mars* (1978). But it was *Halloween*'s success that burst the floodgates, ensuring that variously detailed copies of Carpenter's film dominated the eighties psycho-movie – from *Friday the 13th*, *Prom Night* and *Terror Train* (all 1980) through to *House of Evil*, *The Slumber Party Massacre* (both 1983) and *Friday the 13th – The Final Chapter* (1984). Note, however, that the majority of *Halloween*'s many imitators – for example the four *Friday the 13th* films, to which two more were to be added between 1984 and 1987 – are somewhat gross in comparison with the original, both in style (their use of subjective camera is laughably obtrusive) and in their increasing emphasis on repellant physical detail. *Halloween*, though it remains sufficiently representative to be taken as a prototype here, is a good deal more subtly constructed than most of the period's 'stalk and slash' movies.[5]

Consider, then, *Halloween*'s basic narrative. It can be roughly divided into four phases:

1 A prologue which begins, *Psycho*-like, with the title 'HAD-DONFIELD ILLINOIS', followed by 'HALLOWEEN NIGHT 1963', and which gives us, an extended subjective camera shot representing, as we learn at the sequence's end, the point of view of a young boy (Michael Myers) who spies on his sister as she goes upstairs to make love with her boyfriend. After the boyfriend leaves, Michael dons a mask (the camera's view is appropriately circumscribed by the mask's eyeholes) and stabs her to death. It is at this point that we are allowed to hear his distinctive breathing,

an aural cue later used to much effect. Then, in the film's first non-subjective shot, his parents arrive to find him standing dazed in the garden. In one hand he holds the blood-stained weapon. The whole sequence has taken a little less than five minutes.

2  This brief setting-up section begins with the title 'Smiths Grove Illinois' followed by 'October 30th 1976'. It introduces Loomis, the psychiatrist, and shows Michael's escape from mental hospital as well as establishing that he is extremely powerful and dangerous. The sequence takes almost four minutes.

3  The third and longest section of the film runs over 40 minutes, beginning with the title 'HADDONFIELD' followed by 'HALLOWEEN'. This introduces the film's other major characters: the three girls Laurie, Annie and Lynda, as well as the police chief and two young children, Tommy and Lindsey. Much time is devoted to subjective camera 'stalking' in the residential streets of Haddonfield, first of Tommy and then of the girls, especially Laurie. Michael's presence is repeatedly established by distinctively edgy music, by artificially smooth Panaglide camera movements and by the sound of his breathing.

4  The murderous rampage which fills the remaining 35 minutes falls into two parts. In the opening section Michael hunts and kills first Annie and then Lynda and her boyfriend just after they have made love. Laurie comes looking for them, finds the bodies, and then – in the second and climactic part of the rampage – conducts a running battle with the now apparently indestructible Michael. Though she supposedly kills him several times, he constantly recovers. Finally Loomis shoots him, but even then his body disappears. The film ends with a reprise of the various locations with which he has been associated. He is nowhere to be seen.

Several common features of modern psycho-movies are apparent here. As I have already noted, it is the terrorizing process itself (phases 3 and 4) that lies at the heart of *Halloween*'s narrative, an emphasis which permits and requires only minimal characterization of the psychotic. Not all *Halloween* derivatives leave their psychotic's motives quite as opaque as Michael's – both Mrs Voorhees in *Friday the 13th*, and her son Jason in the sequels, are ascribed some apparent motivation, as is Michael Myers himself in *Halloween II* (1982). But compared with the kind of characterizing concern evident in, say, *Psycho* and *Peeping Tom*, the psychotics of modern terrorizing narratives are more distinguished by their narrative function than by any detail of character and motivation. Even in those few modern psycho-movies that do make some effort to individualize their psychotics, characterization — with the notable exception of *Deranged* (1976) — is far more perfunctory than it once was.

A second representative feature of *Halloween* relates to its settings. Haddonfield's streets and houses are irreducibly prosaic: an everyday background into which the unexplained threat erupts. Of course, some such evocation of 'normality' is common to most horror movies that focus on psychosis rather than madness, but it is also clear that, as the seventies progress, routine psycho-movie settings become more obviously commonplace. The Myers house, for all its aura of desertion and decay, seems a great deal more mundane than, say, the looming Bates residence in *Psycho*, and the small-town suburbs in which the young women are baby-sitting positively exude normality. *Halloween*, like so many modern horror movies, takes place in an essentially familiar physical and social world, with the interesting consequence — again not untypically — that its protagonists can resort to a variety of everyday household tools as weapons: kitchen knives, knitting needles, even a wire coat hanger.

A third much imitated aspect of *Halloween*'s style is its extensive use of subjective camera. From the prologue's tour de force travelling shot we learn to associate a particular kind of camera movement with Michael's point of view, and, subsequently aided by several shots of Tommy and Laurie from over his shoulder (though hardly ever the matching reverse-shot), we establish a general association between certain kinds of imagery and his threatening presence. Add to this the sound of his breathing, and the film has a formidably effective array of devices for promoting tension. What it does *not* do, however, contrary to some claims, is *necessarily* place the viewer in a position of vicarious participation in Michael's stalking activities, offering the (male) spectator the pleasures of observing pursuing, and attacking the film's (female) victims. To argue this case is to assume that subjective camera techniques inevitably identify us with the associated character and his activities, a claim which grossly underestimates the complexity of the movie spectator's relation to optical point of view. While some viewers of *Halloween* might well identify themselves with Michael — no film can defend against determined selective perception — the cultural context of most potential audiences surely makes such identification unlikely. The detail of the movie's narrative, its concern to characterize its principal victims positively, thus constraining us to be on 'their side', as well as the presence of well-established extra-cinematic conventions promoting sympathy with those at risk, mean that *Halloween*'s subjective camera, while certainly contributing powerfully to the growing tension, does so in a context of concerned involvement with the movie's characters.

This is not to say that questions of gender and sex are irrelevant to the film's operation or to modern psycho-movies in general. After all, the majority of *Halloween*'s victims *are* female — as they are in many of its successors — and, in a significant number of these films, women victims are represented in specifically sexual terms. This association has been invoked to support what might be called the 'narrative come-uppance' analysis of modern psycho-movies: the sexually active young women who provide the bulk of the psychotic's victims are, it is argued, represented as recipients of appropriate punishment. They are seen to 'get what they deserve'. As with the use of subjective camera, however, the problem with this line of argument is that it fails to properly contextualize its very general claims.

Although there is, in some cases, a *formal* symmetry between sexual activity and subsequent attack, in practice this is often undercut by other aspects of the narrative. In *Halloween*, for example, all three young women are appealingly characterized — there is no sense that their activities are represented as inappropriate or immoral. They are frivolous, perhaps, but hardly figures who can be seen as inviting their terrible fate. Basically, they are represented as very likeable. And while it is true that Laurie, who is apparently sexually innocent, is the only one with the strength of character to repel the rampaging psychotic, her sexual innocence appears more as another symptom of her underlying seriousness and shyness than as an element in a 'virginity = survival' equation. She succeeds because she alone has untapped reserves of maturity and strength.

On the other hand, terrorizing narratives like *Halloween* do invoke a connection between sexuality and psychosis, and, although there are cases of female psychotics and male victims, the balance of emphasis runs the other way. This is primarily a world of invincible male predators, a feature confirmed by the very distinctiveness of *The Slumber Party Massacre*'s turning of the tables. Thus, however restricted our understanding of the psychotic's motivations, because of the constant sexual references in the cruder *Halloween* clones we are left with the feeling that threatening psychosis *is* sexual in some way and that male aggression and misogyny are significant elements within it. The precise interpretation given to that general disposition depends on the events of the specific film, on the kinds of identification invited by it, and on the expectations brought to it by its spectators. In this context, therefore, it is difficult to generalize across the whole range of modern psycho-movies. It seems likely, for instance, that the sexual content of the highly successful *Friday the 13th* series is of little significance beyond pandering to a particular youth audience's taste for intermittent sexual titillation, just as its increasing emphasis on gory detail — *Friday the 13th* itself is barely a 'splatter movie' compared to some of its sequels — seems to have minimal thematic or narrative connection with anything else. Indeed, many of the youth-focused terrorizing narratives of recent years sacrifice almost all pretence to narrative coherence in favour of an accelerating sequence of shock effects — in *Friday the 13th — The Final Chapter*, no less than 14 killings in 91 minutes.

Although such restricted exercises in teenage jeopardy are easily the most numerous subtype of the modern psycho-movie, they do not quite exhaust it. There is still some room for the traditional psychotic — though increasingly rarely after 1980 — with even an ageing Norman Bates turning up in *Psycho* II (1983). But there is really only one highly successful exception to the *Halloween* pattern in the early eighties, and that film works by adapting the established conventions of the heavily plotted glossy thriller to an overtly sexualized image of psychosis. This is Brian De Palma's *Dressed to Kill* (1980), an up-market shocker casting Michael Caine against type as a murderous transsexual psychiatrist. *Dressed to Kill* was the subject of a good deal of controversy in the early eighties, partly because it was marketed as a mainstream thriller rather than a teen-audience exploitation piece, and partly because it foregrounded some of the more violently misogynistic elements of the psycho-movie.

There is no need here to pursue the detail of the *Dressed to Kill* controversy.[6] Much of it revolved around a version of the 'narrative come-uppance' argument, suggesting that the murder of the film's first identification figure — Kate, played by Angie Dickinson — is presented as a 'punishment' for her active sexuality (she has just made love with a complete stranger) and for her 'provoking' the sexual desires of her psychotic psychiatrist. There are obvious difficulties with such an analysis, not least in understanding precisely how, if at all, we are constrained to read Kate as an emblematic figure representing female sexuality. Such a reading is by no means self-evident or over-determined. What *is* clear about *Dressed to Kill*, however, is that it frames its narrative within a blatant equation of sex with violence. In the movie's opening sequence we are shown Kate in the shower, sensually soaping herself. Her caresses begin to suggest masturbation, and the camera seems to crawl across her body, isolating her breasts, her belly and her pubic area in huge close-ups. There is an aura of lasciviousness about the scene, and as it approaches its apparent climax, both sexual and dramatic, a male figure appears in the steam behind her, violently covering her mouth with one hand while he reaches for her crotch with the other. She screams, the image fades, and then there is a precipitate cut to a shot that tracks in on her having sex with a man whom we subsequently discover to be her husband. He satisfies himself, pats her on the cheek, and gets out of bed, leaving her apparently unsatisfied. The shower sequence, we are forced to conclude, was a sexual fantasy born of her frustration.

Whatever one's detailed response to this somewhat over-heated opening, it clearly frames Kate's character and constructs a certain view of female sexuality as a potential focus for the film. This emphasis is then reinforced by making one of the movie's two main identification figures an up-market prostitute, while the psychotic who pursues her is a transsexual whose 'female' side responds murderously to the experience of 'male' sexual desire. Note that this is not a question of specific narrative implication, a simple formula in which, say, particular actions are followed by appropriate punishments. It is, rather, a general ethos with which the film is imbued. Like many modern psycho-movies, *Dressed to Kill* presupposes the social coherence of a set of loosely formulated ideas about sexuality, violence, repression and misogyny: a culture of sexually grounded disorder which, at the very least, suggests a serious mismatch between male and female sexuality, and in some cases supposes that the one is 'naturally' predatory upon the other.

That said, it is important to emphasize that this 'ideology' is ambiguous, internally inconsistent and unevenly realized in different areas of the sub-genre. Not all psycho-movies are as unabashedly sexual as *Dressed to Kill*, just as few terrorising narratives are as effectively constructed as *Halloween*. What many of these films do share, however, is the generally paranoid emphasis of modern horror movies. Their experts are ineffective, their narratives remain open, and the worlds into which the threatening psyche erupts are the proximate worlds of home, family and peer-group. That this eruption is in some sense sexual is indisputable. But in *precisely* what sense is nothing like as clear.

## The Evolution of the Horror-Movie Psyche

Once again I shall try to map the main features of sub-genre evolution in diagrammatic form. On the whole this task is simpler than in the previous two chapters, partly because psycho-movies have a less complex history, and partly because the genre's portrait of the disordered psyche itself is correspondingly simple. The general pattern is shown in figure 9.2.

The basic division is that already introduced between 'madness' and 'psychosis', and the dotted lines on the psychosis side of the figure reflect the almost total absence of such films prior to the sixties. Madness, of course, is present from the very beginning, but even then − and compared with 'mad' science − it is still only a minor branch on the family tree. Then, after 1960, and in three overlapping phases, horror movie insanity explodes into prominence. First comes the full flowering of the 'madness' tradition, with its melodramatic trappings and woodshed experiences. This is followed by an expanding concern with what I shall call 'characterized psychosis'. Here the psychotic features as a meaningful character, not simply a convenient narrative function, and specific explanations are routinely given for his or her murderous insanity. Then, in the third phase, 'uncharacterized psychosis' predominates. Here the psychotic simply *is*. Given almost no characterizing explanation, his (they are dominantly male) essential function is reduced to that of central mechanism in a terrorizing narrative.

What kind of sense might we make of this? At the beginning of the chapter I observed that horror-movie insanity was, to all intents and purposes, deeply rooted human malevolence made manifest. And so it is, in comparison with the more *external* threats posed in the worlds of mad science and 'secure' horror. At this most general level there is an apparent homogeneity to the genre's conception of insanity. Examine it more closely, however, and it is clear that even the internality of horror-movie insanity varies across the three phases. Thus, 'madness' is fundamentally represented as a form of diffuse

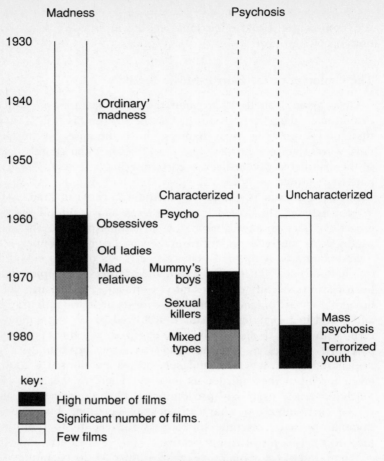

**Figure 9.2   Evolution of horror-movie insanity**

unreason, and in that sense assimilable to, or at least an aspect of, the world of reason. Though the heightened style of movies in this tradition suggests that insanity is rooted in an excess of the passions, in a kind of delirious other world of mad relatives and morbid obsessions, it is a delirium that makes sense only as an absence of reason, and, if it is not simply doomed — as it generally is in such movies — it can therefore be confined. This madness is narratively intelligible, even if it is rarely subject to expert explanation.

'Characterized psychosis', which succeeds it, is also represented as a kind of unreason, if more insidious in that insanity here is concealed beneath a surface of apparent normality. But for all that, it is still subject to reason's sway, still presumed to make sense at some level. Though we may not be able to defeat psychosis, we can hope to understand it — both through the actions of characters within the narrative and by virtue of the structure of the narrative itself. Psychiatry, especially, is presumed to offer *prima facie* plausible explanations, and psychiatric experts exert a kind of control precisely because they provide *post hoc* understanding.[7] In 'uncharacterized psychosis', however, insanity is no longer subject to reason, either as understanding or control. It is now something 'other', something strictly inexplicable, and the once-intelligible psychotic has metamorphosed into an irresistible boogey man lurking within our homes, our nightmares, and our selves.

In effect, the familiar pattern of development from secure to paranoid influences the psycho-movie tradition unevenly. In the 'madness' phase, the paranoid ethos is apparent only in the general internality of the threat, and that only in comparison with what has gone before. But as we move into the period of 'characterized psychosis', the traditional conception of madness — which postulated individual unreason existing in its own distinctive world but alongside our own — gives way to a rather less comfortable view. It is as if our basic presuppositions are changing in their conception of the boundary dividing sane and insane, as if there is an increasingly pervasive cultural disposition presuming that mental instability is a constant potential *within* normality — one still intelligible to us, to be sure, if only through the medium of psychiatric expertise, but more proximate a threat than that posed by traditional madness. Then, with the onset of 'uncharacterized psychosis', normality itself is experienced as untrustworthy and fragile. The threat from the psyche is now entirely unpredictable, unintelligible and altogether ferocious: a material expression of declining faith in the security of everyday circumstances and objects. We have, as it were, progressed from fear of the destructive consequences of uncontrolled 'grand' passions, through fear of repressed desires (though by definition still controllable) and on into terror bred of the collapse of individual and social control. In this world, reason itself is disordered.

What are the terms in which this potential for disorder is constructed? Apart from a growing lack of faith in the power of reason – reflected throughout the genre in the impotence of expertise in the seventies and eighties – the major reference point for the disordered psyche is clearly sexual. In the case of characterized psychosis that is often quite explicit, but even where there is no overt sexual explanation for psychotic behaviour, the now well-established sub-genre conventions of imagery and narrative combine to invoke a diffuse sense of sexuality. We have come to *expect* horror-movie psychosis to have a sexual dimension, whatever the evidence for or against. As with supernature, therefore, sexuality unrestrained – male *and* female – endangers the fabric of everyday normality, putting in doubt our capacity for reasoned control of our selves and the world around us.

Unlike that found in the evolution of horror movie supernature, however, the genre's developing conception of threatening psychosis does not display a double differentiation. The psycho-movie is far more focused and far simpler. As they increasingly take on the attributes of paranoid horror, eighties psycho-movies decline into a kind of lowest common denominator of the terrorizing narrative. The repressed, sexually motivated, misogynistic killers of the late sixties and seventies give way to the terrorizers: much more randomly homicidal figures whose sole purpose appears to be the pursuit and messy elimination of uninteresting juvenile victims.[8] The timing is significant, of course. As with supernature, the most obvious concern with female sexuality is to be found in the seventies, and there is a sense in which these misogynistic psychotics are the mirror image of supernature's lesbian vampires. Both make sense in the context of a culture which is fearful of sexuality and in which traditional sexual roles are undergoing change, and both articulate an essentially male view. But this recedes into the background in the eighties – *Dressed to Kill* is a culmination rather than a beginning – and the youth-in-jeopardy movies presuppose a much more general sense of paranoia.

Indeed, throughout the early eighties the boundaries dividing supernature and psyche are increasingly blurring. *The Evil Dead* (1982), with its quintet of college kids pursued by rampaging Sumerian demons, is nothing if not a terrorizing narrative, while a movie like *The Entity* (1982) pieces together elements of supernature, psychosis and mad science into a thoroughly paranoid story of an all-powerful, invisible rapist. The pattern of the eighties, then, is one of growing mistrust of the everyday and growing interpenetration between the various threatening domains of the horror movie. The psychotic can no longer be located within a world of reasoned discourse because that world itself is insecure; he has lost the motivational specificity of a Norman Bates. Supernature and psyche, now conjointly beyond our grasp and our control, together undermine the most basic order of everyday life, and transform the once secular psychotic into an archetypical product of our worst nightmares — the metal taloned child-killer Freddie of *A Nightmare on Elm Street*. Elm Street's apparently secure family households prove to be no defence, and even ordinary objects — a telephone, a bed — take on a malevolent life of their own. Paranoia reigns, and the suburbs will never be the same again.

## Notes

1 *Monthly Film Bulletin*, 31 (1964), p. 136.
2 For documentation and discussion of this critical response see Ian Christie, 'The Scandal of *Peeping Tom*', in Ian Christie (ed), *Powell, Pressburger and Others* (BFI, London), 1978.
3 Unsurprisingly, this section of *Psycho* has attracted a great deal of detailed attention, often of a psychoanalytic inclination. Perhaps the most elaborate is Raymond Bellour, 'Psychosis, Neurosis, Perversion', *Camera Obscura*, 3/4 (1979) pp. 105–32. There is an outline and discussion of Bellour's analysis in Annette Kuhn, *Women's Pictures* (London, 1982), pp. 96–104. As far as *this* study is concerned, such a detailed reading is neither necessary nor appropriate.
4 The female psychotic is revealingly employed in the highly successful 1987 film, *Fatal Attraction*. Although functioning on the glossy borders of the genre, *Fatal Attraction* features a traditional female psychotic who begins the film as an independent career-woman. Her psychosis receives virtually no explanation, she is represented as sexually voracious and the family that she 'threatens' is rendered as a highly desirable alternative. Few genuine horror films have presented female autonomy and sexuality in quite as rigidly conservative a framework as this. If the eighties have seen a backlash against changing views of women's social role, then the success of *Fatal Attraction* is surely one sign of it.
5 For an interesting discussion of the 'stalker' films see Vera Dika, 'The Stalker Film, 1978–81', in Gregory A. Waller (ed.), *American Horrors: Essays on the Modern American Horror Film*, Urbana & Chicago, 1987. See also Robin Wood's essay in the same volume: 'Returning the Look: *Eyes of a Stranger*' pp 79–85. On *Halloween* specifically see Steve Neale, '*Halloween*: Suspense, Aggression and the Look', *Framework*, 14, 1981.
6 See Giovanna Asselle and Behroze Gandhy, '*Dressed to Kill*', *Screen*, 23 3/4 (1982), pp. 137–43, for a discussion of these issues. See also Annette Kuhn, *Women's Pictures*, pp. 127–8.

7  This clearly resembles the kind of view of madness that Foucault traces as the achievement of the classical age. See Michel Foucault, *Madness and Civilisation*, London, 1967.

8  By 1987–1988 there are some signs that youth-in-jeopardy movies are going into decline.

# 10
## Conclusion: Security and Paranoia

'What *is* the world coming to?' Such is the lament of appalled moralists everywhere on unexpectedly confronting the horror movies of their times. Fortunately for the genre's established audience, these encounters are not frequent, most often occasioned by deliberately manipulated moral panics (encouraged by the popular press and various pressure groups) like that directed at so-called 'video nasties', or by the genre's sporadic successes in the commercial mainstream.[1] But, its patronizing tone apart, the genre outsider's pained response is not entirely inappropriate. It can be quite instructive to ask in what kind of world *could* the horror movie make sense? This is more revealing, certainly, than the conventional media-research inquiry: what are the genre's (adverse) effects on our minds and behaviour? The problem with such 'effects' questions is that they are both atomistic and individualistic. They assume, conceptually and methodologically, that complex fictions can be isolated from the subcultures of which they are a part, and, furthermore, that they are primarily effective at the level of individual psychology. Neither of these claims is self-evident. Fictions are understood and experienced in variable cultural settings, read by audiences in different ways, and can only be explored for their social significance by seeking to understand them in those contexts. That they are significant I do not doubt. But – as the collective incoherence of 50 years of media-effects research suggests – that significance cannot be established in terms of straightforward individual outcomes. If there is an effect it is a 'cultural effect': an effect on the constantly changing cultural envelope within which we live our lives.

So, for example, if the horror movie shares the presumption of most popular film genres that physical or psychological coercion is necessary for successful action, then that is important because it is part of the process whereby this particular cultural pattern is sustained. Yet this indirect, long-term, cumulative effect is unlikely to be apparent in, say, studies seeking to measure levels of aggression as a consequence of individual exposure to particular cultural stimuli. Nor, at the other extreme, does it suggest that the genre is somehow 'to blame' for violence in the wider society. To make such a claim would be pernicious scapegoating, since, other than in isolated and much publicized cases, we simply do not live in a world in which discrete cultural experiences have dramatic measurable effects. We live, rather, in elaborate interlocking systems, the elements of which are in constant interaction.

This is the kind of circumstance I was referring to in chapter 1 when I spoke of the horror movie as an *embedded* feature of our social lives. What that means in this context is that horror movies are neither a direct cause nor an unmediated reflection of their audience's attitudes and activities, although there is a sense in which they are simultaneously both, precisely because they are constituents of the process of producing and reproducing culture. It is essential, therefore, to contextualize the horror movie; to understand genre history as part of a broader process of change[2] – to inquire, in effect, into the kinds of social and cultural worlds within which the genre makes sense. Or, to put it the other way round, if we assume, as we must, that horror movies are intelligible and coherent experiences for their audiences, then we have to ask ourselves what the world must be like for that to be the case.

Indirectly, of course, some such question has informed much of my analysis so far. Thus, in trying to lay bare the general conventions of, say, horror-movie narratives, I am also exploring their conditions of intelligibility. But in this speculative final chapter I want to ask the 'what must the world be like?' question with a slightly different emphasis. One of the distinguishing characteristics of horror movies is that they are implicated in the distinctive subset of cultural patterns through which we construct our understanding of what is fearful to us. That understanding is not psychologically fixed for all human beings. It alters in different historical and social circumstances, for, as Scruton observes, 'fear is a social act which occurs within a cultural matrix.'[3] Horror movies are part of that cultural matrix, both reflecting its character at any given time and contributing to its continuity and change. For their audience they articulate the fearful, directly and indirectly, as well as providing the building blocks out of which people construct the experience of fear itself.

Now there are a number of levels at which this topic might be addressed in relation to the kinds of 'histories' reported in this book. One might usefully look, for example, at the specific fears noted in the 'evolutionary trees' of chapters 7, 8 and 9. In this way, horror-movie representation of radioactivity in the fifties, natural disasters in the seventies or epidemic disease in the late seventies and eighties could be singled out on an *ad hoc* basis and examined in the context of the prevailing concerns of those periods. The risk of that approach is that focusing upon such details obscures global patterns. Here, therefore, I want to ask not about the minutiae of what is fearful, but about the *general form* of the fearfulness that finds expression in the horror movies of different eras, and beyond that, about the social and cultural presuppositions that the genre reproduces and sustains in representing the fearful in the ways that it does. To this end I shall try to set out some of the most generally significant features of the horror-movie histories recounted in this study. They interweave in what I have described as the genre's major developmental pattern: the passage from *secure* to *paranoid* horror.

## Two Worlds of Horror

To further develop the distinction between secure and paranoid horror, it is helpful to construct an 'ideal type' of each form, a summary of the kinds of factors that, taken to their limits, serve to distinguish between these two broad categories. Of course it is unlikely that any single film would encompass every feature of its ideal-typical prototype, and that is anyway not the purpose of the distinction. My aim is strictly analytic. Note, however, that this approach does not negate the variously focused histories of the rest of the book. It seeks to supplement those accounts by drawing out the broadest threads that run through them.

What, then, are the most general characteristics of an 'ideal' film of the secure category? Like all horror movies, the film would pre-suppose a tension between known and unknown; in the secure case, it would do so in relation to a subset of the genre's basic informing oppositions: above all, life and death, secular and supernatural, human and alien, normal and abnormal matter. These contrasts would be clearly counterpoised, their dividing boundary appropriately marked. Such clarity is essential for the proper functioning of secure horror, for only where the boundary between disorder and order is rigorously sustained is it possible to imagine successful human intervention. In secure horror the powers of disorder are always defeated by expertise and coercion, the genre world's authorities — whether those of science or of the state — remaining credible protectors of individual and social order. Though such order is definitionally precarious in the horror movie, human action is always meaningful and potentially effective in the face of the threat, and the threat itself is more likely to be external than internal, and distant rather than proximate. Boundaries can be clearly drawn in relation to an external threat. Internal threats, precisely because they are internal, often blur the distinction between known and unknown, allowing the one to conceal the disturbing co-presence of the other.

Given these basic features of the secure horror universe, it is hardly surprising that its archetypical narrative form is the closed knowledge narrative — the form that dominated the first 30 years of the genre's history. More than any other type, closed knowledge narratives posit a world of effective human action — both in undermining order and in restoring it — and one with clear boundaries between its two domains. Some invasion narratives are similarly endowed, particularly SF/horror films in the fifties and the more orthodox vampire movies of the thirties and forties. As with knowledge narratives, these traditional invasion narratives also permit a wide range of effective action on the part of their experts, who normally operate within a clearly defined division between known and unknown. But invasion narratives are the more flexible, especially when combined with elements of the metamorphosis type. Thus it is that they embrace both secure and paranoid horror, successfully adapting to the demands of these different genre worlds. Knowledge narratives, however, cannot easily adapt to paranoid requirements; their conventions are fundamentally grounded in the basic terms of reference of secure horror.

It is these terms of reference that give rise to our typical modes of involvement and set limits on the ways in which we can relate to a routinely secure horror movie. Inevitably, much of this 'rhetoric of involvement' relates to expertise and to the formal significance of expert characters in the secure horror universe. The mad scientist himself, though the occasion for the disordering impulse, is a primary focus for both sympathy and fear — an interesting ambiguity shared with his often anthropomorphic creations. Things are simpler, of course, where the expert is also the unambiguous hero, as was so often the case in fifties invasion movies, since here all possible modes of character involvement coincide. But, whatever the variation, it is clear that experts and expertise are vital elements in the working of character-based involvement, and that they are most plausibly situated in social settings exhibiting a centre–periphery structure. Those at the centre are conventionally expected to be capable of autonomous action; those at the periphery require the protection of centrally located expertise. Without that socially distinctive locus of authority there can be no reimposition of order and the world of secure horror would not be secure at all.

Our involvement in this world, then, is cast very much in terms of an ultimately successful struggle against disorder. Although secondary identifications can complicate things – for example, those based on the surface attractiveness of classic vampires, or our sympathy for anthropomorphic monsters such as Frankenstein's – the fundamental pattern of our concerns is formed by secure horror's stress on effective expertise, on clear boundaries between known and unknown, on the desirability of existing order and on the significance of our dependence on socially central paternalistic authorities. In such a world the temptations of knowledge, power and – thinly veiled – sexuality must be resisted. Secure horror is secure both in the sense that it presumes an ultimately safe world and that the modes of involvement made available to us are founded on the expectation of final security. As proxy participants we *know* that we will survive to fight another day and that we are appropriately equipped to defeat all kinds of threats. Genuine doubt is almost entirely absent.

In contrast, doubt is everywhere to be found in paranoid horror. Here, human actions are routinely unsuccessful, order far more precarious and boundaries between known and unknown rarely as clear as they might at first seem. The oppositions characteristic of paranoid horror typically include those between conscious and unconscious self, normal and abnormal sexuality, sanity and insanity, collective order and disorder and health and disease. In all these cases the boundary separating the two is far less clearly marked than in secure horror, the disordering unknown often located deep within the commonplace and the threat much more proximate. The unconscious surges up from the seemingly normal self, bringing with it psychopathy and 'abnormal' sexuality; disease spreads in epidemic proportions, striking unpredictably and inexplicably, turning apparently ordered and secure environments into settings for total social collapse. Unsurprisingly, in such a world human actions are ineffectual, and there is a common tendency towards escalating disorder. Expertise is no better a qualification than is everyday common sense, and often those who pose as experts are the least effective of all. In a universe of internal threats and blurred boundaries, a little knowledge can be a dangerous thing.

Here the prevailing narrative form is one based upon metamorphosis of individuals and whole collectivities, usually lacking narrative closure and so implying a continuing cycle of escalation. We, all of us, are at risk in an open metamorphosis narrative, the epidemic characteristics of its collective variant perfectly expressing the basic terms of the paranoid universe. The running battle against zombification, disease or mass insanity reflects the apocalyptic despair so plausible within the assumptions of paranoid horror, a battle which − in its most extreme manifestations − must always be lost. Individually based metamorphosis stories do not quite reach these extremes, yet even without the same potential for collective disorder, most modern psycho-movies clearly belong within the paranoid domain. The explosive surfacing of internal forces, the failure of expertise, the constantly renewed threat, the apparent impossibility of effective action − all the familiar attributes are present. The one thing that is missing is the ultimate disintegration of human order.

Invasion narratives, too, are adaptable to a paranoid context in both individual and collective versions. As I have already observed, the invasion−metamorphosis composite has become the most potent horror-movie narrative of the seventies and eighties, its specific embodiments ranging from demonic possession of the otherwise innocent to mass collapse in the face of parasitic invasion of the human body. However, just as it was the closed knowledge narrative that best represented secure horror, so it is the open metamorphosis type that most nearly typifies the world of paranoid horror.

In such a fictional world, of course, there is no need for a highly developed centre−periphery model of social structure. Paranoid horror is basically victim-centred, and our involvement with character functions accordingly. Everyone is open to attack, and no one stands out as the inevitable locus of successful resistance. Instead, we have no choice but to become involved with characters whose survival is doubtful and who, in the absence of authoritative defenders, are thrown back onto their own resources. In this context the small group is central as a basic unit of defence, and it is notable that the family (or a surrogate family grouping) has grown in significance as part of the paranoid genre's social setting, both as an institution open to metamorphosis or invasion and as a crumbling bastion against outright social disorder. Involvement here, unlike that invited by secure horror, is based on the expectation of ultimate defeat: we can only seek to defer the inevitable, to put up a good fight. Thus, paranoid horror is paranoid both in its inbuilt prognosis of the likely outcome and in its assumption that the roots of disorder are to be found within ourselves and our institutions. It is not just doubt that is ubiquitous in this world: it is self-doubt.

These broad differences between secure and paranoid horror are summarized in table 10.1.

**Table 10.1  Security and paranoia in the horror movie**

| *Secure* | *Paranoid* |
|---|---|
| *Knowledge*      *Invasion*<br>     *(closed)* | *Metamorphosis*<br>*(open)* |
| successful human intervention | failed human intervention |
| effective expertise | ineffective expertise |
| authorities as credible protectors of order | escalating, unstoppable disorder |
| external 'distant' threats | internal 'proximate' threats |
| involvement with expert | involvement with victim |
| centre–periphery structure | family and small group structure |
| clearly marked known/unknown: | diffuse known/unknown: |
| life/death; secular/supernatural; human/alien; normal/abnormal matter | conscious/unconscious; normal/abnormal sexuality; social order/disorder; health/disease |

Given the apparent starkness of the distinctions it is important to underline the typificatory character of the secure/paranoid division, and to emphasize that paranoid horror is still developing. But even thus qualified, this crude distinction does serve to capture a set of contrasts that are central to any understanding both of the genre's development and of its social significance.

Of course, security was not transformed into paranoia overnight; the transition stretches from the late fifties into the early seventies. During these years, as the detailed histories of chapters 4, 7, 8 and 9 suggest, the genre was in a state of flux, so much so that it is extremely difficult to isolate and describe the key strands in sixties horror movies. In effect, then, the developmental pattern that I am suggesting is one of three broad phases, the second of which is essentially transitional. During the first, encompassing the thirties, forties and fifties, the conventions of secure horror dominate the genre, though slightly differently expressed in the fifties than in the other two decades. In the third phase – the horror movie of the seventies and eighties – paranoid horror is increasingly significant, and by the eighties almost all horror movies are showing a strong paranoid inclination.[4] So, what contextual sense can we make of this trend? What more general beliefs underwrite these fictions and render them intelligible?

Early in the development of secure horror, in the thirties and forties, the clearest contextual pattern is one in which fear of the activities of other people is central. But not all 'other people'. Ordinary folk are generally presumed to be reliable. Those who are to be feared are those whose 'abnormal' motives and interests cause them to create something which poses a threat to the 'normal' population. Abnormality, then, is presumed to be easily identifiable, and, given that danger is conceived as arising from the *intentional* activities of human beings, it is also widely assumed that normality can best be sustained by controlling potential deviants. The legitimate forms of control are various. Straightforward coercion is routine and fundamental, but strategies of reform and repression are also significant: reform for the knowledge-obsessed scientists who must be persuaded to see the light; repression of those human desires – for power, for sex – that overcome the norms of appropriate behaviour.

Coercion, reform and repression, then, are the mechanisms which, in this view of the world, ensure conformity and thus restore order. But what kind of order is presumed to be at risk, and in whom is vested the responsibility for its defence? In the initial development of secure horror, the broad assumption is that two interrelated levels of

social order are under threat. The more general of the two is traditional and class-based; a view of the world in which each person fits
into his or her appropriate place. A rigidly stratified social structure
defines the terms in which acceptable social relations may be conducted, and those at the centre are expected to accept the rights and
fulfil the duties of their position. Those with inherited status, the
bourgeoisie, those representing established state authorities and
ordinary people are bound together in a network of mutual obligation.
Within this structure familial order is crucial, and necessarily founded,
it is presumed, in heterosexual romantic love. The parties to this
relationship can be distracted from their proper responsibilities by, in
the case of men, the pursuit of knowledge or power outside the
established structures, in the case of women, failing to repress their
potentially destructive sexual impulses. In short, then, the kind of
world in which this formulation of secure horror would make sense
is a world in which tradition is valued for its own sake, and in which
change at any level is frightening. More than anything else, of course,
it is scientific knowledge that is fundamentally threatening, though
there is also a generalized mistrust of 'new' thinking which serves to
legitimate more specific suspicions about science.

This prevailing fear of social change and innovation is a prominent
feature in the thirties, though a little less significant in relation to
forties horror movies. However, its implicit conservatism is not un-
contaminated by underlying anti-authoritarianism. After all, some
part of our involvement in classic secure horror is grounded in the
pleasures of witnessing authority flouted and rendered fragile, a
feature often reinforced by making the threat itself attractive or
sympathetic. Mad scientists are regularly portrayed as brilliant
obsessives who display a certain crazed charm; anthropomorphic
monsters demand our sympathy; sophisticated vampires can fascinate
us just as effectively as they do their willing victims. Ultimately, of
course, authority triumphs, and preservation of the status quo is
axiomatic in the system of preconceptions within which secure horror
functions. Thus, though these movies may at some level seek to
exploit a tacit antipathy to established authority, they never do so to
such a degree as to put the legitimacy of that authority genuinely at
risk. The threat to prevailing social order is always finally conceived
as more disturbing than is the constraint imposed by that order.

The fifties see some minor alterations in the secure horror universe,
in line with its changing social and cultural context. In particular, as

I have already suggested, fifties horror movies modify the substance of the centre—periphery structure in relation to that decade's popular interest in emerging ideas of meritocracy and 'Mass Society'. In so far as this change presumes a positive evaluation of risky scientific research as the 'price of progress', a widespread acceptance of science-driven social change, and a routinized dependence on scientific expertise as a defensive resource, it suggests a somewhat less inflexible context of fearfulness than that of the thirties. On the other hand, the largely unqualified affirmation of scientists and the military as defenders of social order, as well as the relative lack of sympathetic monsters, presumes an even more unquestioning faith in the legitimacy of established authority in the face of essentially alien threats.

*Alien* threats: there, of course, lies the crucial difference between thirties and fifties secure horror. In the thirties, threatening monsters were predominantly anthropomorphic, many of them volitional products of human intelligence. A degree of ambiguity is intrinsic to our responses to such creations, somewhat tempering secure horror's narrative celebration of authoritative intervention. In the fifties this potential for anthropomorphic ambivalence is much reduced, our way of life threatened by alien invaders with whom we can share very little or by 'invisible' forces which adversely affect the world around us. In this xenophobic universe we can do nothing but rely upon the state, in the form of military, scientific and governmental elites. Only they have recourse to the technical knowledge and coercive resources necessary for our defense. In this respect, then, fifties SF/horror movies teach us not so much 'to stop worrying and love the bomb' as 'to keep worrying and love the state', an admonition which accords perfectly with the nuclear-conscious cold war culture of the period.

Clearly, secure horror can only make sense in the context of a culture and a social world which is confident of its own capacity to survive all manner of threats. What actually poses a threat changes over the three decades, as does the specific character of those responsible for our defence. But the basic reference points remain the same: an essentially hierarchical social order; unquestioning allegiance to the central significance of the traditional family unit; a role division which marginalizes women; a restrictive view of 'proper' sexuality, especially as that applies to women; a conception of social deviance as primarily a redeemable individual failing; a broad anti-intellectual stance; and a general commitment to the legitimacy of established state authorities. Though there are features of the genre that run counter to this traditionalist culture,[5] even they depend on the presupposition that these contextual factors are both cogent and universal – part of an internally coherent social and cultural order in which the secure horror movie is firmly embedded.

Yet in the sixties, the genre, like so much popular culture,[6] was to change quite dramatically. What kind of world must we postulate if we are to make sense of this, the emergence of paranoid horror? I began discussion of the secure horror context with the observation that 'other people' were to be feared, though in the rather special sense that they might have 'abnormal' motives. These deviants were presumed to be easily recognizable, and their deviance, by definition a consequence of individual intentional activity, was therefore open to appropriate techniques of social control. It is this sense of the distinctiveness of deviance, and its potential for containment, that is immediately undermined by paranoid horror. Other people are certainly still to be feared, but now any and all of them pose a risk. However 'normal' friends, neighbours and family may seem, the presumption of paranoid horror is that they might prove unpredictably malevolent and so powerful that resistance is doomed to failure. The world in which this kind of horror makes sense, then, is one which is fundamentally unreliable.

This supposition of unreliability applies at three main levels: individual, group and society. Not surprisingly, it is the unreliable individual which is the most frequently invoked, above all through the theme of psychosis. The psychotic, externally normal though liable to metamorphose into a ferocious killer at any moment, is the emblematic figure of the modern horror movie. There is no question here of social control or redemption. Even with characterized psychotics, the fact that some kind of explanation is offered does not imply any real possibility of prevention or cure, and as the genre develops through the eighties such explanations are anyway increasingly rare. Other people simply cannot be trusted, whatever their social position and apparent respectability. They are frightening because of what lies concealed within, and, since we do not understand the roots of the disordered psyche, any of us may be subject to its terrible influence. This is a view of the world which is not simply paranoid about other people. It fears the unreliability of the self, and doubts the security of our identities as functioning and responsible human beings.

This generalized self-doubt carries over onto group and societal levels. Groups can and do conspire against us, and the institutions to which we were once accustomed to turn for our defence are either ineffective or are themselves implicated in the collapse of social order. The kind of world presumed by this routinized paranoia is strikingly different from that within which secure horror is intelligible. Gone is the sense of an established social and moral order which is both worth defending and capable of defence. Gone, too, is the assumption that there are legitimate authorities who can demand our co-operation in exchange for their protection. Instead we have become either isolated victims of human psychosis, or doomed members of untrustworthy social institutions.

Yet all is not unambiguously hopeless. Though paranoid horror may presuppose our ultimate impotence in the face of increasingly proximate threats, its very elimination of legitimate order releases non-expert, ordinary characters from the bondage, as well as the security, of centre—periphery dependence. Thus for example women, still represented in some areas of the genre in terms of their allegedly threatening sexuality, also achieve a degree of autonomy far beyond that available in secure horror. Or, even more ambivalently, the family and its social surrogates come to occupy a place both as a source of violence, psychopathy and repression *and* as the only institutional defence against the impending apocalypse. In these and other respects, paranoid horror suggests widespread confusion. It is as if we have been cast loose in a world for which we no longer have any reliable maps, in which once-clear landmarks are not what they seem, and in which we know we must seek new shelter or perish.

One way in which such contradictions as these can be made contextually intelligible is by postulating post-sixties erosion of the foundations of social legitimacy in many western societies − the culmination of the 'age of delegitimation'.[7] This feature of what has been variously spoken of as 'late capitalist', 'post-industrialist' or 'post-modern' society can be diversely conceptualized, and I do not propose to enter into the byways of the legitimation debate here. Suffice only to observe that when Habermas writes of a 'motivation crisis' and a consequent 'legitimation crisis', he is arguing that two of advanced capitalism's central patterns of motivation, those that relate to civil legitimation and to the functioning of the privatized family, are being systematically destroyed.[8] It is an analysis that finds a striking parallel in paranoid horror's denial of traditional authority structures and in its evident ambivalence about the status of the family group as both defence and threat.

All this is still in some flux, and the best that one can say at the moment is that, most generally, paranoid horror makes sense in the context of as-yet incomplete social changes. But it is not change itself that is now fearful, as it was in the world of secure horror, but the personal and social confusions that follow in its wake. What is a crisis of legitimation at a social level is a crisis of identity at an individual level. No longer sheltered by the unquestioned values of traditional social order, we find ourselves faced with the fearful prospect of unpredictable social relations in a world now open to the possibility of escalating chaos. In such social circumstances we are obliged to become Janus-faced. In one direction we look into the daylight of a better future, one freed of the restrictions, the repressions and the injustices of past orthodoxy. In the other, we look into the dark at a dimly perceived army of lost souls. It is this vision, this threat of a continuing nightmare, that paranoid horror holds up for our contemplation.

## Notes

1  I say 'fortunately' because such events can have serious censorship consequences without anyone thinking to mount the kinds of public defence common enough with more 'respectable' arts. Thus, several horror movies were withdrawn from circulation on video after the 'video nasties' publicity (among others, *Driller Killer*, *I Spit on Your Grave*, and *Nightmares in a Damaged Brain*), while *The Evil Dead*, already in possession of a BBFC film certificate, was unsuccessfully prosecuted several times. This particular moral panic finally led to a system of certification for video in Britain which has proved significantly more restrictive than that currently applied in the cinema. Ironically, by 1988 this meant that *The Evil Dead* had ceased to be available on video, and, at the time of writing, it seems likely that *The Exorcist* will suffer a similar fate. The latter, of course, was one of those few genre movies that, in 1974, actually crossed the boundary into the commercial mainstream.

2  There are many ways in which such contextualization might be approached. For just two attempts, see James B. Twitchell, *Dreadful Pleasures: An Anatomy of Modern Horror* (New York and Oxford, 1985), and Les Daniels, *Fear: A History of Horror in the Mass Media* (London, 1977). In line with my methodological strategy in this book, I have chosen to examine the most general suppositions of horror-movie narratives. A full account would, of course, demand much wider analysis of twentieth-century popular culture.

3  David L. Scruton, 'The Anthropology of an Emotion', in David L. Scruton (ed), *Sociophobics: The Anthropology of Fear* (Boulder and London, 1986), p. 10.

4  Note that paranoid horror does not exclude comedy. Many eighties horror movies, not least those directed at the American youth audience, quite self-consciously resort to 'sick' or 'black' humour. This pattern − a recurrent feature throughout the genre's history − has been particularly apparent after 1984 as the declining cycle of 'youth-in-jeopardy' movies has run low on invention. Humour, however, does not render the assumptions of paranoid horror any less significant: they remain as central to its operation as they are to other more 'serious' aspects of the modern genre.

5  Most popular genres to some degree allow their audience to 'have their cake and eat it' by satisfying both their desire for affirmation of convention and for resistance to it. This feature has led a number of authors to view popular genres as 'myths' which resolve otherwise irresolvable cultural conflicts. See, for example, Will Wright, *Sixguns and Society* (Berkeley, 1975), and, applying similar methods to a horror movie sub-genre, Vera Dika, 'The Stalker Film, 1978−81', in Gregory A. Waller (ed), *American Horrors: Essays on the Modern American Horror Film* (Urbana and Chicago, 1987) pp. 86−101

6  In invoking popular cultural change in the sixties here I am *not* claiming, as some have, that the period made outstanding positive contributions to our cultures. In retrospect, sixties popular culture seems to me to be both ephemeral and transitional; certainly not the birth of a new age as so many claimed at the time. What does seem clear, however, is that many established popular fictional forms did change significantly during this period, and − though I cannot substantiate it here − in so doing moved in roughly paranoid directions.

7  This phrase is borrowed from Lyotard, though he employs it in a rather different context. See Jean-Francois Lyotard, *The Postmodern Condition: A Report on Knowledge* (Manchester, 1986).

8  See Jurgen Habermas, *Legitimation Crisis* (London, 1976), particularly Part II, chs 6 and 7. Here he argues two theses: 'First, we must demonstrate the erosion of traditions in the context of which these attitudes were previously produced. Second, we must show that there are no functional equivalents for the spent traditions, for they are precluded by the logic of development of normative structures.' (p. 75). I am not convinced that he fully substantiates the second claim.

# Subject/Name Index

# Index of Film Titles